A BOOK OF

THINGS ABOUT

VLADIMIR

ABOKOV

Edited by Carl R. Proffer

Ardis, Ann Arbor

A BOOK OF THINGS ABOUT VLADIMIR NABOKOV

Contents

A BOOK OF THINGS ABOUT VLADIMIR NABOKOV

Larry Gregg

SLAVA SNABOKOVU

Seven years have passed since the publication of Vladimir Nabokov's translation of *Eugene Onegin*. It has been over five years since the hilarious polemics over the translation retreated with a giggle into the well-deserved literary past. Almost three years have passed since the only attempt to assess the work objectively. It would be astute of us, therefore, not to rock the seemingly becalmed boat.

"But. . . ." said the Russian one of us.

A gaunt white-night sunset was framed in a golden gap between indelicate Neoclassical edifices. The remote dims of the gap were eyelashed with strange refractions, and still further, deep in the gap itself, one could distinguish the silhouettes of other, lesser and quite ethereal, edifices in Baroque, Rococo, Slavic Revival, all inundated in Empire. We were in Leningrad, loitering near the still ornate facade of 47 Morskaya (now Herzen) Street. The slender spires on distant Vasilevsky Island and the pale parallelipipeds of ancient monuments took advantage of the gleaming windows to participate in our talk—somewhat in the same way as the Nabokovian iambs did in regard to the reverse tilts of Pushkin's prosody.

"But," said the Russian one of us, "I like it too—but I do think the non-Russian reader ought to be told more what translation is all about."

The American one of us said. . . .

"No," said the Russian one of us, "I don't mean that. I mean the non-Russian reader ought to be told more what *Nabokov's* translation is all about. I mean the *basic aims.* He would want to know what Pushkin's *Onegin* is all about, and what Nabokov was attempting to do."

The American one of us said. . . .

"No, it has not all been said," said the Russian one of us. "We have both gone through it carefully, and so has my wife, and we have not found that it has all been said. There should also be some kind of essay. The non-Russian reader ought to be made to understand that he must read all four beautiful sky-blue volumes (hereinafter referred to as I, II, III, IV, respectively)

11

which contain, among other matter too recondite for quick description: a long introduction of nearly a hundred pages, an almost unbearably literal translation of everything in and near the poem, including rejected variants and extensions, with long stretches of white unprinted paper to indicate omitted or never-composed stanzas (the non-existent lines of these non-existent stanzas are numbered for easy reference), an immensely personal, entertaining, and erudite commentary, two long appendices, one a sort of genealogical novelette dealing with Pushkin's African ancestor, and the other a comparative study of English and Russian prosody (both have appeared separately), and, finally, an index and a facsimile of the last Russian text of the poem to have appeared while Pushkin was still alive, otherwise he would be discouraged and would not bother to read any further."

The American one of us said that an intelligent non-Russian reader could always be told the commentary is inseparable from the translation. The Russian one of us said that a non-Russian reader would not necessarily be an intelligent person. The American one of us said there were non-Russian readers and non-Russian readers. The Russian one of us said that from a Russian's point of view there was only one sort. We both said, well then, let's put together some of the Nabokovisms we've been guffawing ecstatically over behind our hand on this magical white night. After all, what could be more obelusian—even after all these years—than a fictional essay *(vymyslennyi ocherk)* on the translation of the greatest Russian work of Russia's greatest poet by the greatest Russian-American novelist? Written right here, where it all began?

Our essay will of course surge along with such speed and force, such manly and Peterbourgeois beauty will pervade it, and our gift to the non-Russian reader will breathe with such fierce integrity that he will not stop to despair that the curious allusions have a certain structural affinity with the interlacings of our insolent exploit. And if this involuted structure is responsible for seeming to cool somewhat the warmth—and yes!—even the heat of our ardor, we can only say, with an eye to our own defense, that a special feature of our essay is the monstrous but perfectly respectful part that flippance plays in it. We must dismiss once and for all the conventional notion that a fictional essay "should read clearly," and "should not sound like a fictional essay." In point of fact, any fictional essay that does *not* sound like a fictional essay is bound to be comprehensible upon inspection. While on the other hand, the only virtue of a good fictional essay is incoherence and obscurity. After all, the evolution of sense is, in a sense, the evolution of nonsense, and when we consider the innocence of the mental climate wherein we all live, we cannot but notice that a bit of plagiarism is permitted to do for invention now and then.

Before we rememorate the translation, however, we shall have a plot for those of our non-Russian readers who might not have happened to read *Onegin.* As the story begins, the hero, young Onegin, is flying post-haste on his horse to St. Petersburg from the country where he has just buried his uncle "of most honest principles." After a life of penury in the tedious country, he has inherited his uncle's fortune, and as we learn in the course of Chapter One, he is in a hurry to live and a haste to feel the bustle of deceitful society in the capital of old Russia. Onegin, it seems, now has the opportunity to enjoy all the fine things of life he has missed in his youth: balls, ballets, the theater, rich foods, the charms of the fairer sex. In Chapter Two we get a flashback to Onegin's life in the country and the tragic events which led to his unexpected good fortune. We learn that this passionate Byronic hero had been greatly bored with life in the country. With the exception of the poet Vladimir Lensky (very much like Pushkin himself, incidentally), there had been no one—not even his uncle, a wily old duelist—to whom he could confide his longing for a more active life. There were, of course, the local young ladies, and as the work progresses we learn that Onegin had fallen in love with a young girl, Tatyana, who is to all seeming intents and purposes a charmingly innocent maiden, but who is actually a corrupt schemer (as we learn from a careful perusal of the list of her lascivious reading, and as we know from the many fine psychoanalytical studies of her repulsive dreams).

Frightfully envious of her fresh, innocent and wholesome younger sister Olga (VN tells us in one note—and we quite agree— that Olga is the model for the finest young heroines of modern Russian literature), Tatyana sets in motion a crafty intrigue which ends in tragedy for all but herself. She sends a letter to Onegin, declaring her eternal love for him. Although Onegin is promised to Olga, he is led astray by his youth and his thirst for life, and he agrees to meet the calculating young Tatyana in a garden where— with the soft singing of an authentic peasant choir in the background—he is prompted to confess his love. Throughout the autumn and into the winter Onegin falls further under the scheming girl's spell. And finally the trap is sprung. Pained by his young friend's unseemly behavior, Lensky resolves to bring him to his senses. Inviting the strabismic young Onegin to a country get-together at his Auntie Larin's, Lensky tries to reason with him. Onegin, however, leaps to the conclusion that Lensky has designs on Tatyana, and he challenges the hapless poet to a duel. And even though Onegin's uncle pleads with him, reminds him of public opinion, even offers to arrange a friendly breakfast in hope of reconciling the two friends, the hopelessly deluded young man insists on defending his honor. On a cold winter morning (a morning uncannily similar to that on which Pushkin was himself killed), he kills the poet.

And here we realize the tremendous subtlety of Pushkin's irony. For we now understand that Onegin came into his fortune through most unfortunate circumstances. His uncle had died heartbroken and been buried near the martyred Lensky. Returning to Chapter One for a more careful reading, we now discover that there are many mysterious allusions to Onegin's discontent, and from this we realize that he is in search not of idle diversion, but of Tatyana. We realize too that the strange poet who has been pursuing the hero through Petersburg is the ghost of Lensky, still trying to bring his friend to his senses. And of course, Onegin finally does find his enchantress—only to learn that she has married a fat and powerful general. She even (as we may surmise from a careful reading between the lines) has designs on the tsar himself (who, as is well known, had a penchant for Petersburg darlings). Casting his pride to the winds, Onegin writes a letter to Tatyana in which he beseeches her to return to him. But of course the spiteful charmer has no further use for the poor hero, and she rejects him with scornful words. Onegin is thus doomed to a life of eternal wandering in foreign lands (as we know from Tomashevsky's masterful reconstruction of a discarded chapter: III: 365-75). The novel ends—unhappily—at this suspenseful point. Like generations of readers before us, we are fated by Pushkin's untimely demise to speculate as to what he intended to say in this novel which has so happily won him the title of "the father of Russian realism."

But what, the non-Russian reader might ask, has made *Onegin* so important to Russians? *Onegin,* we might reply in a paraphrase of scholiastic subject, is the portrayal of the hero of the time, *l'enfant du siècle* ("child of the century"), the noble Byronic hero corrupted by the evil society of the historical stage in which he lived. He thus takes his rightful place alongside Byron's Childe Harold and Don Juan, Constant's Adolphe, Chateaubriand's

René, and of course N. M. Karamzin's Erast, that other young Russian hero seduced by a sly country maiden. Onegin is thus a representative of his age, a social symbol who proves once again that "a man of most honest principles" is doomed to be the victim of his crass social milieu. The novel in verse is also the first, and perhaps even the most powerful, work of Russian Realism, and this can be seen not only in the true-to-life autobiographical depiction of the poet Lensky, but also in the amount of environmental details, the individualized type-characterizations on a social and national plane, the reflection of contemporary society in the work, the author's progressive attitude, and the nature of the plot. There is a great deal of *byt* or *dejstvitel'nost'*—"authenticity of social reality"—and this can be seen in Pushkin's use of folklore, the folkish, and "national color" which make up most of what is traditionally subsumed under the Russian term *narodnost'*, or "national self-sufficiency." All of these things, and many others, have convinced Russians that *Onegin* is one of the finest works of world literature.

Turning, then, to VN's translation, we suppose we should mention that he worked almost fifteen years—really a whole lifetime—on his version of *Onegin,* and he was a bit piqued when two other English translations appeared months before his own. It was undoubtedly his vexation with this piece of bad luck that prompted him to launch the first barrage of the polemical battle that followed. When his own translation did appear, there was a long silence, while breaths were drawn and dictionaries consulted in nine languages, and then the counter-attack began. Edmund Wilson, Monas, Rosen, Daniels, Brown (one of those three Slavicist Browns, one of whom has been so inconsiderate as to teach at Brown), and even Robert Lowell—one and all let loose with a howl of protest over—of all things—VN's innocuous method of translation. VN replied, someone replied to VN, VN counter-replied, the Pushkin period was reborn in all the glory of its criticism, anticriticism and antianticriticism, and the world of letters became witness to the bright swordplay of an elegantly informed urbane intelligence with facile paraphrasts and tongue-tied scholars. Poor Wilson fell into a trap VN had laid cunningly for him in his commentary; poor Monas asked plaintively, "Where are you, Pushkin?;poor Rosen chortled with glee that VN had missed the beautiful butterfly on the cover of the first edition of *Onegin;* poor Lowell fell headlong into a rude plea to please stop mangling

Mandelstam (and Akhmatova too, please). And so it went, and all to no avail: our pugnacious subject put them down one at a time or all together or, worse yet, by completely ignoring one or two little fellows.

In the opinion of one critic, the work was "a plain, prosy and rhymeless translation." In the opinion of another, "Nabokov's quest for absolute accuracy leads to violent distortions in language and syntax." In the opinion of still another, VN "reduced the sparkling choreography of the Onegin stanza to the dull plod of a schoolboy crib." One poor fellow termed the translation "a spavined pony," while another referred to "Nabokov's aberrations." One critic even had the audacity to suggest that "it only remains for a talented poet like Robert Lowell to take advantage of these translations, and of Nabokov's great commentary, to produce a poem in English that really soars and sings as does Pushkin's masterpiece." In the opinion of one reader, "Nabokov seeks to torture both the reader and himself by flattening Pushkin out" and "Nabokov has surpassed himself in oddity." There were references to "the unnecessarily clumsy style, which deliberately seems to avoid point and elegance." And so it went.

But what is the translation really like? To tell the truth, we have been convinced from our exposure to it that if a truly artistic translation is an impossibility, we would still prefer our own deluded optimism to this result of the literalist method. We are both painfully aware that some of our attempts at artistic fidelity end up as an undignified straddle over the language barrier, but we still believe it is important to try. Such opinions are, however, beside the point, and we find it far more relevant that in dealing with the quality of VN's translation, as in dealing with anything else about him, one should never take things for what they seem to be—even when what they seem to be are what they seem to be. As we intend to show in our own involuted fashion, the merit of the translation does not even enter into the question, and we fear that all those earnest critics were, once again, led off down the path of a little brick house. In fact, we suspect VN even gave them a ride down that way. "Pushkin," VN notes in his Foreword, "has likened translators to horses changed at the posthorses of civilization. The greatest reward I can think of is that students may use my work as a pony." Now how, we ask, could a good Yankee doodle be such a roodle as to take at his face value a man who could say something like that? We shall not. Let us, instead, dismiss the translation *per se* with the following

Onegin stanza, inspired, no doubt, by VN's characterization of the stanza as the poem's "basic brick":

Basically Brick

We recollect an otiose pony,
Onegin on a Yankee steed,
With notes, and puns, and macoroni,
A work of genius high ennuied:
With lines unrhymed and ripe with scud,
Iambic strophe—a crock of crud:
Spondees and tilts, and calques so Gallic
(Wethinks those charming feet are phallic).
"An awkward but accurate translation,"
(We know! We know! Your line won't scan!
But N., reproach us if you can),
With such pedantic adumbration!
We read and think with furrowed brow:
"Who will Nabokov third-rate now?"

This, we think, says all that needs to be said about VN's translation. As for the polemic, we can only say that beneath the unseemly din we seem to have heard feisty Pushkin's voice from on high: "Attaboy, VN, you sonuvabitch!"

As for us, we were attracted by other aspects of VN's work, and we have a cogent question. Is it not curious that so many words have been expended on the translation proper, and so few on the remainder of VN's work? Someone once remarked that reading the translation is akin to taking a ham sandwich to a banquet. We disagree, and would like to suggest that reading VN's translation without a thorough reading of the commentary and other contents of the four volumes is like attending a sumptuous banquet and nibbling on a ham sandwich. So far as we have been able to ascertain, only a few clever fellows seem to have recognized that the translation is relatively unimportant among the contents of this work. It occupies only about two-thirds of the slenderest of these four volumes, and it would have occupied nine pages less had VN not allotted all that white, enumerated space to all those non-existent stanzas. We believe that those who have devoted themselves to the very easily made observations about the ways in which this translation differs from ordinary translations are throwing themselves with great energy at a door behind which VN himself is lurking with a leer, ready to spring it open with a hearty haw-haw-haw. And lest anyone think our hint at foul play is a reproach to our saponaceous subject, let us say once and for all that we believe he is not, like Onegin's uncle, a man of most honest principles. Not, at least, where his critics are concerned. We believe that VN decided long ago that *Onegin* is untranslatable, and so, swallowing his pride like a gorge, he resolved to settle for a literal and deliberately pedestrianated translation which he could revehiculate as only a scholar-translator can hope to do: with a systematic, exhaustive and detail-sensitive commentary. We suspect, in other words, that he was convinced from the very start of his work that if the literalist translator is not satisfied with his version, he can at least hope to amplify it in a detailed note.

We are aware, of course, that when the beauty lost in the conveyance is restored in the commentary, it is seldom in the form of deft imitation of Pushkin's verse, but rather in the whorled, iridescent movement of VN's own prose. But we are still convinced that when the translation, the introduction, the appendices, the commentary, and *all* the other offerings of the work, including even the index, are read together, the non-Russian reader has a fairly good chance of coming to know the Russian *Onegin.* Even this, however, is not what we consider the most important aspect of VN's work. We would like to suggest that the beauty, the elegance, the charm of the work is comprised not so much of the final product as its execution. The words "research" and "scholarship" are disdained nowadays, of course, but there can be no doubt that VN's *Onegin* is not so much a *result* as an *act* of glorious pedantry. We see the work as being partly the echoes of VN's high-school days in this very city half a century ago and partly the outcome of many pleasant afternoons spent in splendid libraries. In art as in science there is no delight without the detail, and it is on the details that VN tried to fix his reader's attention. Let us repeat that unless these are understood and remembered, all "general ideas" (so easily acquired, so profitably resold) must necessarilly remain but worn passports allowing their bearers short cuts from one area of ignorance to another. It is always dangerous to put words into our termaganaceous subject's mouth, we realize, but we are convinced he will never deny our carefully chosen words.

We insist, therefore, that the four volumes of VN's *Onegin* are a joyfully pedantic work of research and scholarship, a work which long before it was published had reached the charmed stage when the quest overrides the goal, and a new organism is formed, the parasite, so to speak, of the ripening fruit. It is a work of research fixed at the stage where VN averted his mental gaze from the end of his work, which was so clearly in sight that he could make out the rocket of an asterisk, the flare of a *sic!* This line of land was, at this point of VN's work, to be shunned as the doom of everything that determined the rapture of endless approximation. The collation of two themes; a precious detail in manners or dress; a reference checked and found to be falsified by incompetence, carelessness, or fraud; the spine thrill of a felicitous guess; and all the innumerable triumphs of *beskorystnyi* (disinterested, devoted) scholarship—this corrupted our dear VN, this made of him a happy footnote-drugged maniac who disturbs the book mites in a dull volume, a foot thick, to find in it a reference to an even duller one. And on another, more human, plane there were the final four volumes lying ahead, those beautiful, incredibly crapulous four volumes of pedantic detail, footnotes, transliteration, cross-reference, allusion, speculation, reconstruction, confirmation, disputation, illumination, celebration—all those joyously detailed pages that only the reputation of an ebullient VN could bully into print.

We feel that we can even explore the genesis of the work without fear of contradiction. We have devoted considerable thought to VN's *modus operandi*—the way in which his mind works— and we have concluded that his *Onegin* began in a way which has not seemed to occur to anyone else. We believe that the work began not as a translation of *Onegin*, but as a viatic study of all of Russian culture. We suggest that VN originally contemplated writing a *Petite Histoire* of Russian culture in which a choice of Russian Curiousities, Customs, Literary Anecdotes and so forth would be presented in such a way as to reflect in miniature *la Grande Histoire*—Major Concatenations of Events, if you please. We like to imagine our VN when he was still at the stage of collecting his materials. And like many good young people we would consider it a treat and an honor to see him pull out a catalogue drawer from the comprehensive bosom of a card cabinet and take it, like a big nut, to a secluded corner and there make a quiet mental meal of it, now moving his lips in soundless commentary, critical, satisfied, perplexed, and now lifting his specious brow where they remain long after all trace of displeasure or doubt has gone, not even lowering them when some fly applies itself, blind fool, to his bald head and is stunned by a smack of his meaty palm. We picture him going in rubber gloves so as to avoid being stung by *amerikanskoe* electricity to the books in the stacks and gloating over them: obscure magazines of the Roaring Sixties in marbled boards; century-old literary monographs, their somnolent pages foxed with fungus spots; Russian classics in horrible and pathetic cameo bindings, whose molded profiles of poets remind our dewy-eyed subject of his boyhood, when he could idly palpate on the book cover Pushkin's slightly chafed side whisker or Zhukovsky's smudgy nose.

But if this is so, our non-Russian readers might well ask, then what happened to that vast history in miniature? And to this we reply: those idle adolescent palpations are what happened to it. Pushkin happened to it, and Zhukovsky, and Batyushkov, and Ryleev, and Katenin, and Bestuzhev-Marlinsky, and Derzhavin, and Delvig, and Kyukhelbeker, and Baratynsky, and Davydov, and Yazykov, and that prince of a fellow Knyazemsky. They, we reply, did away with that petty major history. Simply that the most fascinating of all Russian literary periods, and the most fascinating poet of that period, and the most fascinating work of that poet became the most Major Concatenations of Events. Simply that *Onegin* conquered VN—shot him down in a duel, to put it *à propos*—gave a new direction to his inquiry, turned our footnote-drugged subject into an even more incorrigible Pushkinist. But here VN faced a dilemma. How could he convey Pushkin's *Onegin* into English, thus unavoidably making it his own, and yet allow it to remain Pushkin's? And here, we dare say, he hit upon a device unprecedented in his long and illustrious career: he would use *Onegin* as a document—perhaps even, in his own Englished version, as an inferior document—a document to which he could affix his own imprint fixed forever at that charmed stage when the quest overrides the goal, that stage of the rapture of endless approximation, that stage of all the innumerable triumphs of *beskorystnyi* scholarship, that stage when he dared not—yet finally had to—look ahead to those incredibly beautiful sky-blue volumes of pedantic adumbration. This, we suggest, is the crux of Nabokov's *Onegin*. It is an intensely Nabokovian *Onegin*, which means that it is an agonizingly honest *Onegin*, which means that the non-Russian reader has the opportunity not only to enjoy VN's scintillating erudition, but also Pushkin's sparkling literary fireworks. The Russian *Onegin* is there, we insist, it is there in full *beskorystnost'*, for those who can overcome their undergraduate aversion to "research" and "scholarship" long enough to delve *beskorystno* into a marvelous pedantry.

We confer with our dictionary: "Ped ant·ry (ped ant·ri), n., pl., -ries (-riz). 1. Ostentatiousness, formalism, didacticism, or the like, in the presentation or application of knowledge or learning. 2. A pedantic expression, act, method, etc." No, that's not it. We check further. The term (Ital. *pedante*, used by Montaigne c. 1580, *un pedante*) originally meant "teacher" (and is probably allied to "pedagogue"). That's much better. One variety of pedant, we believe, is the person who likes to perorate, to air, if not to preach, his opinions, with great thoroughness and precision of detail. That, we believe, is what we mean. A fine example of pedantry is, we believe, Pushkin's *Onegin,* that veritable encyclopedia of poetic details and opinions. Another is Nabokov's translation. Pushkin's pedantry was grand and VN's is elegant; the stateliness of the former's is always poetic, and the polish of the latter's is finical occasionally. Erudition—that's it for both. Modesty in the guise of flippance—that's Pushkin's pedantry. *Beskorystnost'* in the guise of arrogance—that's Nabokov's. Research, scholarship, pleasant afternoons in splendid libraries, the joy of a felicitous guess, quiet mental meals, the quest overriding the goal, the sensual pleasure of endless approximation, the delight of the detail—that's it, say we, that's Nabokov's translation, say we.

And so we insist that VN's translation of Pushkin is an act of pedantry, perhaps even an act of that most glorious of all pedantries: potshots at butterfies with cannon. And this, we suggest, is the translation's *basic aim*—what VN was attempting to do. And this is why we are awed that so many critics missed the point of that annoyingly literal method of translation. And this is why we are convinced that the non-Russian reader—if he really cares enough to work—has the opportunity in these four volumes to know the Russian *Onegin.* We believe also that we could demonstrate our conviction, but we realize that any attempt to do so would be tainted by the reader's knowledge that we have already straddled the language barrier from opposite sides. And so we shall not take potshots at this particular butterfly with cannon. Rather, we would like to approach the commentary from another direction—to focus attention on some of the details of the commentary which are important to one or both of us. There are many. We shall make a lip-smacking mental meal of only a few.

A few critics have complained, for example, that VN's commentary is too long. We disagree, for there is much about *Onegin* that VN did not say that could have been said. We find it surprising, for example, that he overlooked the obvious connection between his identification of Onegin's name with the Onega River (II:37: also Lensky-Lena, II:220) and the name of another hero he has Englished—Lermontov's Pechorin—Pechora. It seems to us that this literary coincidence (for there is no connection between Pushkin and Lermontov, of course) might even have served as a pretext for a funny little essay on the two literary characters. Think of it: the deviously winding, sluggish, shallow personality of Onegin-Onega as contrasted to the swift, impetuous, deep personality of Pechorin-Pechora. There could have been a few remarks on the Byronic hero and the child of the age. An adept aside on the contemporariness and naturalness of it all. An extraction of social content from artistic form. . . . Truly, this was an opportunity missed.

We are surprised also—especially when we ponderate VN's admiration for all the elegance, euphony and good taste that the dainty mimic prizes higher than truth—that the clever sound effects of the stanza on Rousseau were overlooked. The orchestration of the last six lines (One: XXIV) is perceptibly sibilated, and it is apparent that Pushkin is "hissing" the eloquent French crackbrain: "Russo . . . poniat' . . . Smel chistit' . . . krasnorechivym sumasbrodom . . . Zashchitnik vol'nosti . . . v sem sluchae sovsem..." Certainly this distinct sound system should have been sensed by our sensitive subject in his scrutiny of such succinctly stated disrespect for the sagacious French eccentric. Of course, we appreciate VN's reluctance to disparage writers of great reputation, and certainly Pushkin's arrogance makes for a grim footnote in the history of Russo-French literary relations, but evidence should never be ignored when poetic beauty is at stake.

The commentary on the similarities between Pushkin's lines on the ball and Baratynsky's verse tale *The Ball* (II:110) is lacking in some relevant details. VN might have at least mentioned Pushkin's parody of Baratynsky's verse tale in the ballroom scene of the *Queen of Spades.* In fact, there was a flurry of parodies of the ball theme in the late 1820s and early 1830s. Pushkin's verses on the theme also set off a flurry of serious thematic responses, and we have always liked the poet-hussar Denis Davydov's brief lyric *NN* (1830):

> She entered—like Psyche, a Peri, literal Peri,
> In languor and shyness, expectant and wary,
> And whispers of rapture careen through the hall,
> And witches detest her, and devils taste gall!

22

The quatrain opening—"She entered"—is a clue that Davydov had Pushkin's lines in mind: "He entered. . . ." And oh, bingo! how those pleasing literary echoes do bound around. On the very next page we find VN tracing the hussars at Pushkin's ball to Davydov's 1817 lyric poem *Song of an Old Hussar* (II:112-13).

In one instance we must agree that VN has said all that can be said, and in precisely the way it should have been said. He gives an ontological interpretation of Onegin's motivation for killing Lensky. Critics have always considered the situation ambiguous, and VN explains this ambiguity on the basis of Onegin's dream-like mental state during the duel.. Why did Onegin kill Lensky instead of firing his shot in the air? Because, VN says, his violations of the duelist's etiquette, which have maddened his opponent, leave him no choice. Yet he makes no conscious decision, and Pushkin never attempts to explain his action. Thus he fires first and shoots to kill, which is quite out of character. Edmund Wilson (*NYRB*, July 15, '65, p.5) charges VN with misunderstanding *Onegin* here. In his opinion, Onegin is evil, he seeks revenge on Lensky "for being capable of idealism. . . When he himself is so sterile and empty. . . . "He cannot stand it that Lensky. . . Should be fired by ecstatic emotion." And so on, and so on. "There are no out-of-character actions in *Evgeni [sic!] Onegin*," Wilson concluded.

Alas, poor Edmund. We realize that "credibility of motivation" has become such a mania of modern criticism that it has been transformed from a fleeting literary value into an artistic universal. But to interpret an early nineteenth-century literary work in terms of a twentieth-century shibboleth is, to put it mildly, an anachronism. Pushkin could not have cared so much as one iota whether or not his reader believed his story or found his characters' action credible. Envy, jealousy, hatred, unconscious desire for revenge? Need we point out that der Herr Professor Siggy Heil was not even a leer in his dirty old daddy's eye when Pushkin wrote *Onegin?* Credible action of plot? The plot of *Onegin* is so unimportant that it could probably be turned upside down without upsetting its true literary values: its racing prosody, its stanzaic articulation, its elegant colonnade structure, the balance of the parts, the switches and swerves of the narrative, the digressions, the transitions, the system of subthemes responding to each other in a pleasing inter-play of built-in echoes—all the fireworks and choreography of Pushkin's sacred play.

If we were tempted to seek out motivations beyond the evidence present in the work itself, we would suggest that Onegin's only motivation in shooting Lensky down was his common sense. A bullet in the gut hurts, and as VN has pointed out Onegin has not been so deprived of his reason as to forget he has placed himself before the gun of an enraged former friend—the most dangerous sort of friend, as Lermontov, who *did* misjudge an angry friend in a duel discovered too late. Whatever the somnolent state of his mind during the duel, Onegin was not so stupid to risk death when an ambiguously aimed shot in the other direction could prevent it. And finally, if there are any lingering doubts as to the correctness of VN's interpretation, we suggest an examination of the ambiguous and dream-like confrontation with death in the execution scene of Pushkin's *Captain's Daughter*. The hero of that work experiences the same dream-like inability to make a conscious decision, the same strangely passive reaction to the terror of violent death.

Bowling along now, we take exception to a few random omissions and correct a few minor errors along the way. The expressions of political plight in meteorological terms, for example, are not peculiar to *Onegin* alone (II:188) "Colder than Winter Nicholas Day" became a popular bit of weather reportage right after the First Nicholas became tsar in 1825. Meteorological allusions are found in many letters, and even published literary works, of the time. The custom has not lost a certain relevance to this very day, and one of us Russians just picked up an unmistakably American item: "Colder'n a witch's tit." The comment on the Russian word *pustynia,* which VN defines as "wilderness," "desert," "vast empty spaces," "remote, sparsely populated place, a provincial hole, backwoods, forlorn place, neck of the woods, backwater" (II:224), might very easily have been associated with the first line of Pushkin's *Bronze Horseman:* "Na beregu pustynnyx voln"—"Upon the shore of sparsely populated waves." The name Lila, Lileta relates not only to Batyushkov's shepherdesses (II:416), but also to the student-poet Yazykov's favorite beer-hall bawd. Which gives us a good pretext to pass on a bit of Yazykov's recently discovered *pornografiia:*

> It passed, that golden time,
> When I was hale and quick,
> And when my youthful muses sang
> The conquests of my haughty prick.

24

That stanzaic opening—"It passed"—brings up some literary echo or other, but we fail to recollect it at this magic moment (speak, memory, goddam it, speak!). This might also be the place to slip in a bit of Pushkin's porno, those lines he wrote to commemorate Tatyana's letters:

> Through her chemise a nipple blackens;
> Delightful sight: one titty shows.
> Tatyana holds a crumpled paper,
> For she's beset with stomach throes.

Our translation, we think, shows that it is possible to translate poetry with some hope of doing artistic justice to the original.

But we digress. We continue. Yes, VN, Russian houses still have large casement windows with two sturdy frames, one of which is removed in spring (II:438). The one here was recently removed and we are gazing out on a balmy late-spring day contemplating that marvelous day when, *beyond any doubt:*

> A Russian branch's shadow shall be playing
> Upon the marble of a hand.

In the note on Bürger's ballad *Lenore* (II:152-54), it is not true that Katenin probably knew the work from a French translation. He had good German. We fail to understand, but are not surprised by, VN's preference for the paraphrast Zhukovsky over the literalist Katenin—especially since Katenin was so notorious for laying about with an axe at his critics or anyone else he considered an oaf and an ignoramous, incompetent, as a linguist and scholar, a low-class person and a ridiculous personality. In the same note, or in any of the other notes on Zhukovsky's translation of *Lenore* (II:330-312, 500-501), it might have been mentioned that he not only paraphrased the original twice (as *Lyudmila* and *Svetlana,* from which latter version petty bourgeois fathers in Russia have taken the name of their favorite daughters ever since), but also translated it (as *Lenora).* Two outright errors! The day of Yazykov's first collected poems is 1834, not 1824 (II:24), and Vasily Davydov was Denis's cousin, not his brother (III:248).

Turning to another aspect of VN's commentary, we indulge in a few comments on word play. We wonder, for example, why it has never occurred to punsters to pronounce Onegin's name is logical English: "one gin." That note on the rhyme *Evgenii-genii* (II:37) reminds us of the notorious translation of the phrase *genial'nyi*

Stalin as "the genial Stalin," the point being, of course, that Russian has an adjective for the word "genius" where English does not and the Russian word seems similar to the English word "genial" but of course we don't have to explain that. VN likes to play with names (so we have been told), and his commentary contains a Chateaubyronic Tolstoevsky—the latter a play on the famous name Gogolevsky. Which reminds us of Kornei Chukovsky's dub for Balmont's exotic translation of Shelley—Shelmont, and of course that brings up the beloved pen-name Korneichuk. We shall resist following Chukovsky's lead by dubbing VN's translation of Pushkin as Nabushkin, of worse yet Nabegin, especially since our non-Russian readers would not be able to appreciate the latter playful attack. Shall we go on? There is VN's Van and Ada Veen's ancestor Prince Zemsky. (We bow to our non-Russian readers Prince *(kniaz')* Vyazemsky, Pushkin's earthy friend.) And then there is Khuyza Freyda, VN's favorite Georgian poet.

Since he mentions it twice, we assume VN must be intrigued by the only single-syllable adjective in the Russian language— "zloi," meaning "mean," "wicked," "evil," "spiteful," as in *Evgenii's zloi genii.* We would like to add another to the language— *vnoi,* as in *vnoi roman,* rhymes with that other gem *liuboi roman,* "Love Story" (II, 278). The word goes well with the Russian exclamation *zloi ty!*—"You're a mean SOB!" *Vnoi ty!* would thus be "You're a mean VNOB!" The verb would be *vnovat',* as in "He VN-ed his critics." The noun would be *van,* defined as "a nattering nabobokov of negativism." As a pretext for filling out the rest of this short paragraph, we would like to play with two more word games. For the first, we would like to dub that omitted stanza describing the night of Tatyana's letter "the nocturnal omission." As for the second, we would like to report a peculiarly Leningradian pun. One of VN's fellow specialists here (a sort of Pushkinist, that is) once purchased a country estate designed in a popular Petersburg style. His colleagues promptly dubbed it *Empir vo vremia chumy,* a play on the Russian title of Pushkin's minor tragedy *Pir vo vremia chumy—The Feast During the Plague.*

As is also well known, VN has a weakness for what he calls "howlers"—those gaffes of translation born out of a too brisk consultation with dictionary, or from no consultation at all. The true howler is thus a joint product of ignorance and self-assurance. An example of a howler is the already mentioned *genial'nyi Stalin.*

Another example is the time an American student looked for the verb "to cross" and found the verb "to cross o.s.," this leading him to a Russian version of the American proverb, "Don't cross yourself by means of a bridge until you come to it." Of course, it can be imagined what Lermontov did with the verse line "Had we never loved so kindly" when he confused the English word "kindly" with the German word "Kindlich." Or what one Russian translator of American black poetry did with the term "black Maria." Or what happened when another Russian translator consulted an American slang dictionary to deal with the British expression "Keep your pecker up!"

But now that we have scrambled through our studies, which were random in matter and in manner, it is time for us to conclude. Once again we must slip off into the ethereal green mists of Petersburg and vanish into the vn-th dimension of our infinite city's ever-expanding concentric circles surrounded by many-chimneyed factories and dressed in soot eternal. We have pursued our two heroes through these pallid white-night streets, down Millionaya, across Dvotsovaya, up Nevsky, over Morskaya, past St. Isaac's, the Synod, the *Kumir* . . . . Now we've lagged behind, now we've scurried on ahead, now we've caught them up, loitered parodistically as they stood chatting, leaning nonchalantly on the parapet, gazing absently across the Neva's opaque luminescence. And that's good, say we, that's damn good, we say.

D. Barton Johnson

CONTRASTIVE PHONOAESTHETICS
or
WHY NABOKOV GAVE UP TRANSLATING
POETRY AS POETRY

INTRODUCTION[1]

This essay is the story of a failure. I am interested in a real, but somewhat nebulous, area that I call contrastive phonostylistics. Phonostylistics, in the sense that I use it, deals with sound patterning in artistic writing—of which poetry is the most striking representative. Sound patterning in poetry, although of some interest in itself, becomes of cardinal import when taken in conjunction with meaning. To me, at least, the essence of poetry lies in the close interlocking of sound and meaning. Words with certain kinds of sounds and sound sequences strike the reader-auditor as being peculiarly appropriate to their meaning. Most poetry readers have an instinctive feeling for example, that the high, bright front vowel sounds, such as [iy] and [ey], are expressive of bright, happy moods, whereas low back vowel sounds, such as [o] and [a], evoke more somber emotions. As an example one might cite the line, "Forlorn! The very word is like a bell."—(with the understanding that a low-pitched tolling bell is meant). There can be no question of the close "fit" between sound and sense here. The interconnections of sound and sense are, of course, much more extensive and elaborate than what has been suggested by this example. Any informed poetry reader with an analytic bent will intuitively note in a given poem particular illustrations of such interconnections. Attempts to formalize these intuitions and set them on a firm theoretical basis have not met with much success. Nonetheless, at least in the case of single poems, the game is certainly worth the candle— if for no other reason than that it is fun and occasionally yields flashes of insight. Why does the poem work? Why are certain parts effective and others ineffective? What are the formal phonostylistic correlates of these successes and failures? The results of such an analysis might be called a phonoaesthetic grammar of the poem.

The translation of poetry is notoriously difficult—so much so that one of the triter definitions of poetry explains it as "That which is lost in translation." The truth of this cliche varies with the kind of poetry being translated. Poetry in which aphorism or metaphor is predominant may survive translation quite well. The hackneyed maxim is much more true as it concerns poetry in which the phonoaesthetic element is preeminent. The interlocking of sound and sense is, at least beyond the most primitive level, probably language specific. The English "forlorn" with its concentration of sonorous liquid consonants and low labialized vowels, has a certain phonetic resonance reinforcing its meaning. These supporting phonetic qualities are conspicuously lacking in one of its Russian counterparts *pokinutyj.* How does *"Pokinutyj!* The very word is like a bell." strike you?—or, to be a bit more fair, *"Pokinutyj! Slovo samo—kak kolokol."* A bit better, but still a poetic disaster. All this is by way convincing us of something we know already. Translating poetry is very difficult and is made even more so by the language specific nature of the interworking of sound and meaning. Nevertheless, poetry is translated—rarely by the author, more usually by a translator, and occasionally by a translator in conjunction with a poet. A number of intruding factors must be considered at this point. Does the author know the second language well enough to judge the translation? Usually not. Does the translator really understand the poem? Is he aware of the sound/meaning interplay; Is his command of his native tongue adequate to the task, i.e., is he as gifted a wordsmith in his own language as the poet of the original is in his own? If a second poet is involved, has the translator fully conveyed all aspects of the original to him? Is he a good poet? And so on. All of these reservations might be lumped under the heading "The Translator as Traducer." In almost every case, when we read a translated poem we are responding to and evaluating something quite different from the original poem. Hence, a contrastive phonoaesthetic study of most translated poems and their originals is a futile exercise.

I am interested in trying to establish the correspondence, if any, between the phonoaesthetic systems of Russian and English. For such an undertaking, a single piece of content, a poem, must be examined in its phonetic realization in each of the two languages. Are the sound/sense interlockings of the original conveyed in the translation? Sometimes? Occasionally? Never? Are the association of certain sound patterns and certain types of mood or meaning the same or different in the two texts? If different, is the correspondence consistent? The translator stands as a barrier to a meaningful examination of any of these problems. There is only one situation in which the variables introduced by the translator can be held constant. The condition that must be met is that the poet must be a master stylist in both the language of the original and the language of the translation. If this situation prevails, then and only then can we assume that the phonoaesthetic correspondences or non-correspondences which we find may be due to differences in the internal resources of the respective languages rather than to the vagaries of the translator.

Nabokov presents such a rare case. He is unquestionably a master of both Russian and English and has translated some of his own work from Russian into English and vice-versa. As you know, Nabokov has in the last twenty years undergone a change of philosophy on translation. Since most of his more recent translation work (most conspicuously the *Onegin* translation) has been in the literalist morpheme-by-morpheme vein, it was necessary to find something in which poetry is translated as poetry.

The sonnet which I have chosen is the closing paragraph of Nabokov's last Russian novel—*Dar "The Gift"* (1935-1937). The English version of the novel was published in 1962 and, although the translation was done by Michael Scammell, Nabokov notes in the foreword that he himself did the "...various poems and bits of poems scattered throughout the book."

By way of preliminary comment we might note that this translation starts at an even more severe disadvantage than most—quite apart from technical poetic considerations. The Russian poem exists against the background of the closing stanzas of Pushkin's *Evgeny Onegin,* which it parallels in both form and meaning. Thus the Nabokov sonnet evokes an immediate and powerful resonance in every Russian reader. The English translation exists chiefly within the context of Nabokov's novel and lacks this much more profound cultural setting in the mind of the reader. Thus the English translation inevitably and unavoidably suffers from what we might call "poetic culture shock"—to recoin a phrase.

The basic structure of the *Onegin* stanza is three quatrains plus a concluding couplet. Thus the quatrain is the basic poetic unit or framework in that most of the poetic effects are internal to that unit. It is largely, but not entirely, self-contained as a formal unit and will serve as the focal point of much of our discussion.

ANALYSIS

The opening sentence, [prashcháj-zhykn'íga]!,and its English counterpart, /gud-bay, may buk/!, already provides food for thought. Why not "Farewell" instead of "Goodby?" "Farewell" is stylistically certainly more closely equivalent to *proshchaj* than is "goodby" and is no less suitable from the point of view of mettrics since both words are iambs. In this case, assonance and allit-eration have conspired to force the choice of the more prosaic "goodby." The Russian line is relatively spare in its internal sound patterning: [shch], [j], [zh] with a faint feeling of assonance through the recurring /a/'s. The English /gud-bay/ (as opposed to "farewell") permits a much richer sound mix within the context of the sen-tence. The vocalic pattern of /u/ /ay/–/ay/ /u/ displays an envelop-ment of the two /ay/'s by the /u/'s. The two iambs are auditory mirror images of each other. This pattern is duplicated and inten-sified in the adjacent consonants: /gud-/ is to /buk/ as /-bay/ is to /may/. In terms of sound classes, /gud-/ and /buk/, with their re-spective initial and final velars, are near inversions of each other and they envelope the rhyming labial syllables /-bay/–/may/. One further point contributing to the choice of /gud-bay/ is that of the identity of the stressed vowels in the Russian and English [-shcháj] and [-bay]. The only other point of phonetic similarity between the two is the velar /k/ of /buk/, which echoes the two velars of /kn'íga/. Thus in the short sentence at hand (as in the poem as a whole), it is clear that the internal phonetic qualities of the English line outweigh any attempt to duplicate the sound effects of the Russian.

The remainder of the first line of the original—/dl'a vi-d'én'ij/ is only weakly linked to the earlier part in its sound structure by the repetition of the /i/ of /kniga/ in /v'id'en'ij/. The /e/ of the rhyme syllable stands alone in the line not echoing any prior oc-currence. The counterpart English, on the other hand, displays both striking internal assonance and strong phonetic ties to the first half of the line. Internally, the English (in contrast to the Rus-sian /a/ /a/-/i/ /e/) shows /ay/ /oh/-/u/ /ay/ closely paralleling the earlier /u/ /ay/ /ay/ /u/ in its symmetry and externally reevokes the dominant /ay/ sound of the first sentence, thus phonetically bridging the gap between the two sense units.

Before proceeding to any examination of the comparative po-etics of the second sentence, a word is in order about the semantic correspondence of the two lines "Dlia vidénij otsróchki smértnoj tózhe nét" and "Like mortal eyes, imagined ones must close some day." There are two points to be made here. The general sense of the Russian text which we might paraphrase as "There is no deferment of death" is replaced in the English by the at once more concrete and yet metaphorical "eyes must close." At first one might assume that this metonymic substitution is due to the metrical exigencies of translation, but we shall see that this is done consistently throughout the English text. The second point concerns the implicit comparison suggested in the Russian text, but made overt in the translation. Both the Russian and the English texts say "There is no deferment of death for fictive beings." The single Russian word "tozhe" implies the comparison "Just as there is no such deferment for real beings." The English text makes the inferred comparison explicit in its phrase "Like mortal eyes." As in the foregoing case, the English with its spelled out comparison is more concrete.

The second line [at-sróch-ki sm'ért-naj tó-zhi net] is poetically a strong one displaying an especially effective correspondence of sound and sense. In terms of assonance, the line falls into two matching reinforcing halves, i.e.,

    1st half   /a/ /ó/ - /i/ /é/
    2nd half   /a/ /o/ - /i/ /e/

The line which speaks of the deferment of death or continuance of life is built on a series of continuant consonants (/s, ch, s, j, zh/), but ends abruptly with a denial of continuation reflected semantically by /n'et/ and phonetically by the consonant stop /t/, which gives an air of finality to the sentence, especially following the sequence of continuant consonants. This interpretation of the interlocking of sound and sense may seem strained at first glance, but the impression is strengthened by comparison with the English translation, which likewise has an abundance of continuant sibilants "imagined ones must close some day." The English sentence, which unlike the Russian is positive in its formulation, terminates in a vowel glide rather than the abrupt stop of /n'et/. The glide is supported semantically by the hazy indefinite "someday," which lacks any counterpart in the Russian. The continuant effect of the sibilants is enhanced by the repeated nasal continuants /n/ and /m/, whereas the latter labial is obtrusively reinforced by the stressed labialized complex vowel nucleus of /klowz/.

The third line /s-ka-l'én pad-n'í-m'it-sa jivgénij/ is the stanza's only specific reference to the object (and source) of Nabokov's tribute to Pushkin. Phonetically the line is built upon the stressed syllable sequence /l'en/ - /n'im/ - /g'en'/ and also relies (as did Pushkin) on the euphonious characteristics of /jiv-ge-nij/ with its inverted sequences of /jiv/ and /n'ij/ encompassing the stressed syllable. Allowing for the syntactic transpositions, the English is a model translation. The reasons for the substitution of *Onegin* for /jivg'en'-ij/ are fairly obvious. For one, the English form of /jivgén'ij/, Eugene, is a syllable shorter and for the other, the general English reader would have even less chance of recognizing an allusion to Eugene than he might to *Onegin*.

The concluding line of the first Russian quatrain up to the final iamb makes its phonetic effect by the succession of /a/'s framed by the surrounding dental consonants. The fifth and sixth syllables constitute an internal grammatical rhyme with the same syllables in the preceding line, i.e., /ji-tsa/ and /m'i-tsa/. Also adding to the effect here, I think, is the soft blurry sequence /l'a-ji/ inset amidst the hard opening and closing iambs /na/, /ud/, and /pa-et/. This phonetic phenomenon accords well with the misty remoteness evoked by the root /dal'/—one of the favorite words of Russian romantic poetry of the early nineteenth century. In this line as in its rhyme mate, line 2, the open syllable flow of the line /na-u-da-l'a-ji-tsa/ is sharply cut off by the dental stop of /pa-et/.

The English line is vocalically more diverse, but this impression is somewhat overcome by the recurrence of the stressed /ey/ in syllables four and eight. As in line two, the sibilant sequence (/z, s, z/) tapers off into the final stressed vowel glide /ey/ in contrast to the more final note of /paét/ in the Russian. Also worthy of remark here is the internal rhyme of /strowlz/ and /klowz/ in the sixth syllable of lines two and four respectively. The choice of "strolls away" in the face of the Russian /udal' ajitsa/ is also of interest. For one thing, it seems to reflect a consistent preference for more specific meanings in the English text as compared to the Russian. Phonetically, /strowlz/ with its long vowel glide very well conveys the slow leisurely sense evoked by /udal'ájitsa/. Further, while /udal'ájitsa/ represents a soft phonetic intrusion into the somewhat abrupt feel of the Russian line, the English /strowlz away/ is of a piece with the much more flowing feeling of the English line.

Finally, a word about the overall rhyme pattern in this first quatrain of the Russian and its English counterpart. The initial rhyme set of the Russian consists of the beautifully matching /v'id'én'ij/ and /jivg'én'ij/, with their soft feminine endings trailing off after the stressed syllable. The abrupt sentence final masculine rhymes /n'et/ and /pa-et/ of line 2 and 4 stand in vivid contrast to them and serve as highly effective contrastive elements which express negation and finality, both phonetically and semantically. The sound quality of the English end-rhyme carries, it seems to me, quite another flavor. None of the rhyme words either semantically or phonetically convey abrupt finality. It is also noteworthy that the English sentence of line two is positive in contrast to the Russian original. Thus the English reader will, I think, enter the second quatrain with a less definite feeling of the demise of the poet's creatures. In semantic support of this phonoaesthetic assertion we need only point to the final "net" of line two in contrast to the English "some day."

Quatrain I sets the theme. The second and third quatrains continue and develop that theme. We noted the phonosemantic finality of the preceding Russian quatrain. The most casual reading of the second quatrain cannot but impress one with an overwhelming impression of continuant sibilants.

/i fs'ó z slúx n'i mo — zit srá zu/
/ras stát sa smú — zi kaj, ras ská zu/
/dát za mir ét   ...   sud bá samá/
/ji's'ó zv'i n'it,.../

The lingering sibilants are a phonetically highly effective expression of the central idea of the quatrain, i.e., continuation of the lives of fictional characters beyond the printed page. This alliterative interlocking of sound and sense forms a framework for a rhyme pattern much richer than that required for the quatrain. The usual pattern for the second quatrain of the *Onegin* stanza is AA bb (CC dd within the context of the whole stanza). This particular quatrain, however, shows, in addition, a striking and consistent internal rhyme pattern at midline. Observe:

1.	i	fs'ó	zi	slúx	a
2.	n'i	mó	zit	sr ázu	b
3.	ras	st	át	sa smú(z)	a
4.	zi	kaj	ras	sk ázu	b
5.	d át	za	m'i	r'ét.	c

6.	s ud'	bá	sa	má	d
7.	j i	s'ó	zv'i	n'it	c
8.	i	dl'a	u	má	d

The iambic tetrameter quatrain can be restructured into an eight line group in iambic dimeter with the new rhyme pattern abab, cdcd. Within this new tighter scheme the stressed second syllable of the first foot more palpably displays the striking repetition:

1.	i	fs'ó	zi
2.	n'i	mó	zit
3.	ji	s'ó	zvi

Also note that the proposed distribution of the line based on the internal as well as the external rhyme pattern more closely coincides with the natural syntactic and semantic segmentation of the passage. /Za-m'i-r'et'/ and /zv'i-n'it/ both become line final as well as clause final, thus eliminating the (to me at least) disruptive caesuras in the second and fourth lines. The last dimeter of the reformulated quatrain is a run-on line which signals a transition in both sound and sense to the next quatrain. Particularly noteworthy in this transition function is the repetition of the stressed /má/ syllables of /u-ma/ at the end of the second quatrain and in the first stressed syllable of /vn'i-ma-til'-na-va/ at the start of the new quatrain.

The English of the second quatrain is a pale reflection of the Russian original. Casual inspection reveals two serious lapses—one metrical and one stylistic. Perhaps it is simply that Nabokov and I speak different dialects of English, but the "right now" at the end of line one seems to me to be deplorable. Granted that it probably exists mostly to fill out the line (as does the /srazu/ of the Russian text), but it is of a very different lexical level from the rest of the section and, for me at least, it grates badly. The second lapse is perhaps more serious. One of the most fundamental rules of iambic accentual-syllabic verse is that the final foot of a line must not deviate from the iambic pattern. The pattern must be _ ́ as in "of fate," not trochaic, as in "vibrate," which is what we unhappily find in line four. (The choice is to exercise poetic license and give final stress—/vaybréyt/.)

35

The sibilant continuants, which form the skeleton of the Russian text, are supplanted in the English version by the /t/ sound which gives quite a different effect.

The rich internal rhyme pattern of the Russian is not at all in evidence. The only internal pattern to catch the ear is the refrain of the "tale," "fade," and "fate" of line three. This phonetic recurrence plays an important role in establishing a bond between the different sense and syntactic units separated by the caesura in the middle of line three. More remotely it affords an echo of the "some day/ away" rhyme of the first quatrain and the "vibrate" concluding the second quatrain.

Although the translation is admirably accurate except for the not undesirable extension of the quatrain's message to coincide with its formal termination, there are some points worth comment. Here again we find a Russian term of general meaning /slux/ replaced by a more specific (but metaphorically used) English word—ears.   /Sud'ba/ grows into "the *chords* of fate," in which the "chords" pick up and echo the "music" of line two. The concise and elegant /jishchó zvenít/ becomes the cumbersome "continues to vibrate."

The third Russian quatrain further develops the stanza theme but lacks the intricate internal rhyme pattern of the foregoing section. The only pattern that I note for this quatrain as a whole is the not very significant fact that the first and last vowels of each line are identical. Only /i/ and /a/ occur in these two positions and in syllables three, four, and five. With a single exception, only syllables two and six show other vowel sounds. Of the individual lines, the third is phonetically the most striking with its recurrent /pra-dl'on-nij/. The /a/ of /pr'i-zrak/ also seems to foreshadow the line final ending of /bi-t'i-já/. The fourth line begins a pattern of sibilant alliteration (/s'/, /j/, /z/, /ch/, /s/, /c/) that continues to the end of the poem and nicely parallels the continued existence of the fictional characters beyond the last pages of the book.

The English does not attempt to reproduce the sound effect of the Russian. The opening line with its "obstruction" and "sage" for *granicy* and *um vnimatel'nyj* seems to be a case where the requirements of meter and rhyme have forced some unhappy choices on the translator.* If the first two lines of both the original and the translation strike the reader as indifferent, the

---

* Here again we note the English has replaced the intangible Russian *um* with the concrete English *sage*.

final two lines of the two texts represent a significant success. Due to the very different grammatical structure of the two languages, a close one-to-one translation of the Russian is impossible. If nothing else, consider the problem of translating *prodlyónnyj prízrak sinéet.*

Prodlyónnyj is translated by "extend" as *prizrak* is by "shadows." From the point of view of phonoaesthetic equivalences, however, the match is more nearly between *prodlyónnyj* and *shadows.* A similar, but somewhat weaker, case can be made for "world" which semantically translates *bytija* but the sound equivalent is *prizrak.* (I could argue this on the shared R sound but it seems too strained.) Continuing our argument, the phonoaesthetic correspondent or translation to *prodlyónnyj prízrak* is "shadows of my world." This suggestion is, of course, beyond proof but it would be interesting to know if it corresponds to the intuition of the bilingual reader.

The last line of the English is also successful as a translation of a structurally difficult Russian passage. The sense of the verb *sinéet* "shows blue," which lacks a direct English equivalent, is shifted to the translation of the colorless Russian *chertoj* "limit" to fuse with it into the "skyline" of the English text. The blended word /skaylayn/ also functions as the phonetic centerpiece of the line with its iterated /ay/ bridging syllables four and five. The line initial /b/ and final initial /p/ also contribute their effect while the /-yahnd/ of /biyyahnd/ phonetically, as well as semantically, continues the /-end/ of /ekstend/. The English quatrain has in translation acquired a pair of verbs which while lacking in the original add a certain distant alliteration to the new text—/egzists/ and /ekstend/.

The concluding couplet of the original stanza stands out sharply against the phonetic background of the three quatrains. All four of the stressed vowels are /a/ and this sound accounts for all of the 16 syllabics, while the remaining five are all /i/. Linquists sometimes speak of maximal vowels or maximal consonants. This reflects the fact that some vowels are more vocalic than others depending the energy input compared to the energy output. In these terms /a/ is more vocalic than /i/, which is close to the consonants in its degree of closure—specifically to /j/, the most vocalic and least consonantal of the consonants. /K/ is the most consonantal consonant. Thus /k/ and /a/ represent points of maximum contrast in the Russian sound system. It is thanks to this contrast that the final couplet is so forceful (as compared to the foregoing) for it is built on the opposition of these two maximally opposed sounds.

/*kak* záv-tra-shn'i-ji a-bla-ká /
/i n'i *kan*-chá - ji-tsa stra-*ká*./

In the first line we note the internal rhyme sequence /kak/ and /blak/ and the assonance sequence /zav/, /tra/, /-bla/. The second line interposes an alliterative series of voiceless sibilants (/ch/, /s/, /s/) between the /ka/ of *kanchajitsa* and of *straka.* It is also of interest that syllables five through eight share the same vowels in both lines. Finally, we observed in the first quatrain the phonoaesthetic effect of ending a negative sentence with a stop. The closing line represents a negated negation—/n'i kan-chá-ji-tsa straka/—the line does not end, i.e., it continues. The sonnet ends with a maximally closed consonant followed by the maximal continuant—the stressed vowel /a/. The negative sentences of the first quatrain ended in the closed syllables /n'et/ and /pa-et/ while the final positive line of the poem ends with the open continuing syllable in /a/. It is perhaps too far-fetched to suggest a parallel between the high energy stop /k/ with its continuant /a/ and the end of the work of art with the continued life of its characters?

The English is both a poor shadow of the Russian and a pallid thing in its own right. The internal harmony of the first line consists of a sequence of labial consonants /b/-/m/-/m/ in conjunction with a number of labialized complex nuclei /uw/, /ah/, /ow/, /oh/. The final line faintly echoes its Russian source with the alliteration of /duz/ and /freyz/. In contrast to the Russian the lines fail to harmonize with each other or to contrast with the earlier sections of the poem.

CONCLUDING COMMENTS

Should we call the translation a success or a failure? From the point of view of information content the translation is certainly admirable. Syntactically—likewise. With two or three exceptions the English syntax matches the Russian almost metrical foot for metrical foot. In terms of meter the correspondence is good (excepting /váybreyt/) and noting the restriction of the English to masculine only lines. The rhyme pattern is faultless. Yet the English text is clearly a weak poem in its own right and, I think, unsuccessful as a translation. It generally neither succeeds in transplanting the phonoaesthetic effects of the original nor in supplanting them with parallel (but not similar) effects of its own as dictated by the key English morpheme. It is precisely in these areas of sound patterning and sound/sense interplay that the translation fails.

At the beginning of our discussion we suggested that *inter alia* poetry translation probably fails because of the variables introduced by the translator. If only a bilingual poet translator of equal brilliance in both languages could be found, perhaps the phonoaesthetic sense/sound units might somehow be conveyed from one text to another. Nabokov probably comes as close to meeting our ideal of the virtuoso poet-translator as we are ever likely to see; and although there are strikingly successful points, he does not on the whole succeed. We can, I think, draw one further generalization from our examination of the translation. The phonoaesthetic density of the translation is vastly inferior to that of the original. Such effects found in the translation are indigenous to the English text—not inspired by those of the Russian. Almost no direct correspondences can be demonstrated.

The cautious reader may pause here. Perhaps one language is inherently richer in its potentialities for sound patterning. Or perhaps Nabokov's English poetry style is not on a level with his English prose. I started my research for this essay using a very different set of texts in which the original language was English. The opening chapter of Nabokov's *Lolita* is in metered prose and can only be described as a stylistic *tour de force.* Close inspection of the first paragraph shows an intricate pattern of alliterations which are based on the consonants of the name Lolita. In Nabokov's own Russian translation not only are these effects lost but no effort is made to duplicate and/or parallel them. The Russian is flat and prosaic. Thus it is not the direction of translation, Russian to English or English to Russian, that is responsible for the unhappy result. Phonoaesthetic effects are impossible of systematic transfer from one language to another. The extent to which phonostylistic and phonoaesthetic effects are responsible for our overall impression of style is a good index of how badly a translation (even by our ideal translator) is apt to fail. For a number of years Nabokov has been a forceful advocate of what he calls the "servile path" in translation, i.e., absolute literal translation. Our investigation demonstrates at least one of the reasons for this conversion. Indeed, if one of the greatest stylists of modern literature, a man bilingual from earliest

	1	2	3	4	5	6	7	8	
1.	Про- Good-	щай by	же my	кни- book!	га! Like	Для mor-	ви- tal-	ден- eyes,	ии
2.	От- I-	сроч- mag-	ки ined	смерт- ones	ной must	то- close	же some	нет. day.	
3.	Ско- O-	лен ne-	под- gin	ни- from	мет- his	ся knees	Ев- will	ген- rise—	ий--
4.	Но But	у- his	да- cre-	ля- a-	ет- tor	ся strolls	по- a-	эт. way.	
5.	И And	все yet	же the	слух ear	не can-	мо- not	жет right	сра- now	зу
6.	Рас- Part	стать-ся with	с the	му- mu-	зы- sic	кой, рас- and	ска- al-	зу low	зу
7.	Дать The	за- tale	ме- to	реть; fade;	судь-ба the	са- clouds	ма of	fate	
8.	Е It-	ще self	зве- con-	нит, tin-	и ue	для to	у- vi-	ма brate;	
9.	Вни- And	ма- no	тель- ob-	но- struc-	го tion	нет for	гра- the	ни- sage	цы
10.	Там, где Ex- ists	по- where	ста- I	вил have	точ- put	ку the	я: end.		
11.	Прод- The	лен- sha-	ный dows	при-зрак of	my	бы- world	ти- ex-	я: tend	
12.	Си- Be-	не- yond	ет the	за sky-	чер- line	той of	стра- the	ни- page,	цы
13.	Как Blue	зав- as	траш- to-	ни- mor-	е row's	об- morn-	ла- ing-	ка, haze—	
14.	И Nor	не does	кон- this	ча- ter-	ет- min-	ся ate	стро- the	ка. phrase.	

childhood, cannot successfully translate his own poetry, then who can?

[1]Phonetic and/or phonemic transcription is necessary for an accurate analysis of poetic sound patterning due to the considerable gap between Russian spelling (or its transliteration) and the actual pronunciation of a text. The same holds for English. Since some of the specialized type needed for such transcription is not available for this book, it has been kept to a minimum. Where its use was necessary, unavailable symbols were replaced by other characters affording a somewhat peculiar but adequate transcription.

For the convenience of the reader, the Russian and English texts of the poem are given in parallel syllable against syllable.

Ludmila A. Foster

NABOKOV IN RUSSIAN EMIGRE CRITICISM

Even before his return from Cambridge University to Berlin in 1923, Vladimir Vladimirovich Nabokov started publishing poetry in the Russian émigré press in Berlin and Paris. For example, three of his poems were printed, under the pseudonym V. Sirin which he used until World War II, in the first "thick journal," *The Future Russia (Griadushchaia Rossiia,* Paris), which folded in 1920 after the publication of only two issues. After Nabokov turned to prose, over a period of twenty years his serialized novels (with the exception of the first two) and his short stories appeared in the periodical press, primarily in journals, before they were published in book form, although some of his short stories and many poems were also printed in newspapers. His two major plays were published in journals and never appeared in book form.

In this article I shall survey the reaction of Russian émigré critics to Nabokov. My survey, which is based on the *Bibliography of Russian Emigré Literature, 1918-1968,*[1] will include reviews and articles published in Russian in the émigré journals or included in books; newspaper criticism, erudite as some of it has been, will remain outside the scope of this study. To avoid "cutting a bilingual author in two," to borrow a phrase from Professor Wiktor Weintraub's recent paper,[2] I shall proceed chronologically, discussing the reactions of the critics to Nabokov's Russian works, as well as to his English writings.

Nabokov's first books were translations of Romain Rolland's satiric novel *Colas Breugnon (Nikolka Persik,* Berlin, 1922)[3] and Lewis Carroll's famous *Alice in Wonderland (Asia v strane chudes,* Berlin, 1923). They did not elicit any comment from the critics. His first two collections of poetry, *Gornii put' (The Empyrean Path)* and *Grozd' (The Cluster,* both Berlin, 1923), were summarily dismissed in the Berlin bibliographic journal, *Novaia russkaia kniga (New Russian Book,* No. 1 and No. 5 / 6), as "a boring book" and "a very boring book" respectively. The reviewers accused Nabokov of repeating in form the worn-out cliches of nineteenth century Russian poetry, and of limiting his themes to petty details ("melochi").

Every major émigré journal, however, reviewed his first novel,

Mashen'ka (Mary, Berlin, 1926). Mikhail Osorgin, himself a writer and a publicist, wrote in the prominent Paris *Sovremennye zapiski (Contemporary Notes,* henceforth designated by SZ, 1926, No. 28) that Nabokov ably described the émigré milieu ("byt"), with rare simplicity, and in good literary Russian, in spite of some unsuccessful expressions. After retelling the plot of *Mashen'-ka,* and observing that the positive, strong hero was not convincing, Osorgin welcomed the absence of political and civic themes in the novel. The eminent literary scholar, Konstantin Mochul'sky, writing in the Paris *Zveno (The Link,* 1926, No. 168), discussed the two stylistic levels of the novel, one of which presents the pitiful reality, the other—the beautiful dream world of the past. Nabokov did not succeed in creating a strong and significant hero and because of that the novel does not evoke the feeling of tragedy. Although Nabokov writes with a "literary ability," the book reads without any excitement. Another critic, N. M. P-k (possibly Mel'nikova-Papoushek) in the Prague *Volia Rossii (Russia's Freedom,* 1926, No. 5) praised Nabokov's intention to elucidate the psychological aspects of the hero and of the plot, but concluded that this intention was poorly carried out, perhaps due to the lack of experience on the part of the young author. In the Brussels *Blagonamerennyi (The Well-Intentioned,* 1926, No. 1), A. (today Archbishop John of San Francisco) also spoke of the human depth ("glub' cheloveka") towards which the author's attention and love were directed. Saying that the types were not successfully created, A. was in general quite enthusiastic. He praised the absence of action and of a movie-type plot, and placed Nabokov within the Dostoevsky tradition of the "reality of the spirit."

Korol', dama, valet (King, Queen, Knave, Berlin, 1928) with its German heroes evoked Mikhail Tsetlin's reflections in SZ (1928, No. 37) on the difficulty of being an émigré writer in a foreign country. The main interest of the novel is not in its plot, but in the way the author so artfully presents the automatism, the "soulless-ness" of contemporary people. The poetics of the big city remind Tsetlin of Dostoevsky's and Bunin's (the story "Petlistye ushi") Petersburg. The striving towards expressiveness at any cost makes the novel definitely an experiment in literary expressionism, in the fashion of Leonid Andreev.

In reviewing also in SZ (1930, No. 42) the short story and

poetry collection, *Vozvrashchenie Chorba (The Return of Chorb,* Berlin, 1930), Tsetlin wrote that because Nabokov's work was so much outside of the Russian literary tradition, critics tended to search for foreign influences. The intensity of emotion in the stories fascinates the reader, but they are somewhat weaker and more artificial than the novels. Tsetlin repeated his opinion and elaborated upon Nabokov's similarity to Leonid Andreev, who also showed a predilection for life's tragic ugliness. G. Kh. (G. D. Khokhlov) in *Volia Rosii* (1930, No. 2) saw Nabokov's departure from the Russian tradition specifically in that Nabokov did not attempt to write "as in reality" ("chtoby bylo kak nastoiashchee") and that the personality of the author and his artistic devices are obtrusive. Both reviewers agreed that the poems in the collection were worse than the prose.

The *Defense (Zashchita Luzhina)* was the first of six novels to be serialized in the SZ. When it was published in a separate edition (Berlin, 1930), Al. Novik (another pseudonym of G. D. Khokhlov) maintained in SZ (1931, No. 45) that the convincing image of Luzhin as a "living person," made the novel Nabokov's biggest success. The description of his childhood is given with an unerring vision and completely nontraditionally; in Russian literature there had never been such a childhood. Khokhlov was the first to note that the chess game was a form of artistic creativity for Nabokov's hero. This art had in the end "drained" Luzhin's soul.

The Paris literary journal *Numbers (Chisla),* which welcomed many young writers and which was not averse to modernism, began to appear in 1930. Why this journal from its very beginning until its end was hostile to Nabokov, who qualified on both counts, has remained a mystery to me.[4] In the first issue, Georgy Ivanov, the dean of Russian poets abroad, wrote a survey article, discussing all of Nabokov's then-published work. Actually, there was no objective or critical discussion, but only a personal attack. Ivanov was merciless and rude, labelling Nabokov not only an "imitator" of cheap French and German bulk literature, but also a "literary impostor" and a pushy, banal journalist who was merely technically deft. "Nobody has written like that in Russian" commented Ivanov about *The Defense.*

Ivanov was immediately answered by Professors Gleb Struve

and Nikolai Andreev. Struve, also surveying Nabokov's work to date, wrote in the Paris newspaper *Rossiia i slavianstvo (Russia and Slavdom*—the only exception to journal articles cited in this survey, May 17, 1930) that Nabokov was the biggest gift of the emigration to Russian Literature. Nabokov depicted realia in a totally new way; behind the familiar world he revealed an illusory, one-dimensional existence. In this manner of description Nabokov did not imitate either Russian or foreign writers. Defending Nabokov against accusations of "un-Russianness," Struve admitted only one feature of Nabokov's which he considered outside the Russian literary tradition: the absence of love for man, of pity, and of positive characters. Professor Andreev's article was published in *Nov' (Virgin Soil,* October, 1930) a Tallin journal for young writers.[5] Calling Nabokov the most "whole" ("tsel'-nyi") and interesting representative of the new Russian prose, Andreev underscored Nabokov's success in synthesizing Russian literary tradition with Western innovations, and in combining Russian concern for psychology and Western fascination with plot and perfection of form. In his survey he gave a detailed analysis of each book, discussing its poetics in a scholarly fashion.

Even though Nabokov's next novel, *Podvig (Glory,* Paris, 1932) portrayed a Russian émigré milieu, Mikhail Tsetlin in SZ (1933, No. 51) continued to speak of the novel's "peculiarity" against the background of the Russian literary tradition. In an amusing way, forgetting that he himself had done so, Tsetlin complained that "someone had compared Nabokov to Leonid Andreev," a poor comparison, since Andreev's ideas, soul searchings, and problems provided ample material for the critics, while Nabokov would probably never become a favorite with the critics. While admitting the significance of Nabokov's grasp of memory, his original vision, and his style which is an end in itself ("samot-sel' "), Tsetlin rather capriciously accused the book of not being a *Bildungsroman,* dismissing the possibility that the author might not have intended to write one. *Numbers* (1933, No. 7/8) again printed a highly negative review, this time by Vladimir Varshavsky. He said that Nabokov was frequently compared to Bunin [?], but Bunin was the last of the Mohicans, while in life victory belongs to more petty and tenacious people, like Nabokov. Continuing to speak in generalities, Varshavsky described the novel as talented, but to no end ("Ni k chemu"), void of any teaching ("zhizneucheniia net"), a simple presentation of the raw material of immediate perception of life.

The last issue of *Numbers* (1934, no. 10) remained true to its custom of criticizing Nabokov; Yury Terapiano accused *Camera obscura (Laughter in the Dark,* Berlin, 1933)[6] of being external, of viewing people and life itself from the outside. Nabokov lacks the internal dimension; his characters and their actions are not motivated by anything except the whim of the author. Nabokov's sharp three-dimensional vision annoyingly glides past the essence of man and only demonstrates the author's inner emptiness. The fact that all this is expressed with such stylistic glitter only increases the disappointment. In SZ (1934, No. 54) Mikhail Osorgin praised the literary qualities of *Camera obscura,* but also repeated the generalities about Nabokov's "un-Russianness," i.e., an absence of burning Russian questions and problems in his works, an absence of linguistic and stylistic experiments so common in Russian writers, and a complete absence of nature descriptions. Osorgin praised the composition of the novel, but declared its plot (as well as the plots of other Nabokov novels) devoid of spiritual values.

In 1934 Mikhail Kantor devoted an article in the literary almanac *Vstrechi (Encounters,* No. 3) explicitly to the role of memory in Nabokov's works. Kantor noted the dual attitude of the critics towards Nabokov: some praise him with reservations, and others censure him with respect. Memories play a decisive part in the plots of *Mary,* "The Return of Chorb," *The Defense* and *Glory.* Nabokov's entire literary arsenal, his similes, metaphors, metonymies, etc., is of a mnemonic origin. His conclusion was that memory played a primarily illustrative function, and limited the author's perception of the world to its sensuous, external manifestations, thus cutting his works off from the spiritual wellspring.

As if attempting to show the critics how to write *literary* reviews, Nabokov published, also in SZ (1936, No. 61) a brief article about Mark Aldanov's *Peshchera (The Cave,* 1936). He discussed the artistic composition of the book, analyzed several examples of Aldanov's stylistic   devices, and citing a few images and events of the plot as illustrations, he praised Aldanov's power of observation of detail. This review was Nabokov's only venture in the fiction review pages of a Russian journal, and it apparently remained unheeded.

Writing about *Otchaianie (Despair,* Berlin, 1936) in another

Paris almanac, *Krug (The Circle,* 1936, No. 1), Professor Wladimir Weidlé praised Nabokov's verbal novelty and singled out the theme of creativity as central to all Nabokov's works. Nabokov's heroes are symbols of an artist, a poet who creates his own world. The failure of their creation causes despair in many of Nabokov's heroes. The consistent presence of this basic motif is enough to forbid us to treat Nabokov as only a superficial virtuoso of technique.

After the serialization of *Priglashenie na kazn' (Invitation to a Beheading)* was completed in 1936, Professor Petr Bitsilli wrote a long article for SZ, (1936, No. 61), entitled "Vozrozhdenie allegorii" ("The Rebirth of Allegory").[7] Looking for stylistic similarities, his usual approach, he tried to establish Saltykov Shchedrin—particularly the grotesque and the illusory qualities in his writing—as Nabokob's literary parallel. *Invitation* is a utopia as well as a u-chronia: it presents the world in general, and Cincinnatus is the Everyman. He and the other characters in the novel are embodiments of ideas, and therefore they are allegorical figures, i.e, they can be retold in other words. (Unfortunately, Bitsilli does not elaborate upon the ideas embodied in these figures.) The rebirth of the allegoric art, which presupposes a certain separation from reality, is characteristic for our time.

When *Invitation to a Beheading* was published in a separate edition (Paris, 1938), Bitsilli reviewed it for SZ (1939, No. 68). This time he concentrated on the frequently repeated stylistic peculiarities, in order to approach the understanding of Nabokov's leading idea, his vision of the world. Nabokov uses many stylistic devices, such as alliteration and word-play, to renovate a word, to make it more expressive, as well as to reiterate its meaning. Another device Bitsilli discussed was the transposition of qualities which pertained to one logical category to another, in order to revive an image, or to illuminate an event of the plot from a different angle. Without using the word "synesthesia," he demonstrated how Nabokov employed the various levels of reception to achieve a single effect. Bitsilli further maintained that this transposition existed also on the compositional level, that Nabokov rendered the real in an estranged, "renewed fashion" and the fantastic in a matter-of-fact tone and diction. Such mixture contributed to the dominant feature of Nabokov's works—the feeling of unreality and senselessness in the surrounding world. In conclusion, Bitsilli discussed the main themes of the novel—"life is a dream" and "man is a prisoner"—and he felt that Nabokov developed them with great consistency and had achieved excellence. Even though Professor Bitsilli did not note the surrealistic elements in *Invitation,* in general his analysis of Nabokov's style was most elucidating and scholarly.

The other reviewers of *Invitation,* Sergei Osokin and B., clung to vague generalities in condemning the novel. Osokin rejoiced in *Russkie zapiski (Russian Notes,* 1939, No. 13) that for the first time Nabokov could be traced to the Russian literary tradition to Gogol's "The Nose"—and Leonid Andreev's *Moi zapiski (My Notes).* While individual episodes are well written they are not connected with each other, at times they are even contradictory and unnecessary, and themes, serious in themselves, are treated wtih inexcusable frivolity. Osokin expressed the hope that Nabokov's method of writing with external acrobatics and internal schematization would not remain his permanent form. In the short-lived Paris *Gran' (The Facet,* 1939, No. 1), B. called *Invitation* a study ("etiud") for two reasons: thematically it is a study of a mental illness, and stylistically it is not completed, because the reality it presents does not fit in to our normal conception of life and is therefore unconvincing.

In 1938 Nabokov also published his two major plays and a collection of short stories. The first play, "Sobytie" ("The Event") appeared in *Russian Notes* (1938, No. 4). Vladislav Khodasevich, famous poet and the *maitre* of Russian literature abroad, reviewed in SZ (1938, No. 66) its performance by the Russian Theater in Paris. He found the play well cast and staged, and remarked that it was well received by the large audiences. Khodasevich analysed several plot situations and motifs which reminded him of Gogol's *The Inspector General,* although in most cases it was a negative parallelism. Besides the genuine artfulness of its text, the play introduced new staging and acting devices. Lidia Chervinskaya, writing in *Circle* (1938, No. 3), repeated the critics' commonplace of unconvincingness and complained that it was impossible to find the essence of the play.

The collection *Sogliadatai (The Eye,* Paris, 1938), said S. Saveliev in *Russian Notes* (1938, No. 10), contained two of Nabokov's best works: the novel (?) *The Eye* and "The Aurelian." The tragedy of Smurov's "soullessness" in *The Eye* is presented so well, that this non-living person ("ne zhivoi chelovek") actually evokes sympathy in the reader. Nabokov's other novels do not reach this level, they can be compared to tapestries in which petty detail abounds, but the author is not able to synthesize them into one whole.

The other play, "Izobretenie Val'sa" ("The Waltz Invention"), was also published in *Russian Notes* (No. 11, 1938). It was being prepared for the stage, according to Field, when the war broke off its production.[8] SZ (No. 69, 1939) printed an article by M. K. (possibly Mikhail Kantor), in which the author used the play as a trampoline for philosophical musings, obviously prompted by the political situation of the time. Beginning with a discussion of the general situation of uncertainty and unpredictability in twentieth-century Europe and the influence of society upon individuals, M. K. analyzed the types of Evil in the world (sin and vice) and the nature of potential and actual dictators in terms of a manifestation of the Antichrist. One of such manifestations he considers to be Waltz, who is the more real for being artistically convincing. Waltz is a successful crossing of Khlestakov with Bela-Kun; in him are united the terrible and the ridiculous. Waltz's invention has been accepted by people today, and the only salvation is for people to exorcise it.

This was the last review of Nabokov before World War II broke out. Throughout the years there had been a division between Nabokov's "friends and foes," who were to some extent aligned by journals. It is curious to note that the staid and traditional SZ and *Will of Russia* remained steady supporters of Nabokov, while the more explicitly literary and the literary avant-garde journals remained predominantly hostile to him.

Furthermore, Nabokov completed the serialization of his last Russian novel, *Dar (The Gift,* in my estimation his most successful work), in 1938 in *SZ;* but the novel was never reviewed in a Russian journal, nor was it even published in a separate edition until 1952. The events of World War II and Nabokov's move to the United States do not seem to be sufficient explanation for this negelect of *The Gift* by Russian critics.

During the war, when Nabokov's English books began to appear, two short reviews, both of them highly laudatory, were published in the New York *Novyi zhurnal (The New Review).* Maria Tolstaya (1942, No. 2) discussing *The Real Life of Sebastian Knight* (Norfolk, Conn., New Directions, 1941), defended Nabokov against the earlier critics' accusations of "un-Russianness" and cold and superficial brilliance. She mentioned as central to his works the theme of creativity and the tragedy of the artist, the secondary role of the plot with regard to the narration, and the excellence of Nabokov's English. She expressed regrets that there was no Russian original of this novel.

Professor Georgy Fedotov praised Nabokov's discussion of stylistic problems in *Nikolai Gogol* (Norfolk, Conn., New Directions, 1944) in *The New Review* (1944, No. 9). Perhaps in order to underline Nabokov's "Russianness," Fedotov insisted on tying Nabokov to the Gogolian tradition of Russian literature. Both authors were creators of imaginary worlds, he said, but Nabokov's negation of Gogol's ethical content marks the difference between their kinds of art.

The collection of Russian poetry *Stikhotvoreniia (Poems, Paris, 1952) received three brief, but complimentary reviews, one of which appeared only in 1955 *(Grani [The Facets], 1952, No. 16, Opyty [Experiments], 1953, No. 1 and Vozrozhdenie [Renaissance], 1955, No. 37).

Since 1939 these five reviews were the only references to Nabokov in Russian émigré journals. Then a "deluge" of no less than four major articles concerning his artistic production as a whole suddenly appeared.

Khodasevich's posthumous *Literaturnye stat'i i vospominaniia (Literary Articles and Memoirs, New York, 1954) included a chapter on Nabokov, which was written in 1937. Khodasevich says favorably that Nabokov is primarily an artist of form, and one of his books, *Invitation to a Beheading,* is built entirely upon the interplay of devices. The life of the artist and the life of the device in the artist's consciousness seemed to Khodasevich to be the main themes of Nabokov beginning with *The Defense.* The figure of the artist is usually estranged by being presented as a chess player, a scheming businessman, etc.

Georgy Adamovich, who before the war wrote primarily in newspapers, included a chapter on Nabokov in his book of literary reminiscences, *Odinochestvo i svoboda (Loneliness and Freedom,* New York, 1955). Adamovich followed the prewar critics in saying that Nabokov was brilliant, but behind this constant effort to surprise there was a dry and deadening sadness. His main thesis was that Nabokov described a dead world, full of despair, and devoid of any Eros, in its highest and purest sense. In spite of his similarity to Gogol, his frivolous attitude to his themes and even to truth and simplicity put Nabokov outside of Russian literary traditions. In his poetry, however, Nabokov was the only real poet who succeeded in learning from Pasternak.

By 1955 Varshavsky, who had been so intolerant of Nabokov in *Numbers,* seemed to have partially revised his opinion. Concentrating upon *Invitation to a Beheading,* admittedly his favorite Nabokov book, he wrote in *Opyty (Experiments,* 1955, No. 4)[9] that from the formal point of view, Nabokov's prose was the only glamorous success of the younger émigré generation. With the exception of the individualistic Cincinnatus, all the characters of the novel resemble the stereotyped automatons of Socialist Realism, they are shadows without any humanity, who move in an automated, future society.

The fourth general discussion of Nabokov's work was the chapter in Professor Gleb Struve's book, *Russkaia literatura v izgnanii (Russian Literature in Exile,* New York, 1956), to date the only comprehensive study of émigré literature. Professor Struve presented a brief and objective survey of criticism, which he thought had been rather capricious and unjust at times to Nabokov, and added his own evaluations of Nabokov's work and a few personal reminiscences. The basic attitude of Professor Struve remained benevolent and laudatory as it was in his 1930 article.

Nabokov's Russian memoirs, *Drugie berega (Other Shores,* New York, 1954), received a brief mention in *Renaissance* (1955, No. 39) by Nikita Maier, who declared that personal life should not be thrown open for the wide reading public, and that only a person infinitely sure of himself could do so. The reviewer did not mention Nabokov's nostalgia for Russia and the past or the artistic skill which he used to recreate this past.

Vesna v Fial'te (Spring in Fialta, New York, 1956) was Nabokov's last Russian book. It contained stories written before the war and published in the periodical press. Reviewing it in the Frankfurt *Facets* (1957, No. 33), A. Kashkin tried once again to establish Nabokov's literary predecessors and maintained that the collection presents a new type of short story, in which the plot is in the background and in the foreground there is the picture, the mood, the change of scenery. The story "The Destruction of Tyrants" is most representative in this respect.

The English original of *Lolita* (Paris: Olympia, 1955) was not mentioned in Russian journals until 1959 at which time three critics wrote about it. Nikolai Armazov *(Grani,* 1959, No. 42) and Vladimir Zlobin *(Vozrozhdenie,* 1959, No. 85) both writing in Europe, stressed the sociological aspects of the book, and pointed to Nabokov's satire on contemporary society. Professor Nina Berberova, herself a member of the "younger émigré writers' generation," presented in *The New Review* (1959, No. 57) a detailed and in-depth literary analysis of the book's poetics and themes and briefly discussed Nabokov's other work. She praised Nabokov without the usual reservations about his "un-Russianness" and without any attempts to trace his Russian mentors.

The second edition of *The Real Life of Sebastian Knight* (New York, 1960), was briefly reviewed in the Munich literary almanac *Mosty (Bridges,* 1960, No. 5). The anonymous author remarked upon the difficulty of writing creatively in a foreign language, stressing the fact that Nabokov had already earned a prominent place in American literature.

Yakov Gorbov reviewed the French translation of *Pnin* (Paris, 1963, originally New York, 1957) in *Renaissance* (1963, No. 134). He stressed Nabokov's "Russianness" which was immediately obvious in this English novel. The personality of Pnin, his past, his motivations, and even the etymology of his name strongly reflect the Russian cultural tradition. The book would have been even more impressive and suggestive had it been written in Russian.

After this one there were no more reviews or articles until the end of 1968, the last year covered by my survey. The volume of postwar Russian criticism of Nabokov was drastically smaller, and with the exception of Professor Berberova's study, the articles were much briefer. Nor was there any alignment of "friends and foes" by journals, as there had been before the war. The reviewers were in general friendlier and most of them stressed Nabokov's "Russianness" in his English works.

The total number of reviews and articles on Nabokov in the émigré journals is 31; incidentally, the same number as on Mark Aldanov, the historical novelist, who like Nabokov, was once considered for the Nobel Prize. Other émigré authors received more attention from the critics; for example, 64 journal articles and reviews were devoted to Ivan Bunin, the first Russian Nobel Prize winner, 47—to the "teller of tales," Aleksei Remizov, and 38—to Ivan Shmelev, to name just a few. Nabokov, I think, has suffered both numerically and qualitatively. Most of the articles about him were rather superficial; many judged his work by extraliterary criteria.

Many critics used a basic formula: talented, brilliant stylistically and formally, BUT "un-Russian." The "un-Russianness" although it was used normatively, was, however, an indefinite quantity, which encompassed a multitude of "sins" from an inability to touch the heart of the reader, to an absence of verbal experimentation, conceived as peculiar to Russian writers. Reading the criticism in chronological order reveals no particular change in the critics' attitudes; his admirers praised him with certain reservations, and his enemies scolded him, while still paying tribute to his talent and the brilliance of his style.

I am forced to make the conclusion that Nabokov's contribution to Twentieth-Century Russian literature has not been adequately analyzed or appreciated by Russian émigré critics. But, because Russian critics and scholars in the Soviet Union are rather limited in their interpretations of Nabokov this task falls upon the Western critics and scholars, whether Russian or of other nationalities.

NOTES

1. Compiled by Ludmila A. Foster (Boston: G. K. Hall, 1971), 2 vols.

2. "Some Aspects of the Relations Between Polish Renaissance Literature and the West," presented at the AAASS meeting (Denver, March 1971).

3. Erroneously quoted in the Bibliography.

4. Andrew Field [Nabokov: His Life in Art (Boston, 1967)] sees Ivanov's motive partly as revenge for Nabokov's unfavorable review of a novel by Ivanov's wife, Irina Odoevtseva.

5. Since most issues of this journal are virtually unobtainable, I am indebted to Professor Andreev for sending me a photocopy of his article.

6. Field gives the publication date as 1932; in the Bibliography I give an estimated date of 1932, but the novel was still being serialized in 1933, and the two reviews give 1933 and 1934 respectively.

7. Translated into English in the TriQuarterly, No. 17 (1970).

8. TriQuarterly, No. 17 (1970).

9. And the following year he included an expanded version of this article in Chapter Four of his book Nezamechennoe pokolenie (The Unnoticed Generation), New York, 1956.

10. For more detail, including an English translation of the entry on Nabokov in the Kratkaia literaturnaia entsyklopediia, see Ellendea Proffer, "Nabokov's Russian Readers," TriQuarterly, No. 17 (1970).

Stephen Suagee

AN ARTIST'S MEMORY BEATS ALL OTHER KINDS:
AN ESSAY ON *DESPAIR*

Like all of Sirin's novels that he has translated, the 1965 edition of *Despair* is an autonomous production of the accomplished novelist Vladimir Nabokov. In creating his English version, the author points out that he has revised not so much his original translation of 1936 as the novel itself. The formidable English prose that resulted from this process is well suited to Hermann, who is self-conscious, clever, and a prig. Like Nabokov he is super-confident of his writing skill, and like Nabokov he acknowledges the powers of memory. On the other hand, Hermann is insane. He exalts a shabby murder as an artistic masterpiece, he is absurdly ignorant of his wife's adultery, and he really believes that he can be in two places at once. Sooner or later it occurs to the reader that Hermann constantly jumbles reality and unreality. The question provoked by this state of affairs—*i.e.,* what in the world of the novel is real or reliable?—is ultimately an improper one. Hermann's problems, although they make for a fascinating novel, will always be simply Hermann's problems.

The narrative itself becomes quite murky at times, as in Tarnitz, but the words on the page cannot be anything but real— and the words belong to Hermann. The general characteristics of his style are apparent: first person narration with occasional anacolutha and aposiopeses, tortuous sentences interspersed with fragments, a sensitivity to colors and details, vigorous metaphors, parodies of novelistic devices, and so forth. "I have grown much too used to an outside view of myself, to being both painter and model, so no wonder my style is denied the blessed grace of spontaneity " (p. 29). Style is the man, and Hermann is definitely self-conscious. Nevertheless, he is largely ignorant of how his own mind works. Many of the details that he dwells on, the objects that enrich the texture of his novel, are suspiciously phallic—a fact that Hermann never notices. Yellow posts, silver pencils, sausages, cigarettes, and a treacherous walking stick parade through his manuscript, imparting to it the atmosphere of an absurd priapic nightmare.

The yellow post is prominent throughout the novel, chiefly

because Hermann keeps calling it to our attention. It is a landmark of the murder site, but it is also a guide to Hermann's "artist's memory," which after all is the genuine author of the book. He first notices the post on a summer jaunt to Ardalion's sylvan lot. In recounting this episode, Hermann says that he "recognized" the yellow post, then reconsiders, "perhaps the glance that I gave it was quite an indifferent one," and concludes, "but all the same, today as I recall it, I cannot separate that first acquaintanceship from its mature development" (p. 45). He recalls that an eerie sense of *déjà vu* pervaded that first encounter, and in describing the yellow post as skullcapped with snow, he inadvertently fore-glimpses the woods on the day of the murder. Indeed, he has trouble keeping the summer scene in focus, mentioning also a bare birch and patches of snow, until he points out that not he, but his "impatient memory," is the real author. That is, his memory disregards temporal sequences and compresses distinct events into a single impression. This little scene in Ardalion's wood is by no means a mystical omen, and it is more than a simple literary fore-shadowing; it is tangible evidence of memory's power to reshape the past.

Since the whole novel (except for the last two chapters[1]) is written in retrospect, we know that Hermann's memory might at any moment be playing similar tricks—whether he knows it or not. In addition, more drastic instances of delusion—his misunderstanding of the dissociation and his belief in the false double—totally discredit Hermann as a reporter.

Sometimes, however, an outside world seems to penetrate his illusions. He fancies himself a criminal of genius, but it is another phallic object, Felix's walking stick, that turns triumph into trite failure. Since Hermann does not realize the stick's perfidy until the final, unplanned, chapter, the proleptic associations between stick and failure are, so to say, the unconscious interpolations of his artist's memory. The stick-theme is nicely introduced while Hermann is making fun of his "bird-witted" wife, "We discovered one day that to her the term 'mystic' was somehow dimly connected with 'mist' and 'mistake' and 'stick,' but that she had not the least idea what a mystic really was" (p. 33). The retrospective reader, thumbing back to this passage after finishing the book, happily notes that Hermann, in his smugness, overlooks the portentous association of stick and mistake and general murkiness.

There is, however, a further difficulty with the stick. In chapter three, Hermann has a dream, which transforms the hypnagogic impression of a cane striking a lamppost into a walking stick knocking roadside trees. This is the first time in the novel that Felix is depicted with a walking stick—but is it a prophetic dream, or mnemonic afterthought, or something else altogether? When the doubles meet beneath the bronze statue in Tarnitz, Hermann picks up the stick and notes that it is engraved with the owner's name and home city. At this point it would seem that the stick has solidly entered the world of objects, were it not that the whole Tarnitz episode presents a special problem, which I shall describe later on. Briefly though, the town of Tarnitz is a kind of illusion within the book, composed of tantalizing clues and meaningless repetitions. We may assume that the stick itself is no illusion, but to do so leaves unexplained its precise role in this shadowy interlude.

The stick next appears on the day of the murder, and an extremely careful reader is free to notice that Hermann overlooks it when he is tidying up the scene of the crime. Moreover, Hermann's nifty little Icarus issues an unheeded onomatopoeic warning. ("Ick," says the car, twice in fact, but its owner persists in his fatal oversight.) When he flabbergastedly realizes his error, Hermann again mentions his artist's memory—"a curious thing! Beats all other kinds, I imagine." Whatever, precisely, an "artist's memory" might be, it can at least notice and record details of which its possessor is not conscious. Possibly it is one device that Nabokov uses to smuggle in the "derisive mirages" alluded to in his foreword. In any case, it is tempting to say that Hermann is preoccupied consciously and unconsciously with phallic objects, and that they embody his most humiliating failures. Indeed, there is much more of this questionable evidence.

It is clear that something is peculiar about Hermann's sex life. He imagines that he is making love with his wife when he is not; he is incapable of admitting that he has been cuckolded by her; he is squeamish of lip kisses. In this respect, it is amusing to note that cigarettes suggest his sexual problems. He manages to talk quite smugly about his domestic set-up—Ardalion being a minor nuisance in comparison to devoted wife, neat car, plush flat, and "accommodating stomach"—but he can do so only by being hilariously thickheaded. In chapter six, Hermann calls on Ardalion and finds Lydia there in her cousin's bed, languorously smoking the hackneyed post-coital cigarette. Despite such a stock situation (which Hermann, as a connoisseur of literary cliches, should have immediately suspected), despite Lydia's bold riddle, despite the helter-skelter arrangement of Ardalion's clothing—indeed, despite dozens of hints throughout the book—our hero remains in the dark.

On the other hand, he often feels vaguely dissatisfied, as for example on the eve of his Tarnitz journey, when it is something about his exclusion from the activities of the other two that makes him melancholy:

> So they went on for a good while, talking now of their cards and now about me, as though I were not in the room or as though I were a shadow, a ghost, a dumb creature; and that joking habit of theirs, which before used to leave me indifferent, now seemed to me loaded with meaning, as if indeed it were merely my reflection that was present, my real body being far away (p. 75).

On this occasion Hermann happens to be smoking. Lydia is also smoking, as she is nearly every time that Hermann sees her with Ardalion. In the novel there are at least twenty references to cigarettes and their appurtenances, and nine of these involve Hermann's perceptions of Lydia and Ardalion. Hermann only notes Lydia's smoking when Ardalion is present in thought or in flesh. Moreover, none of the other cigarette references are accidental. Most of them show how Hermann uses cigarettes to placate or cajole his double. Just before the murder he rejects as being in bad taste the idea of offering his victim a cigarette, and thus severs one of the palpable bonds between them.

At this point we might be tempted to speculate. Hermann cannot face up to his sexual problems, cannot acknowledge Lydia's infidelity. He suppresses everything, but his artist's memory, true author of the tale, naturally notices those phallic details that symbolize his frustrations. Therefore, if cigarettes represent the sexual triangle, perhaps Hermann doles them out to Felix in order to regain a feeling of power. The conclusion is reached by noting that a gun barrel, with its "puff of smoke hanging in midair" (p. 181), is suspiciously similar to a certain cigarette, with its "puff of smoke that slowly stretched out in midair..." (p. 65)—and we have fallen into one of those traps that Nabokov loves to set, for "Freudists" and for everybody.[2]

And yet there are too many repetitions of sticks, and cigarettes, and so forth, to dismiss them all as ornamental jokes. Consider the birch tree whose forked trunk keeps popping up in a variety of locations. Birch trees are first mentioned in a general way, in connection with Lydia's ignorance of the term "mystic"; the birch is the only tree she can identify because it recalls her native Russian woodland. Later, when Hermann, Lydia, and Ardalion first visit the lakeside lot, Hermann notices "a Y-stemmed couple of inseparable birches," which is in turn twinned by its reflection in the lake. He notices another double-trunked birch in Tarnitz; two girls are playing marbles beneath it. A second mention is made in Tarnitz of a double-trunked birch, but it is unclear whether it is the same tree that shelters the marble-shooters. In any case, it is identical to the one that grew near Hermann's former Moscow residence. Unfortunately, we know little of Hermann's life in Moscow. After more than four years' internment in a Volgan village, he was stranded in Moscow for three months, and during that time he met and married Lydia, whose favorite tree is the birch. Thus, by starting with Lydia and proceeding to the lake, to Tarnitz, to Moscow, and finally to Lydia again, the artist's memory has drawn a circle around the reader, suggesting as it does so that birch trees must have something to do with Hermann's marriage, or with the theme of reflections, mirrors, and doubles.

Clearly, Hermann is not in control of what he chooses to call his artist's memory, and it is up to us as readers to make what we can of all these mysterious repetitions and intercombinations. We can try to sort real from unreal, but since we must use as a reference the document of a self-deluding neurotic, the task is futile. A visit to Tarnitz will be enough to discourage the most meticulous literary detective.

During the war Hermann was interned as a German subject in a fishing village on the Caspian Sea, near Astrakhan and the mouth of the Volga. It was after this confinement that he spent those three months in Moscow, whence he migrated to Germany. The Saxon town of Tarnitz—which must come from the German verb *tarnen,* "to veil"—is composed from scraps of Hermann's Russian past. Shortly after his arrival there, he looks out of his hotel window, and the view of its courtyard evokes an hallucination: a familiar Tartar is showing a blue carpet to buxom Christina Forsmann, whom Hermann "had known carnally in 1915," in that Volgan village. He knows that this is an illusion but cannot discover the "kernel" around which it is formed. He dismisses his uneasiness; after all, everything in that hotel room is bound to resemble vaguely something seen long ago in Russia. He goes outside. Here too, transplanted bits of his past begin to haunt him. A fishmonger's sign recalls another fishmonger of the same name; a bronze Herzog resembles the Bronze Horseman of Petersburg; a painting in a pipe shop might be one of Ardalion's. The ubiquitous birch grows in a familiar setting.

It occurs to Hermann that he will not find Felix in Tarnitz "for the simple reason that he was a product of my imagination, which hankered after reflections, repetitions, masks..." (p. 80). One is tempted to agree with him, and yet the doubles do meet, so that Hermann thinks no more of the uncanny resemblances. After they have chatted and dined, they walk in darkness to Hermann's hotel. The clouds covering the moon curl "like astrakhan,"[3] and in his room, there returns the "sensation of something very familiar." Later that night he abandons Tarnitz—and Felix temporarily—but its mystery remains unexplained. Eventually, that mystery reaches out from Tarnitz, as if to reclaim our hero.

Likening himself to an adolescent masturbator determined to give up his habit, Hermann has tried to return to a healthy, bourgeois life. But he succumbs to the temptation provided by Felix's letters, and writes back to arrange a rendezvous by the yellow post. Inexplicably, he cannot bring himself to drop his letter into a mailbox. Looking around for help, he espies "two little girls playing near me on the pavement: they rolled by turns an iridescent marble, aiming at a pit in the soil near the curb" (p. 134). He selects one of the girls and gives her the letter to mail. Throughout this episode—or properly speaking, throughout his recollection of it—he remains ignorant of the parallel recorded for the reader's contemplation by his artist's memory. In Tarnitz, while wandering about on his way to meet Felix, Hermann had stepped out of the wind to light a cigarette. He stood on a sheltering porch and noticed "two girls playing marbles; rolling by turns the iridescent orb... in order that the marble should trickle into a tiny pit in the ground under a double-trunked birch tree..." (p. 79).

Such patterns as this one, which ought to have a meaning, simply have none. As a result, they create a world as it appears to someone so vexed and anxious that his heart itches. Of a piece with this anxiety is the oppressive bafflement felt by a reader who has to rely on such murky clues in order to figure out what must have happened during Hermann's Russian period. At any moment some horrible truth is going to burst forth and Hermann, possibly ourselves as well, will not survive the upheaval. Nothing like this happens of course. The hints and echoes invite us to look for a profound secret, but we can never penetrate their tangled surface simply because Hermann does not tell us enough.

Any trace of the outside world that does creep into Hermann's narrative proves maddeningly inadequate. For example, Orlovius, along with unnamed others, testifies that Hermann used to write letters to himself (p. 201). The use of the plural is surprising; so far we know only that Hermann showed him one letter, Felix's third. Perhaps Orlovius simply does not know what he is talking about. But if the earnest fellow is lying, we must wonder why. If he is right, if Hermann composed that letter in one of his twenty-five hands, then we can only guess how much of Hermann's complicated plot is pure fancy.

The perfection of the double is certainly fanciful. After the murder Hermann boards a train. He examines Felix's passport and is troubled to find that its photograph does not resemble himself "closely." Then he reflects, "here was the real cause of his being so little aware of our likeness: he saw himself in a glass, that is to say, from left to right, not sunway as in reality" (p. 183). But is not the very opposite true? Felix, the vagabond who avoided towns and houses, and who seldom slept under a roof, would rarely have seen a mirror in his adult years. But he did carry his passport with him. Its photograph would at least depict him "sunway," although not necessarily as in reality. On the other hand, Hermann has only recently begun avoiding mirrors, which used to surround him. It is he who is accustomed to seeing himself as in a glass. Perhaps Felix is the double of Hermann's mirror image. That would make even more appropriate the novel's frequent references to mirrors, and would also account for such gestures by Hermann as shaking Felix's right hand with his own left, so as to mimic the effect of a mirror.[4] Finally, Hermann, who is used to his own mirror image, becomes angry rather than enlightened when he sees his passport photo printed in the newspapers: "...on [it] I indeed look like a criminal, and not like myself at all, so maliciously did they touch it up" (p. 203).

In the end, we cannot decide what is real and what unreal. Nor can we discover why Hermann is insane. But these questions are improper anyway. The essential thing is how the artist's memory associates objects and events, how it shapes *Despair* itself. In this novel, self-conscious style combines with secret patterns to produce a world impervious to final explanations. Yet by inviting us to discover its hidden meaning, that world asserts its own autonomy. The novel as it exists is the only reality, and its great achievement is to create formally the eerie anxiety that torments its narrator.

Because *Despair* does arouse, rather than assuage, the appetite for final explanations, we are likely to fault either the novel itself of our own powers of detection. This is a natural result of Nabokov's method of narrating, yet we find ourselves continuing to puzzle over this untraceable hint, or that bogus clue, as though we had overlooked something vital. On the other hand, some commentators have missed the point utterly. Nabokov rightly calls "silly" an article in which Sartre talks quite earnestly about "rootlessness," revolt, society, and Nabokov's spiritual and artistic "ancestor" Dostoevsky.[5] Equally wide of the mark is Claire Rosenfield, who suggests that Nabokov employs the theme so congenial to Mann and Dostoevsky, that of the double, because Felix somehow represents Hermann's suppressed counterpart, and that, moreover, Hermann is driven by a "lust for immortality" common to musicians, poets, and "primitives."[6] But it is obvious that Dostoevsky, as novelist and as mystic, is parodied rather than emulated; and as for doubles, libidoes, alienation, and eschatology, there is nothing in the novel to indicate that we take such flapdoodle seriously.

Fallacies such as these result from trying to read the novel discursively and without a sense of humor. *Despair* is like all of Nabokov's novels in that it requires a different method of reading. Each time we read we collaborate in a creation, and the peculiar brand of pleasure is in watching how a world is constructed. In order to collaborate we must be alive to patterns of details, because it is these patterns that make Hermann's world so tauntingly impenetrable. It is not necessary, however, to spot every secret repetition, or to pursue each clue to its baffling *cul-de-sac*. The literary tricks are fun in themselves, but they take their ultimate value from the smoothly-running, self-sufficient universe they help to create.

NOTES

Page references to *Despair* follow the citations in the essay. I have used the Capricorn paperback edition (1970); the pagination is identical to that of the 1965 Putnam hardback.

1. In chapter ten, the original plan of Hermann's book is disrupted and he is compelled to add a chapter. The tenth chapter begins to narrate events that took place after Hermann started writing his manuscript, and the eleventh lapses first into diarism, and then on the last page, into a second-by-second account of Hermann's announcement.

2. Here is a fuller description of the gunshot: "I remember various things: that puff of smoke, hanging in midair, then displaying a transparent fold and vanishing slowly..." (p. 181). When Hermann makes his first solo visit to the eventual murder spot, he smokes a cigarette: "I looked at the little puff of smoke that slowly stretched out in midair, was folded by ghostly fingers, and melted away" (p. 65). Apart from the obvious fact that Nabokov is having fun, what do we make of this—omen? artist's memory? enchanted woods? symmetrical universe? It is as hopeless as the two little marble-shooters.

3. These curling clouds (p. 101), along with the Tartar's blue carpet (p. 77), reappear on the railroad platform at Ardalion's departure (p. 145). The astrakhan is on a collar, and the blue carpet has become a blue mackintosh.

4. When they meet in Tarnitz (p. 83), Hermann "shook his right hand with my left." After discovering Felix near Prague, Hermann returns to his hotel, approaches his mirror—and there is Felix (p. 24). Nothing is conclusive in this novel, but it is plausible to suggest that the strongest resemblance exists between Hermann-in-the-mirror and Felix-in-the-flesh—sunway.

5. Jean-Paul Sartre, "Vladimir Nabokov: *La Meprise*," in *Situations I,* (Librairie Gallimard, 1947), pp. 58-61.

Although this article (originally published in 1939 and later reprinted) is remarkable for its author's carefree invocation of weighty ideas, a more serious error is summed up in this assertion: "M. Nabokov (est-ce timidite ou scepticisme?) se garde bien d'inventer une technique nouvelle. Il raille les artifices du roman classique, mais pour finir il n'en utilise pas d'autres."

6. Claire Rosenfield, "Despair and the Lust for Immortality," in *Nabokov: the Man and His Work,* L. S. Dembo, ed. (University of Wisconsin Press, 1967), pp. 66-84.

INVITATION TO A BEHEADING AND THE EYE

A Review Article by P. M. Bitsilli

The work of Vladimir Nabokov, who wrote his nine Russian novels under the pen name V. Sirin, has been the subject of several volumes of criticism and of a great many critical articles. Most of this study has been done on his English novels or on English translations of his earlier Russian works. American critics have remained largely ignorant of the critical assessment of Nabokov's Russian works by émigré Russian critics. One might note in particular the criticism of V. Khodasevich, G. Adamovich and P. Bitsilli.[1]

Petr Mikhailovich Bitsilli (1879-1953), an émigré scholar who lived in Bulgaria between the two world wars, wrote a number of valuable studies of Russian authors, particularly—Dostoevsky and Chekhov. Of all of the émigré criticism, Bitsilli's is the most perceptive on Nabokov's style and particularly so in the following review-article. It should be of particular interest to non-Russian reading critics that many of the stylistic traits typical of Nabokov's mature English style are present in his earlier Russian work.

The translation of a critique of style offers special problems. Much of Bitsilli's stylistic commentary focuses on alliteration and assonance, two elements which ill lend themselves to translation. It is manifest that an observation about alliteration and assonance in a Russian sentence is meaningless when the reader is looking at an English translation of that sentence. Consequently I have retained the original Russian illustrative sentences in transliteration (and supplied stress marks) so that the reader without Russian can at least have some idea of what the critical commentary has reference to. I had intended to give Nabokov's own (or approved) translation of the relevant sentences. A comparison, however, of Nabokov's English renderings showed that the translator had attempted (or sometimes not attempted) to give a parallel English stylistic paraphrase rather than an exact transfer of alliteration effects. Indeed, the latter is foredoomed to failure. Consequently, in those Russian sentences where particular phonetic effects are being discussed I have given my own literal translations with some effort to duplicate the Russian phonetic effect. In cases

63

where such effects are not involved I have given the translations found in the standard author-approved English translations.

A final note. In the second (and less successful) part of his article Bitsilli attempts a philosophical exegesis. It appears that he is contrasting the Russian terms *real'nost'* and *deistvitel'nost'*, both of which are usually translated as "reality." I have attempted to duplicate this distinction by the terms "reality" and "actuality" respectively.

D. B. J.

P. M. Bitsilli

V. NABOKOV'S *INVITATION TO A BEHEADING*
AND *THE EYE*. A Review Article Translated
from *Contemporary Annals,* No. 68
(Paris, 1936) by
D. Barton Johnson

When one rereads an author straight through that one has
previously read at great intervals, it is easier to notice in his work
certain constantly recurring stylistic characteristics and through
this to draw nearer to an understanding of his guiding *idea—*
in the full sense of this word, i.e., his vision of the world and of
life—insofar as "form" and "content" are identical in the case
of the writer in question. One such feature of Sirin's work is his
peculiar sort of "word play," the play of like-sounding words:
"... I kak *dym* ischezáet dokhódnyi *dom...*" "*... and like smoke
vanishes the lucrative estate...*" *(The Eye),* —as well as a multitude
of similar combinations in *Invitation to a Beheading;* combinations
of words with the same number of syllables and rhyming with each
other— "... Ot negó pákhlo muzhikóm, tabakóm, chesnokóm"...
"he smelled of muzhik, tobacco, and garlic..."; or word groups
which are "symmetrical" in regard to sound— "... v pes'ei *máske*
s *márlevoi* pást'yu..." *(pm—mp)* "...wearing a doglike mask with a
gauze mouthpiece..."; cf. also"...*K*artîna li *k*isti krutógo kolor*ista"*
"... is it the painting of the brush of the abrupt colorist—"; alliterations plus assonances— "test', opiráyas' na trost'..." "the father-
in-law, leaning on his walking stick..."; "Tam tamózhnie kholmý
tomlénie prudóv, támtam dalékogo orkéstra..." "There, the local
hills, the languor of the ponds, the tom-tom of a distant band...";
"blevál blédnyi bibliotékar'..." "the livid librarian was vomiting...";
—or as many more such cases as you like. It seems as if the author
himself is alluding to his own mannerism when he speaks of the
novel that Cincinnatus is reading where "there was a page and a
half long paragraph in which all of the words began with p." But
here it is as if he were making fun of himself, consistent in his
striving to maintain the tone of irony; in another place, speaking
in the name of Cincinnatus, he provides a foundation for this
verbal device: "...sensing how words are combined, what one must
do for a commonplace word to come alive and to share its
neighbor's sheen, heat, shadow, while reflecting itself in its

65

neighbor and renewing the neighboring word in the process..." The device which I have noted is only one of the means of bringing a word to life, of making it more expressive, of forcing one to *hear* its sonority. But the sonority of a word is connected with its *sense:* "shelestiáshchee, vlázhnoe slóvo *schást'e,* pléshchushchee slóvo, takóe zhivóe, rúchnoe, samó ulybáetsia, samó pláchet..."—"the rustling, moist word 'happiness,' a plashing word, so alive, tame, itself smiling, itself crying..." *(The Eye).* "Here too is the interesting word 'konéc' 'end.' Something like a 'kon' 'horse' and 'gonéc' 'herald' in one..." *(Ib.)* Cf. also in *Invitation to a Beheading:* "Tupóe tut, podpërtoe i zápertoe chetóiu 'tvérdo', tëmnaia tiur'má... dérzhit meniá i tesnit" "The *d*ull *tut* 'here" propped up and locked up by its pair of "t's," the *d*ark *d*ungeon, ... holds and constricts me."[2] Thus it is that words which have similar sounds speak about something common to all.

Of course, there is nothing new here in essence—since in the wide use of bold metaphors, in the transfer, for example, of physical qualities to concepts expressing psychic qualities: "... zadúmalas' zhénskoi oblokóchennoi zadúmannost'iu *(The Eye)* "... she sank into meditation with a feminine meditativeness which leaned its head on one elbow" or to concepts engendered by the perceptions of one category, of qualities relating to the perceptions of another category: "bárkhatnaia tishiná plát'ya, rasshiryáyas' knízu, sliválas' s temotói "the velvet quiet of her dress flaring at the bottom, blending with the darkness" *(Invitation to a Beheading).* Here the verbal indications of separate perceptions are combined so that instead of (discrete-DBJ) perceptions, a single integral impression is imparted to us. Similar stylistic wonders can be found as early as Gogol, and, subsequently, in a number of other writers. The whole point is in the *function* of these devices which is displayed by the degree of boldness in their utilization. In this regard, Sirin, it seems, goes farther than anyone before him—inasmuch as such audacities are met in his work in contexts where they strike one by their unexpectedness: not in lyric poetry, but in "narrative prose," where, it would seem, attention is directed toward the "usual," the "everyday." In Sirin's case this is connected with the composition where fantasy, the imaginary world, somehow creeps in where we do not expect it. No matter how often this happens, as in *Invitation to a Beheading,* we do not at all expect it because

66

just at the time it occurs, the tone of narration is deliberately "low-keyed," calm, such as that in which one customarily narrates the commonplace. Nor is the introduction of fantasy into the vulgar commonplace new: it is found in Gogol, in Saltykov, and still earlier in Hoffmann. But once having intruded, the imaginary world becomes primary in their works; the fantastic motif is elaborated in detail in each bit of the narration so that the commonplace constitutes, as it were, the framework or the backdrop. In Sirin the elements of fantasy and reality are intentionally mixed; all the more in that it is precisely the "impossible" that is narrated *en passant* just as are everyday trivialities upon which one's attention does not linger: "The footmen... briskly served the food, sometimes even leaping across the table with a dish (somehow resembling a Chagall painting) and everyone noticed the polite solicitude with which M'sieur Pierre took care of Cincinnatus." One could adduce as many such examples as one likes. Sometimes, again by means of the merest verbal hints, even that which relates to "actuality" assumes the character of some kind of stage prop: "Lunúuzhé ubráli i gustýe báshni kréposti slivális' s túchami" "The moon had already been removed and the dark towers of the fortress blended with the clouds." At first this seems to be some sort of delirious perception of actuality. But if you read anything of Sirin, through to the end, all at once, so to speak—particularly *Invitation to a Beheading*— it turns itself inside out. One begins to perceive "reality" as "delirium," and "delirium" as "actuality." Thus the "word play" device performs the function of the reconstruction of an actuality concealed by the usual "reality."

All art, like culture in general, is the result of the effort to free oneself from actuality and utilizing, nonetheless, the empirical data as *material,* to rework them so as to touch another, an ideal, world. But these data are perceived and conceived as real existence, as something having their *own,* albeit very nasty *meaning* and as something, even though very nasty, none the less *established* and this means, in and of itself, from a certain point of view, also "normal." Sirin shows customary reality as a "Whole collection of various negations," i.e., of absolutely absurd objects: "All sorts of such shapeless, mottled, holey, spotted, pockmarked, knobby things..." In such a situation the essence of creativity is the search for "an unintelligible and distorted mirror" in the reflection of which "an unintelligible and distorted object"

67

would be transformed into "a marvelous, shapely image." Wherein lies this illusoriness, this unreality "of our vaunted reality, of our bad dream," where only "from without penetrate the strangely, absurdly changing sounds and images of the actual world which flows beyond the periphery of consciousness" (the words of Cincinnatus)? In that the "I" is not free in it—and *cannot* be free, for man is not born of his own free will, ("... I am here through an error—not in this prison, specifically—but in this whole terrible striped world..." *ib.*). And if one is not M'sieur Pierre, for whom life is reduced to "delights, amorous, gastronomic, and so on, he is obligatorily Cincinnatus, who, wherever he finds himself, ultimately returns ever anew to his death cell.

But again: the theme "life is a dream" and the theme of man/prisoner are not new; they are well-known universal themes and they have been touched upon in world literature a multitude of times and in the most diverse variants. But in no one's work, so far as I know, have these themes been exclusive nor have they been worked up till now with such consistency, and with such perfection conditioned by this consistency, with such mastery of reinterpretation of the stylistic devices and compositional motifs going back to Gogol, to the Romantics, to Saltykov-Shchedrin and to Jonathan Swift. This is because no one has been so consistent in the elaboration of the *idea* underlying this theme. "Life is a dream." Dream, as we know, has long been considered the brother of Death. Sirin follows this path to its end. Precisely, that life is death. This is why, after the execution of Cincinnatus, one of the three Fates standing by the scaffold bears off *not him* but "the tiny executioner," "like a larva" in her arms; Cincinnatus, on the other hand, goes to a place where, "judging by the voices, stood beings akin to him," i.e., "impenetrable" Leibnitzian monads "which have been deprived of windows," pure souls, inhabitants of the Platonic world of ideas.

I have already had occasion to express the opinion that the art of Sirin is the art of allegory. Why is the executioner "tiny as a larva" at the final moment? Because, probably, M'sieur Pierre is that which is proper to the Cincinnatian monad in its earthly embodiment and because he [M'sieur Pierre—DBJ] *was born* together with it and is now returning to the earth. Cincinnatus and M'sieur Pierre are two aspects of "man in general," the *everyman* of the medieval English "street drama," of the mystery play. The "M'sieur Pierre" element is present in every man while he lives, i.e., while he sojourns in that state of the "bad dream," of *death,* which we consider life. To die for "Cincinnatus" means precisely to exterminate from himself "M'sieur Pierre," that impersonal, "universal" element which therefore is *nameless* as it is embodied in a second variant of M'sieur Pierre, (in the hero of the story) *Khvat* "A Dashing Fellow" *(The Eye)* who in just such a way refers to himself as "we," or by the provisional name "just—Kostya."[3] But, of course, life is *not only* death. In *The Gift,* in the touching story "Breaking the News" *(The Eye),* Sirin is, as it were, not in agreement with himself. But every person has moments when that very same feeling of unreality, of the meaninglessness of life, envelopes him and which in the case of Sirin serves as the dominant motif of his creativity—amazement mixed with terror before what usually is perceived as something comprehensible in and of itself, and as a dim vision of something "real" lying beyond all this. It is in this that we find Sirin's Truth.

---

1. The interested reader may find a survey of such work in Ludmila A. Foster's "Nabokov in Russian Emigre Criticism" in this volume.

2. The full force of this sentence is untranslatable. I have substituted *d's* for the alliterative *t's* except for the critical case of *tut* (pronounced *toot)* "here." In the Russian word the *t's* envelope and imprison the melancholy "oo" sound. There is a further untranslatable word play here based on *tverdo* which has both the meaning of the adverb "firmly" and also that of the Old Slavonic name of the letter *t.* Hence that part of the phrase may be understood as "locked up firmly" or "locked up by a pair of t's" in reference to *tut* "here."

3. This story and the subsequently-mentioned "Breaking the News" were published in a collection entitled *Soglyadatai (The Eye)* (Paris, 1938). The collection included the title novella plus a number of short stories. The translated novella was published separately under the title *The Eye.* Both of the stories have recently been republished in Nabokov's *A Russian Beauty and other Stories* (New York: McGraw-Hill, 1973).

Anna Maria Salehar

NABOKOV'S *GIFT:* AN APPRENTICESHIP IN CREATIVTY

Writing in 1937 Vladislav Khodasevich, an early critic and admirer of Nabokov-Sirin observed that although Nabokov's heroes to date had been businessmen and chessplayers, Nabokov's books really had been about "the life of the artist and the life of the device in the consciousness of the artist."[1] Had Nabokov indeed created a writer-hero, Khodasevich speculated, the novelist would doubtlessly have represented both the man and his creation, presenting a novel within a story. Nabokov had, the critic implied, eschewed a man of letters as his main character, because the requisitely complex plot clearly "necessitated on the part of the reader a certain knowledge of the writer's craft."[2] Unwittingly,[3] Khodasevich succinctly described both the structure and the quintessence of *The Gift* a few weeks before the novel began to be serialized in *Sovremennye Zapiski (Contemporary Annals).* Almost as if responding to an uncanny challenge, Nabokov sought to turn what Khodasevich presumed an obstacle to the appearance of a book about a writer, namely "a certain knowledge on the part of the reader of the writer's craft," into the objective of his newest novel. For Nabokov structured this, his last novel written in Russian, as a medium through which the reader must participate in every phase of literary production like a vicarious apprentice.

In *The Gift* Nabokov has presented to us a psychogram, perhaps a notebook, of Fyodor Godunov-Cherdyntsev, a young Russian émigré author living in Berlin. The "journal," it appears, contains free-flowing ruminations, self-observations, and personal letters all sandwiched between creative writing. Among this eclectic material we find a biography of the nineteenth century critic Nikolai Chernyshevski, an unfinished monograph on Fyodor's father, and several poems based on Fyodor's childhood, to which, on a second reading, Cherdyntsev appends *explications de texte,* personal evaluations or, occasionally, a pseudo-review. In addition to these self-evident works, Andrew Field has noted that the journal entries embody a number of "autonomous,"[4] "tenuously connected short stories":[5] "Fyodor's romance with Zina Mertz, vignettes of émigré literary life... the imaginary discourses on Russian literature, and the strange death of [Fyodor's acquaintance] Yasha Chernyshevsky."[6]

But there is yet another literary piece lurking in *The Gift:* "the love poem to Zina," as Nabokov points out in his introduction to the English edition.[7] That such a poem exists is not obvious to the reader, the novelist's assurances notwithstanding. However, once detected, the poem is clearly more than the "hub of Chapter Three," to use Nabokov's own term. It comes to be the core of the novel as well. For as the reader identifies the evolving verse he experiences Fyodor's artistic workshop in operation and gains insight into the material of poetry and the nature of Fyodor's gift. In the process the reader is embroiled in the provocative, but formidable question: why does the poet create—because he desires to express 'something' or because he is driven to write by the power of the word, i.e., rhythm and rhyme?

Our poet Fyodor recalls that as a teenager he was impelled to compose verses by the technical challenge of producing rhythms and rhymes. Under the influence of Andrei Bely's studies on prosody, he became a "wordsmith" trying to imitate the patters of pyrrhic feet which Bely had discovered in the works of great poets. As a neophyte Fyodor compiled a card file of words, lending themselves to specific meters and rhyme clusters. These "rhymescapes," as he called them, grew of their own accord into poems on predictable subjects. For instance, "Svechi, plechi, vstrechi, and rechi (tapers, shoulders, meetings, and speeches) created the old-world atmosphere of a ball at the Congress of Vienna or on the town governor's birthday " (p. 164). In retrospect Fyodor characterizes this workshop poetry as "an ugly, crippling school" (p. 165). He remembers trying to verbalize emotions aroused by a beautiful young girl:

> The agitation which seized me, swiftly covered me with an icy sheet, squeezed my joints and jerked my fingers... But at that moment, in a hasty clumsy attempt to resolve the agitation, I clutched at the first hackneyed words available, at their ready-made linkages, so that as soon as I had embarked on what I thought to be creation, on what should have been the expression, the living connection between my divine excitement and my human world, everything expired in a fatal gust of words... (p. 165).

In experiencing this conflict between word and vision Fyodor has displayed what might be considered a sign of creative maturation. We recall that such real-life renowned poets as Tiutchev and Blok allude to a similar fatality and futility of expression in their mature works. Tiutchev in "Silentium" formulated it as "Mysl' izrechennaia est' lozh' " (A thought uttered is a lie); while Blok in "Khudozhnik" ("The Artist") compares creating to killing ("Tvorcheskii razum osilil—ubil").

When a poet reaches the stage where he is no longer satisfied with the "game" of rhyme and rhythm, what then becomes the mode of his thinking? Nabokov answers this question by allowing us to look into Fyodor's reverie which "suddenly began to speak with a human voice":

> Nothing in the world could be better than these moments. Love only what is fanciful and rare; what from the distance of a dream steals through: what knaves condemn to death and fools can't bear. To fiction be as to your country true. Now is our time. Stray dogs and cripples are alone awake. Mild is the summer night. A car speeds by: Forever that last car has taken the last banker out of sight. Near that streetlight veined lime-leaves masquerade in chrysoprase with a translucent gleam. Beyond the gate lies Baghdad's crooked shade, and yon star sheds on Pulkovo its beam. Oh swear to me— (p. 168).

Here Fyodor is interrupted by a phone call. Dashing back to bed he once again sinks into a euphoria:

> What shall I call you? Half-Mnemo*syne* [sic]? There's a half-shim*mer* [sic] in your surname too. In dark Berlin, it is so strange to me to roam, oh, my half-fantasy, with you. A bench stands under the translucent tree. Shivers and sobs reanimate you there, and all life's wonder in your gaze I see, and see the pale fair radiance of your hair. In honor of your lips when they kiss mine I might devise a metaphor some time: Tibetan mountain-snows, their glancing shine, and a hot spring near flowers touched with rime. Our poor nocturnal property—that wet asphaltic gloss, that fence and that street light—upon the ace of fancy let us set to win a world of beauty from the night. Those are not clouds—but star-high mountain spurs; not lamplit blinds but camp-light on a tent! O swear to me that while the heartblood stirs, you will be true to what we shall invent. (p. 169).

This flow of seemingly unrelated thoughts halts abruptly when Fyodor's landlady returns home from market, disrupting his mood and the silence of the apartment. Fyodor gets up to dine with the family. After a day crammed with tutoring, visiting bookstores, and puzzling over a chess magazine, Fyodor waits on a deserted street to meet his girl, who, it turns out, is the

72

landlady's daughter Zina Mertz. As he stands in the darkness illumi-
nated only by a streetlight, fences, kitchen gardens, and coal-
houses assume a new aspect, and Fyodor again allows his thoughts
to ramble:

> Waiting for her arrival. She was always late—and always came by
> another road than he. Thus it transpired that even Berlin could be
> mysterious. Within the linden's bloom the streetlight winks. A dark
> and honeyed hush envelopes us. Across the curb one's passing shadow
> slinks: across a stump a sable ripples thus. The night sky melts to
> peach beyond the gate. There water gleams, there Venice vaguely
> shows. Look at that street—it runs to China straight, and yonder
> star above the Volga glows! Oh, swear to me to put in dreams your
> trust, and to believe in fantasy alone, and never let your soul in
> prison rust, nor stretch your arm and say: a wall of stone (p. 189).

At this juncture Zina arrives:

> She always unexpectedly appeared out of the darkness, like a shadow
> leaving its kindred element. At first her ankles would catch the light:
> she moved them close together as if she walked along a slender rope.
> Her summer dress was short, of night's own color, the color of the
> streetlights and the shadows, of tree trunks and of shining pavement—
> paler than her bare arms and darker than her face (p. 189).

Although one is immediately struck by the poetic phraseology—
translucent gleam, honeyed hush, flowers touched with rime—of
Fyodor's far-flung, exotic musing, it is not immediately evident
that these excerpts from his stream of consciousness contain a
thread of coherence and even a structural relationship. Ultimately
the careful reader recognizes that these thoughts are expressed in
rhythmic prose which can be divided into lines of iambic penta-
meter and organized into stanzas. Once rendered in poetic form,
images and allusions are more easily discerned and associated.

(I)

> Love only what is fanciful and rare:
> What from the distance of a dream steals through;
> What knaves condemn to death and fools can't bear.
> To fiction be as to your country true.

73

Now is our time. Stray dogs and cripples are
Alone awake. Mild is the summer night.
A car speeds by: Forever that last car
Has taken the last banker out of sight.

Near the streetlight veined lime-leaves masquerade
In chrysoprase with a translucent gleam.
Beyond the gate Baghdad's crooked shade,
And yon star sheds on Pulkovo its beam.

Oh, swear to me—

(II)

What shall I call your? Half- Mnemo*syne?*
There's a half shim*mer* in your surname too.
In dark Berlin, it is so strange to me
To roam, oh my half-fantasy with you.

A bench stands under the translucent tree.
Shivers and sobs reanimate you there,
And all life's wonder in your gaze I see,
And see the pale fair radiance of your hair.

In honor of your lips when they kiss mine
I might devise a metaphor some time:
Tibetan mountain-snows, their glancing shine,
And a hot spring near flowers touched with rime.

Our poor nocturnal property—that wet
Asphaltic gloss, that fence and that street light—
Upon the ace of fancy let us set
To win a world of beauty from the night.

Those are not clouds, but star-high mountain spurs
No lamplit blinds, but camplight on a tent.
O swear to me that while the heartblood stirs,
You will be true to what she shall invent.

(III)

Waiting for Her Arrival

Within the linden's bloom the streetlight winks.
A dark and honeyed hush envelopes us.
Across the curb one's passing shadow slinks:
Across a stump a sable ripples thus.

The night sky melts to peach beyond the gate
And water gleams, there Venice vaguely shows.
Look at that street—it runs to China straight,
And yonder star above the Volga glows!

Oh, swear to me to put in dreams your trust,
And to believe in fantasy alone,
And never let your soul in prison rust,
Nor stretch your arm and say: a wall of stone.

(IV)

She always unexpectedly appeared
Out of the darkness, like a shadow leaving
Its kindred element. At first her ankles
Would catch the light. She moved them close
                    together
As if she walked along a slender rope.
Her summer dress was short, of night's own color,
The color of tree trunks and of shining pavement—
                    paler
Than her bare arms and darker than her face.[8]

As he verbalizes these poems, Cherdyntsev, now in his twenties, no longer gropes for rhythms or rhymes. Nor is the subject of his verse dictated by the technical aspects of poetry as had been the case earlier. Rather, images repeat themselves in all four poems and are fixed in synonymous, but varied phrasings. The words create a steady rhythm. Just how spontaneous and indigenous rhythmic word-flow is to Fyodor's thoughts can be seen from the fact that in describing his landlady's return from market, Fyodor continues to think in rhyme:

At midday the peck of a key (now we switch to the prose-rhythm of Bely) was heard, and the lock reacted in character clacking; that was Marianna (stopgap) Nikolavna home from the market; with a ponderous step and a sickening swish of her mackintosh she carried a thirty-pound netful of shopping past his door and into the kitchen. Muse of Russian prose-rhythm! Say farewell to the cabbage dactylics of the author of *Moscow* (p. 169).

This stream of thoughts is not a poem, however, since the dactylic units can not be systematically grouped into lines.

Why are some of Fyodor's "rhythmic thoughts" divisible into

lines of verse, while others remain prose? Nabokov does not provide a clear answer to this question, but perhaps a partial explanation can be found by examining the area of poetic subjectivity
and the genesis of Fyodor's thoughts. The prose-rhythm passage
describing Marianna Nikolavna is a reflection, an *otobrazhenie*, of
physical reality which has filtered through Fyodor's creative mind
with little or no transformation. The content or substance of the
four poems, however, is far better described by the term
izobrazhenie, a representation of reality as conjured up by Fyodor.
A close study of the four poems will help to articulate the difference between these modes of thought.

Although Fyodor composes four poems in form, in essence
he has created one completed poem (Poem IV) and three variants
of a second (Poems I, II, III or Poem I-II-III). Or, if we heed
Nabokov's introductory remarks, we may indeed consider that we
have only a single poem comprised of two parts. Poem IV differs
from the rest, but is readily linked with them since it is clearly a
description of Zina coming towards Fyodor, who is waiting in the
street. Poems I, II, III are more complex. They are constructed of
the same images (a star, a linden tree, a streetlight) and have
similar references to Zina, fantasy, and an exotic foreign land. As
we will see, in addition to uniting the three poems, these recurring
images and allusions relate to prose which Fyodor created before
them and even to some which he will compose later.

Let us consider the sources and implications of the various
repetitive elements. The linden or lime-tree, which appears in all
three variants, is most obviously the tree standing near Zina and
Fyodor's trysting spot. As such it is an element of *otobrazhenie*,
a reflection of external reality. But the tree may be further
associated with pre-war Berlin, famous for its lindens and the
street named for them: Unter der Linden. By alluding to mythological characters in Poem II, Fyodor tacitly encourages us to seek
further explanation of imagery in mythology. We find that in Slavic
mythology the lime-tree *(lipa)* was considered female, and women
seeking good crops sacrificed wood of the lime-tree to Perun, the
Slavs' equivalent of Zeus.[9]

Frazer tells us that Mnemosyne is the goddess of memory,
mother of the Muses by Zeus. The italicized syllables which
Nabokov has so conspicuously brought to the reader's attention
are, of course, decoded to give Zina (-syne a sound imitation)
Mertz (half of shim*mer* is -mer).[10] The name Zinaida, for which

Zina is the diminutive, itself means "daughter of Zeus."[11] Thus if Zina is half Mnemosyne and daughter of Zeus at once, she must be one of the Muses, and we seem justified in concluding that she must be Fyodor's Muse of Poetry: She has, after all, inspired at least four poems. Furthermore, in Poem IV we find that Zina's dress is the color of a tree trunk, again bringing to mind the linden. Because of the linden's general mythological assocation with Zeus and women, and its specific connection with the trysting spot, the color of Zina's dress, in addition to Zina's link to Zeus through her name, we seem justified in regarding the linden as a recurring symbol for Zina.

Nabokov has said the poem in Chapter Three is a love poem to Zina, but she is not its sole subject. Fyodor's father figures in the verses as well. His symbol is the star. In the three variants we find: "yon star shed on Pulkovo its beam" (Poem I); "star-high mountain spurs" (Poem II); "a star beyond the Volga glows" (Poem III). This poetic star, possibly evoked by a real star Fyodor sees as he thinks, moves eastward in his mental vision. First he views it over Pulkovo, a village outside St. Petersburg, the city where the Cherdyntsev's had lived. The allusion to the star-high mountains conjures up the Tien Shan range of Asia. (The Urals are not sufficiently high to be termed "star-high.") The phrase "beyond the Volga" once more brings to mind Siberia. The elder Cherdyntsev, the reader will remember, disappeared in Asia nine years earlier on a lepidopteral expedition which had originated in Petersburg. There are yet other implied references to Konstantin Kirillovich. The metaphor describing Zina's kiss, "Tibetan mountain-snows, their glancing shine and a hot spring near flowers touched with rime," auto-plagiaristically echoes a description of a Tibetan morning in Fyodor's biographical sketch of his father: "night frosts were so bad that in the morning flowers were filmed with rime..." (p. 133). "Lamplit blinds" dissolved into camplight on a tent of the scientist's encampment, while the allusion to Venice and China (Poem III) resurrects the image of Marco Polo, an image which Fyodor had developed in the biography (p. 136). Baghdad, on the other hand, can be associated with the lepidopterist with less assurance. This city may be a subliminal reference on Fyodor's part to one of the routes his father might use in an escape from Russia, or perhaps, it is merely another of the unique places like Tibet, Siberia, and China which might have attracted him.

Fyodor's *idée fixe* of being loyal to fiction or fantasy can be interpreted in two ways, both of which are associated with his father. First, the young writer maintains that his father's death is a "fiction" (p. 150). By tenaciously clinging, as he does, to the belief that the elder Cherdyntsev is alive, Fyodor is being faithful to fiction. We can also interpret "fiction" as denoting the world of the poet's imagination, the reality created by his mind. A writer, Fyodor feels, should bear allegiance only to the country of his thoughts, to that which he composes (p. 187). Cherdyntsev is thus unable to devote himself completely to anything or anyone else—note even when he is in love (p. 190). Fantasy is his world, his life. Fyodor terms himself "a seeker of verbal adventures" (p. 151) and confesses that he abandoned the biography because he could not bring himself "to hunt down my own fancies on my father's collecting ground" (p. 151). We are led to believe that young Cherdyntsev consults scholarly source materials and individuals who had known his father so that his portrayal of the lepidopterist's life would be accurate and objective. According to Fyodor, his father had cautioned him about making observations:

> When closely—no matter how closely—observing events in nature, we must in the very process of observation beware of letting our reason—that garrulous dragoman who always runs ahead—prompt us with explanations which then begin imperceptibly to influence the very course of observation and distort it: Thus, the shadow of the instrument falls upon the truth (p. 343).

Yet the vivid "eye-witness" description of Tibet and China are obviously Fyodor's fabrications since he was not permitted to participate in the expedition! Fyodor's way of "seeing" is alien to what his father would have considered good observation. One perception prompts Fyodor to make an association which, in turn, leads to a new idea or image far removed from the original observation. The shadow of the artist most definitely falls upon the objective truth for the artist transforms objective reality into the truth of his personal vision. This is the reason that Cherdyntsev can not complete the biographic sketch. Fyodor may permit himself to impinge upon his father's physical reality, but he cannot bring himself to encroach upon the reality of his father's thoughts. "I fervently try... to divine the current of his thoughts, and I have less success with this than with my mental visits to places which I have never seen" (p. 131). Had he infringed upon his father's thought process, Fyodor would have destroyed the man by creating him in the likeness of his (Fyodor's) own inner world. Still another explanation for Fyodor's inability to present his father's thought will become clear as we explore the nature of our artist's gift.

The multi-faceted images of Zina and Konstantin Kirillovich are, then, forms of *izobrazhenie.* Incorporated in these images or adjacent to them in the poems are elements of *otobrazhenie:* the car (Poem I), the bench (Poem II), the streetlight (Poems I, II, III), the linden, and the star to name but a few examples. These are fragments of the physical world which Fyodor sees as his mind whirls, sorting memories and feelings in his subconscious. The case of prose-rhythm description of Marianna Nikolavna returning from market has a similar explanation. When the front door of the apartment opened, the flow of subliminal thoughts and associations ceased, but Fyodor's mind kept functioning on a poetic frequency. The result is a rhythmic-prose *otobrazhenie* of the incident rather than a poem.

This abundance of element from the physical world in Fyodor's verse helps supply the key to the essence of our poet's gift: seeing in a special way. Scrutinizing Cherdyntsev's verse once more, we recognize that his symbols and allusions are purely visual. Note the preponderance of words like: Radiant, glossy, shine, shimmer. From other "stories" in the "notebook" we find that color is a consuming interest of Fyodor's. He is so sensitive to hue that he must characterize tones as reddish-gray, dove-gray, cinder-gray; sky-blue, smoke-blue, dim-blue; chrysoprase, emerald. We learn, further, that Cherdyntsev possesses synesthetic hearing. The sound of the "a" of the four languages he speaks vary in color from "lacquered black to splinter gray—like different sorts of wood," while the "ch" is "a mixture of burnt-sienna and sepia," and the "s" is "luminous sapphires" (p. 86).

Fyodor's gift extends beyond the bounds of color into the realm of perspective. His descriptions of the physical world have a twist in them as we might expect: "In its garden a young chestnut tree, still unable to walk along and therefore supported by a stake, suddenly came out with a flower bigger than itself" (p. 71). Or, "A golden, stumpy little butterfly, equipped with two black commas, alighted on an oak leaf, half opening its slanting wings, and suddenly shot away like a golden fly" (p. 347). In a third instance a plane flying at night becomes "a broach with three rubies gliding over the dark velvet" (p. 374). The gift of sight pertains to Fyodor's mind's eye as well. As he rereads his book of poems Fyodor "sees" them:

> Now he read in *three-dimensions* (italics are mine—AMS), as it were, carefully exploring each poem, lifted out like a cube from among the rest... (p. 21).

For Fyodor the ultimate in perception is found only in death, when our soul is liberated from "the eye-sockets of the flesh and [we are transformed] into one free eye, which can simultaneously see in all directions."[12] This liberation would allow the artist "supersensory insight into the world accompanied by... inner participation " (p. 322). Since Fyodor does not yet possess this ability to participate in anyone else's world, he can describe only what he "sees" either physiologically or in his mind's eye. This suggests a second explanation why he is unable to simulate his father's thoughts.

As we noted Poems I, II, III are a conglomerate of bits and pieces from Fyodor's subconscious. It is not surprising, therefore, that the same symbols and images continue to intrude upon the poet's thoughts right up to the end of the novel. At one point, while he is trying to fall asleep, Cherdyntsev mulls over the star: "the crystal crunching of that Christian night beneath a chrysolitic star" (p. 364). The nine iambic feet do not satisfy him. Still on this same frequency Fyodor's mind pursues the image in a new way: "A falling star, a cruising chrysolite, an aviator's avatar " (p. 364). Next we enter into a dream, presented to the reader as reality, in which Fyodor's father arrives in Berlin to be reunited with his wife and son secretly. A few days after this dream, Zina's parents move from Berlin conveniently, but unknowingly leaving the two lovers living alone in the same apartment. Walking home with Zina to the deserted flat for the first time, Fyodor composes what might be considered tonic verse which, presented as prose, ends the penultimate paragraph of the novel:

> Will it really happen tonight?
> Will it really happen now?
> The weight and the threat of bliss
> When I walk with you like this,
>
> Ever so slowly,
> And hold you by the shoulder,

Everything slightly sways,
My head hums, and I feel

My head hums, and I feel
Like dragging my feet,
My left slipper falls off my heel.

We crawl, dawdle,
Dwindle in a mist—
And now we are almost all melted...

And one day we shall recall all this—
The lindens, the shadow on the wall,
And a poodle's unclipped claws tapping
Over the flagstones of the night.

And the star, the star.
And here is the square
And the dark church
With the yellow light
Of its clock. And here
On the corner, the house.

[p. 377]

The linden, symbolizing Zina, the star representing his father, the darkness, and a light haunt Fyodor to the end.

In his introduction to *The Gift* Nabokov ponders "how far the imagination of the reader will follow the young lovers once they have been dismissed." The last paragraph of the novel which the author has revealed (p. 11) to be an Onegin Stanza in prose, echoes this question: "the cords of fate / itself continue to vibrate; / and no obstruction of the sage / exists where I have put The End: / the shadows of my world extend beyond the skyline of the page..." (p. 378). In so ending Nabokov nudges the reader, who by this time has completed his vicarious apprenticeship, to become a creator. Zina and Fyodor will play any scene like obedient puppets if only the reader will build the set and provide the script.

What *The Gift* discloses, then is the anatomy of one poet's creativity. In Fyodor's case its central nerve is the writer's remarkable ability to see the objective world in a way different from most people, coloring it with memory, emotional attachments, and elements of fancy. The poet transforms the surrounding, physical world into a new, for him, more real world. He creates this world spontaneously, subconsciously. The technical challenges of describing this world, specifically rhythm and rhyme, no longer figure in the process of creation any more than writing down the words does. While a word may set into motion a chain of ideas ("Noticed" once grew into a poem on Russia, pp. 41 and 68) our mature poet is no longer preoccupied with words as the building blocks of expression. He thinks in images. In the final analysis this is not a disclosure original with Nabokov. In 1905 Alexander Potebnya pointed out: "Poetry, as well as prose, is first and foremost a special way of thinking and knowing... (which permits) an economy of mental effort."[13] Victor Shklovsky described this economy as "thinking in images."[14] His term *ostranenie* (making strange), furthermore, implies that the artist sees in a special way. The point is, however, that Nabokov does not merely describe how an artist creates. He has done more. He has contrived to expose that fragmentary, unique process of seeing and thinking, which, when articulated and committed to paper, is called writing poetry.

NOTES

1. V. Khodasevich, "On Sirin," trans. M. H. Walker, *Triquarterly* (Winter, 1970), p. 100.

2. *Ibid.*

3. The note to "On Sirin" in *TriQuarterly* indicates that Khodasevich had not yet read *The Gift* when this article appeared in *Vozrozhdenie,* the Paris émigré daily, on February 13, 1937. However, on January 30, 1937, *Vozrozhdenie* reported a literary gathering ("An Evening of V. V. Sirin") at which Khodasevich made introductory remarks similar to the contents of "On Sirin." Nabokov read excerpts from *The Gift* at this evening. It is not clear from either the newspaper report or Khodasevich's critique just how familiar he was with Nabokov's novel prior to its serialization. It is, however, possible, he had read it in manuscript form.

4. Andrew Field, *Nabokov, His Life in Art* (Boston, 1963), p. 214.

5. *Ibid.*

6. *Ibid.*

7. Vladimir Nabokov, *The Gift,* trans. Michael Scammell and Vladimir Nabokov (New York,1963). All further page references in the text are to this edition.

8. This blank verse confirms Bely's conviction that "there is no line of distinction between poetry and artistic prose." Quoted by V. M. Zhirmunsky in "On Rhythmic Prose," *To Honor Roman Jakobson,* (The Hague, 1967), p. 2367.

9. James Frazer, *The Golden Bough* (New York, 1923), p. 61.

10. The Russian original makes this clue even more self-exposing: polu-Mnemo*tsine* and polu-*merts*anie, rendering "To Zina Mertz." On the whole, all Sirin's verbal cleverness is masterfully preserved in the English edition.

11. Flora Loughead, ed., *The Dictionary of Given Names with Origins and Meanings* (Glendale, Calif,, n.d.), p. 234.

12. This "quotation," attributed to the Frenchman Delalande's *Discours sur les ombres,* is found in Alexander Chernyshevski's diary which imperceptibly creeps into Fyodor's "notebook." In the introduction (p. 6) to the English edition of *Invitation to*

a Beheading (New York, 1959) Nabokov indicates that Pierre Delalande is his invention.

13. Alexander Potebnya, *Iz zapisok po teorii slovesnosti* (Kharkov, 1905), p. 83, quoted by V. Shklovsky in "Art as Technique," *Russian Formalist Criticism,* trans. L. T. Lemon and M. J. Reis (Lincoln, 1965), p. 5.

14. V. Shklovsky, *op. cit.,* p. 5.

D. Barton Johnson

SYNESTHESIA, POLYCHROMATISM, AND NABOKOV

Synesthesia is one of the more exotic byways of the human experience. Like most nebulous phenomena, it is more easily illustrated than defined. One of the most vivid and precise descriptions of a synesthetic experience is that of Albert Hofmann, the Swiss chemist who first synthesized LSD.

> On arriving home I lay down in a dazed condition with my eyes closed. There surged upon me an uninterrupted stream of fantastic images of extraordinary plasticity and vividness and accompanied by an intense, kaleidoscopelike play of colors. I felt a marked desire to laugh. I had great difficulty in speaking coherently, my field of vision swayed before me, and objects appeared distorted like images in curved mirrors. The faces of those around me appeared as grotesque, colored masks. I had a clear recognition of my condition, in which state I sometimes observed, in the manner of an independent, neutral observer, that I shouted half insanely or babbled incoherent words. Occasionally I felt as if I were out of my body. All acoustic perceptions (e.g., the noise of a passing car) were transformed into optical effects, every sound evoking a corresponding colored hallucination constantly changing in shape and color...[1]

This is a classic description of synesthesia—the intermixing of the output of the normally discrete sense modalities. Three kinds of intersensorial blends are described: photisms—intense, detailed, colored visions with closed eyes; phonisms—verbal hallucinations; and chromesthesia—the conversion of acoustic perceptions into colored visual effects.

Synesthesia is by no means restricted to drug-related experiences or to psychotic states, although much of the recent literature that mentions synesthesia (usually *en passant*) stems from the current widespread interest in hallucinogenic drugs. Synesthesia manifests itself in varying degrees among otherwise normal people. Chromesthesia, in particular, is noted fairly commonly among children but tends to die out with maturation.[2] Occasionally, however, the phenomenon survives into adulthood. The Russian composer Scriabin not only possessed colored hearing (as chromesthesia is sometimes called) but actually wrote music for which he orchestrated an accompanying colored light show. Roman Jakobson has reported one highly developed case in which the subject, a thirty-two-year-old Czech, gifted in both music and painting, exhibited a complete set of color correspondences for all of the Czech vowels and consonants.[3] Although chromesthesia is the most commonly discussed form of synesthesia, there is another type which is much more widespread—that of hypnagogic visions. These are the simultaneous auditory and visual hallucinations which sometimes drift through the mind in the drowsy state just preceding sleep. Psychological synesthesia is a well-attested phenomenon with a clinical history of over 250 years.[4]

Literary synesthesia (as opposed to psychological) manifests itself as a metaphor of the senses that involves the application of words and images, which are normally appropriate to the description of one type of sense perception, to the description of one type other type of sense perception. A familiar example is Kipling's "The dawn comes up like thunder" in which the cataclysmic violence and abruptness of a natural sound phenomenon is ascribed to the tropical sunrise, a light phenomenon. A simpler and perhaps more tasteful example is the title of Voznesensky's new book, *Ten' zvuka (The Shadow of Sound),* an intersensorial blend of *ten' sveta* (shadow of light) and *ekho zvuka* (echo of sound). Literary or verbal synesthesia is at least as old as Western literature (it is found in Homer) and, doubtless, a great deal older.[5]

Literary synesthesia became a subject of intense interest late in the last century largely through its cultivation by the French symbolists. The most famous exemplification of literary *audition colorée* is Arthur Rimbaud's 1871 sonnet "Voyelles" which begins:

> *A noir, E blanc, I rouge, U vert, O bleu: voyelles,*
> *Je dirai quelque jour vos naissances latentes:*
> *A, noir corset velu des mouches éclatantes*
> *Qui bombinent autour des puanteurs cruelles...*

The remaining stanzas give a set of colored images evoked by the respective vowel sounds. Contemporary critics attacked the device of literary synesthesia with a ferocity that now seems amusing. The German critic Max Nordau, for example, asserted that synesthesia is:

> ...an evidence of diseased and debilitated brain activity, if consciousness releases the advantages of the differentiated perceptions of phenomena, and carelessly confounds the reports conveyed by the particular senses.

It is a retrogression to the very beginning of organic development. It is a descent from the height of human perfection to the low level of the mollusc. To raise the combination, transposition and confusions of the perceptions of sound and sight to the rank of a principle of art, to see futurity in this principle, is to designate as progress the return from the consciousness of man to that of the oyster.[7]

This passage, although more strident in tone, is typical of many critics' reaction to synesthetic transfer in at least two ways. Firstly, the author sees synesthesia as a diseased condition—which it certainly is not—and, secondly, he fails to distinguish between synesthesia as a psychological phenomenon and synesthesia as a purely literary artifice—simply another type of metaphor which is in no way dependent upon its psychological counterpart. Intersensorial metaphors, at least in their less extravagant forms, are far from uncommon in everyday speech. Indeed in many cases they have become standard figures of speech or cliches in which we no longer see their synesthetic basis. We describe, for example, the sound of the human voice in visual terms (silver, golden), kinesthetic terms (heavy), tactile (velvety, soft, warm), or even in gustatory terms (bitter). We habitually speak of loud colors and dull pain.[8] This sort of synesthetic metaphor is universal and its role in language has been summed up by the eminent psycholinguist Roger Brown with his observation that "Many, perhaps all, languages make metaphorical extentions of their vocabularies of sensation.[9]

In his autobiography *Speak, Memory* Nabokov discusses his own synesthetic gifts at some length.[10] From early childhood on, Nabokov was subject to mild hallucinations. These fell into two categories—hypnagogic visions and chromesthesia. The hypnagogic visions are limited to those brief transitional periods between waking and sleeping and are both aural and optical in nature. These are described as being conveyed by "a neutral, detached anonymous voice, which I catch saying words of no importance to me whatever—an English or a Russian sentence, not even addressed to me, and so trivial that I hardly dare give samples, lest the flatness I wish to convey be marred by a molehill of sense" (33). These aural mirages have visual, often grotesque, counterparts in which Nabokov sees "projected, as it were, on the inside of the eyelid—gray figures walking between beehives or small black parrots gradually vanishing among mountain snows, or a mauve remoteness melting beyond moving masts" (34). Chromesthesia, unlike hypnagogic visions, is a function of the waking mind, and is described by Nabokov in much greater detail.

Nabokov reports that he first became aware of his own chromesthetic gift while playing with a set of colored alphabet blocks. In the course of building a tower with the blocks, the six-year-old boy remarked to his mother that the colors for the various letters were "all wrong." It turned out that his mother also had letter (sound) /color associations and that some of the toy block letters had the same hues for her as for her son (but different from those assigned by the toy manufacturer) [35]. Once aware of the boy's synesthetic gift she encouraged his sensitivity to visual stimulation in various ways. Herself an amateur painter, she showed him the magical results of blending colors. At bed-time the child was allowed to play with masses of her jewelry which seemed to him hardly inferior to "the illumination in the city during imperial fetes, when. . .giant monograms, crowns and other armorial designs, made of colored electric bulbs—sapphire, emeralds, ruby—glowed with a kind of charmed constraint..." (36). Drawing and painting lessons were part of the boy's early home education.

As Nabokov himself notes, colored hearing is not an entirely apt name in his case since the concurrent color response is not keyed exclusively to a sound unit. He remarks that "the color sensation seems to be produced by the very act of my orally forming a given letter while I imagine its outline" (34). This suggests that in addition to the sound itself the physiological facts of articulation are an element in the process. Other references indicate that as a child Nabokov was particularly sensitive to the physical shape of letters—both written and printed. In describing his new French dictation notebook, he recounts "...delighting in every limb of every limpid letter. . .with exquisite care I would inscribe the word *Dictée...*" (105). Or in speaking of his first reading primer (which was in English, not Russian), he notes that its four protagonists "now drift with a slow-motion slouch across the remotest backdrop of memory; and akin to the mad alphabet of an optician's chart, the grammar-book lettering looms again before me" (80). It is of interest that Nabokov describes the relationship between the later Russian and the earlier English variants of his memoirs as that of capital letters to cursive (DB8). The influence of letter shapes is also mentioned by Nabokov in discussing his reaction to them in different languages. He notes that the slightest difference in the physical shape of a letter representing the same sound in different languages also alters its color impression. In particular, Russian letters representing the same sound but formed differently from their Latin counterparts are generally distinguished by their duller tone (DB 26-27). Thus the Russian П is described as "gouache" green whereas the Latin 'p' is characterized as "unripe apple" green—a brighter shade. This particular example is instructive in another regard for it established that sound rather than letter shape is the primary determinant of hue since the Cyrillic П and Latin 'p' have basically the same color (green), although the letter shapes are quite different. That still other sense modalities are involved in the correspondences is suggested in the Russian variant of Nabokov's autobiography where in reference to Cyrillic letters he reports that their "color sensation is formed by palpable, labial, almost gustatory means. In order to determine thoroughly the hue of a letter, I have to savor the letter, let it swell and radiate in my mouth while I imagine its visual design" (DB26).

Taken together these observations indicate that Nabokov's sound (letter) / color correspondences are dependent on a variety of factors: sound, articulatory physiology, letter shape, and perhaps taste. All of these contribute in some measure to Nabokov's color responses. In his memoirs Nabokov gives in detail his color associations for each sound and/or symbol of the two alphabets, English and Russian. Much of interest can be said about the linguistic and structural aspects of Nabokov's sound/color correspondences, but here we wish to focus the discussion on the more "literary" aspects of his synesthesia, i.e., its aesthetic and thematic implications and its role in his creative psychology.

An examination of Nabokov's work provides us with a number of examples of synesthetic images. One of the earliest and most vivid is afforded in

> The recollection of my crib. . .which brings back. . .the pleasures of handling a certain beautiful, delightfully solid, garnet-dark crystal egg left over from some unremembered Easter; I used to chew a corner of the bedsheet until it was thoroughly soaked and then wrap the egg in it tightly, so as to admire and re-lick the warm, ruddy glitter of the snugly enveloped facets that came seeping through with a miraculous completeness of glow and color. But that was not yet the closest I got to feeding upon beauty (24).

In Nabokov's account of the room of his childhood French governess, Mademoiselle O, he writes that "it was imbued with a *heavy, enuretic odor.* In that sickening mist, reeking, among other *woolier effluvia,* of the *brown smell* of oxidized apple peel, the lamp burned low and strange objects glimmered upon the writing desk" (107, my italics). In this passage there are no less than three synesthetic images—one "a heavy...odor"—a petrified metaphor which serves as a defining context for the "live" figures "woolier effluvia" and "brown smell." Thus weight, texture, and color are all attributed to an odor. In recalling a reunion with Mademoiselle O many years later he writes, "She turned to me with a *dazzled look* of *moist wonder* and bliss in her eyes" (116). This would appear to be built on the transposition of the adjectives in an implicit phrase "moist look of dazzled wonder." "Moist look" is, of course, itself an ossified synesthetic image just as "dazzled wonder" is a cliche but by transposing the two epithets Nabokov achieves a fresh synesthetic image of great effectiveness. A similar transformation is evident in the example: "...she was so enchanting that it even brought tears to one's eyes, and even at the merest thought of her, a moaning, awful salty night would well up in me."[11] The implicit "salty tears" yields "salty night" while the effect is further enhanced by "moaning" as an attribute of "night." Another passage in *Speak, Memory* depicts a violent downpour which "was reduced all at once to oblique lines of *silent gold* breaking into short and long dashes against a background of subsiding vegetable agitation" (216). Here a substantivized adjective is metonymically substituted for "rain" thus transforming an underlying source phrase "silent golden rain" into "silent gold."

The poem *Voluptates Tactionum* is wholly built on an image of sound/touch interplay.[12] "When you turn a knob, your set/Will obligingly exhale/Forms, invisible and yet/Tangible—a world in Braille." Nabokov goes on to explore the erotic possibilities of his invention.

One of the most extended uses of synesthetic imagery occurs in the 1945 poem *An Evening of Russian Poetry.*[13] The speaker (Nabokov?) is giving a talk on Russian poetry to an American women's circle:

My little helper at the magic lantern,
insert that slide and let the colored beam
project my name or any such-like phantom in

Slavic characters upon the screen.
The other way, the other way. I thank you.
On mellow hills the Greek, as you remember,
fashioned his alphabet from cranes in flight;
his arrows crossed the sunset, then the night.
Our simple skyline and a taste for timber,
the influence of hives and conifers,
reshaped the arrows and the borrowed birds.
Yes, Sylvia?
"Why do you speak of words   .
when all we want is knowledge nicely browned?"
Because all hangs together—shape and sound,
heather and honey, vessel and content.
Not only rainbows—every line is bent,
and skulls and seals and all good worlds around
like Russian verse, like our colossal vowels:
those painted eggs, those glossy pitcher flowers
that swallow whole a golden bumble bee,
those shells that hold a thimble and the sea.
Next question.

The chromesthetic representation here is so explicit as to be almost clinical—the colored beam of Cyrillic characters, the discussion of the shaping of the Greek letters and then their reshaping into the Cyrillic, and finally the linking of shape, sound, and color in the rainbow-curved colossal Russian vowels.

The foregoing examples notwithstanding, synesthetic imagery, although used to brilliant effect, is comparatively rare in Nabokov's work. Although sense-blending metaphors are not common, Nabokov does utilize a wide range of discrete sense perceptions in his descriptions. In depicting a scene the entire panoply of the senses may be brought to bear, e.g., "Using a candle flame (diluted to a deceptive pallor by the sunshine), I had been engaged in transforming dripping sticks of the stuff into gluey, marvelously smelling, scarlet and blue and bronze-colored globs" (58). Here we have light quality, texture, smell, and significantly, a complex of colors. Color and particularly color groupings are an important aspect both of Nabokov's view of the world and of his literary style. Polychromatism is, in fact, a far more evident aspect of his style than chromesthesia. Perhaps the most frequently recurring complex color image in *Speak, Memory* is that of the rainbow—both natural and artificial as refracted through a prism. A few examples: in his last glimpse of his childhood love, Colette, "...there was, I remember, some detail in her attire . . . that reminded me of the rainbow spiral in a glass marble. I still seem to be holding that wisp of iridescence...." (152). This image is evoked again in "a colored spiral in a small ball of glass. This is how I see my own life" (275). Elsewhere, we read of "...a pleasantly supercilious, although plainly psychopathic, rotary sprinkler with a private rainbow hanging in its spray above gemmed grass" (304). Of his father, Nabokov writes, "I viewed his activities through a prism of my own, which split into many enchanting colors the rather austere light my teachers glimpsed" (186). Even more frequent are descriptions of rainbow-like color spectra —although often without explicit reference to the underlying rainbow image. The young Nabokov's governess showed him the art of selecting autumn maple leaves and arranging them into "an almost complete spectrum (minus the blue—a big disappointment!), green shading into lemon, lemon into orange and so on through the reds and purples, purplish browns, reddish again and back through lemon to green..." (97). Similarly, he tells of his mother's passion for hunting the "tawny edulis, brown scaber, red aurantiacus" and of her spreading them out on a white garden bench "while the sun cast a livid gleam just before setting, and there. . .her mushrooms would lie, very colorful. . .viscid fawn cap. . . .base of a dark-stippled stem" (43-44). The color spectrum occurs again in a passage on: "Colored pencils. Their detailed spectrum advertised on the box but never completely represented by those inside..." (Nabokov then details the special properties of each pencil) [101].

In Nabokov's Victorian, albeit Russian childhood, upperclass homes made lavish use of stained glass window decoration and Nabokov often mentions particular color patterns in describing such dwellings. One of the most persistent color motifs in *Speak, Memory* (and not uncommon in Nabokov's other works) is that of stained glass window-panes. The family town house front door had stained glass with a tulip design (92). A more significant occurrence of the stained glass motif describes Mademoiselle O's French readings to the Nabokov children on the glass-enclosed veranda of their country house. Nabokov writes of the pleasure of listening to Mademoiselle O "distilling her reading voice from the still prism of her person" (105).

But the most constant source of enchantment during those readings came from the harlequin pattern of colored panes inset in a whitewashed framework on either side of the veranda. The garden when viewed through these magic glasses grew still and aloof. If one looked through blue glass, the sand turned to cinders while inky trees swam in a tropical sky. The yellow created an amber world infused with an extra strong brew of sunshine. The red made the foliage drip ruby dark upon a pink footpath. The green soaked greenery in a greener green. And when, after such richness, one turned to a small square of normal, savorless glass, with its lone mosquito or lame daddy longlegs, it was like taking a draught of water when one is not thirsty (106-107).

The stained glass motif culminates in a passage about a pavilion located on the family country estate. The pavilion sits midway on a small bridge which rises over a ravine "like a coagulated rainbow" and has "wine-red, bottle-green, and dark blue lozenges of stained glass" that "lend a chapel-like touch" (215). This pavilion plays a key role in Nabokov's artistic and emotional development in that it serves as the point of genesis for two of the ruling passions of his life and is closely connected with a third: these are literature, love and lepidoptera.

Nabokov's first venture into literature was as a poet.

In order to reconstruct the summer of 1914, when the numb fury of verse-making first came over me, all I really need is to visualize a certain pavilion . . . I dream of my pavilion at least twice a year. As a rule, it appears in my dreams quite independently of their subject matter, which, of course, may be anything, from abduction to zoolatry. It hangs around, so to speak, with the unobtrusiveness of an artist's signature. I find it clinging to a corner of the dream canvas or cunningly worked into some ornamental part of the picture (215).

It was in this pavilion that the fifteen-year-old Nabokov waited out a brief but violent wind and rainstorm:

The storm passed quickly . . . . Beyond the park, above streaming fields, a rainbow slipped into view; the fields ended in the notched dark border of a remote fir wood; part of the rainbow went across it, and that section of the forest edge shimmered most magically through the pale green and pink of the iridescent veil drawn before it: a tenderness and a glory that made poor relatives of the rhomboidal, colored reflections which the return of the sun had brought forth on the pavilion floor. A moment later my first poem began (216-17).[14]

The pavilion also figures as the scene of Nabokov's initial meeting with his first love whom he refers to as Tamara, "to give her a name concolorous with the real one" (229). Thirty-three years later Nabokov describes their first meeting as taking place on "August 9, 1915, to be Petrarchially exact, at half-past four of that season's fairest afternoon in the rainbow-windowed pavilion" (230). The pavilion has still other strong associations for Nabokov. His early butterfly collecting was centered on the grounds of the country estate where the pavilion stood. It is certainly not without significance that Nabokov chooses to comment on the close etymological relationship between 'pavilion' and 'papilio,' the Latin word for butterfly (216). The pavilion also functions on a more abstract, purely esthetic plane in the formal structure of Nabokov's autobiography. It is in the pavilion that the numerous polychromatic images (e.g., the imperial illuminations with jewel-like monograms and designs of colored lights, the colored pencils, the autumn leaves, the mushrooms, the recurrent stained-glass descriptions, etc.) blend back into the rainbow motif whence they all originated. The pavilion is one end of Nabokov's esthetic rainbow.

We initiated this discussion of polychromatism in Nabokov's work by noting its connection with synesthesia. There is, of course, no necessary tie between the two phenomena. The association of the two is justifiable only insofar as it is possible to show them to be linked in Nabokov's mind. This association can be demonstrated with certainty. The expanded 1966 English version of Nabokov's memoirs (but not the earlier English or Russian variants) has an index which is, at certain points, as much esthetic as practical. In addition to the factual entries for names, places, and books, there are also a few general thematic entries. Scanning the index we find, among others, the following entries: Colored hearing, Stained glass, Jewels, and Pavilion. Thus most of the constituent elements which enter into the rainbow motif are given, although there is no index entry for Rainbow. The connection between these polychromatic entries and Colored hearing or chromesthesia is quite clear. The reader who consults Colored hearing is referred to Stained glass and thence to Jewels and Pavilion. The Jewels entry, via a cross-reference, leads the reader back to Stained glass. In other words, Colored hearing (chromesthesia) is the primary entry and may take the reader to associated secondary topics. The latter do not, however, point back to Colored hearing. This associational chain constitutes one proof of the connection between the elements of the rainbow motif and synesthesia.

The rainbow motif is still more important in another context. It plays a central role in establishing synesthesia as a critical element in Nabokov's esthetic canon and his creative consciousness.

English-speaking children sometimes learn the prismatic rainbow colors and their sequence by a simple mnemonic device: the name Roy G. Biv—an acronym formed from red, orange, yellow, green, blue, indigo, violet. The primary rainbow consists of the seven indicated colors with red at the top and violet at the bottom. Thus the initial letters of the color names are read from top to bottom to get the acronym. Nabokov coins his own acronymic 'words' for his Russian and English rainbows but does so in the context of his own synesthetic color/sound correspondences. For Nabokov, the first (i.e., topmost) rainbow color, red, is correlated with the Russian letter 'В' [v];[15] the second rainbow color, orange, with 'Ё' [jo] ; the third, yellow, with 'E' [je] ; green, with 'П' [p] ; blue, with 'C' [s] ; indigo, with [K] ; and violet with '3' [z]. On the basis of these chromesthetic correspondences Nabokov's Russian rainbow acronym is ВЁЕП CK3 [vjojepskz]. The discussion of the colors of the Russian letters and sounds and the Russian rainbow 'word' is in the Russian version of his autobiography, *Drugie berega (Other Shores,* pp. 26-27). The presentation of the parallel English information is found in the 1966 *Speak, Memory* (34-35). There is at no point a confrontation of the two sets of data. The English equivalent to ВЁЕПCK3 [vjojepskz] is KZSPYGV. This acronym is formed in the same way as its Russian counterpart but in reverse order: violet is 'K'; indigo, 'Z'; blue, 'S'; green, 'P'; yellow, 'Y'; orange, 'G'; and red, 'V' . The relationship between the two rainbow words is more clearly demonstrated in the following.

Russian	*English*
B Ё E П C K 3	K Z S P Y G V
R O Y G B I V	V I B G Y O R
e r e r l n i	i n l r e r e
d a l e u d o	o d u e l a d
n l e e i l	l i e e l n
g o n g e	e g n o g
e w o t	t o w e

The Russian and English rainbow acronyms are in reverse order vis-à-vis each other. They are, within the limits imposed by the somewhat different sound/color correspondences of the two different languages, mirror images of each other.[16] Why should the Russian chromatic rainbow acronym reflect the color sequence red, orange yellow...violet, whereas its English counterpart displays the backward ordering violet, indigo, blue...red? If there is any single aspect of Nabokov's work that is indisputable it is that his constructs are never random. It is not by chance that the colors reflected in his Russian and English rainbow words are antithetically ordered.

Nabokov in addition to being a man of letters is also a natural scientist of some repute. His interest in nature, his acuity of observation, and his knowledgeableness are immediately evident to the reader of his work. It is in this area that we must seek an answer to the mirror image rainbows. There are, in nature, two kinds of rainbows—primary and secondary. A primary rainbow is one "in which the rays are refracted on entering each drop, reflected from its interior surface, and refracted again on emerging and in which the red is seen on the outside of the bow."[17] A secondary rainbow is one "that is above, concentric with, and near but somewhat larger and fainter than a primary rainbow and . . . differs . . . in that there are two internal reflections and the red is seen on the inside edge of the rainbow." Nabokov's Russian rainbow acronym ВЕЁПСКЗ (red, orange, yellow, etc.) corresponds to the bright primary rainbow with red at the top, whereas his English KZSPYGV corresponds to the "larger fainter" rainbow with red (i.e., V) at the bottom. The arrangement and relationship of the mirror image rainbows is illustrated in figure A.

The rainbow motif runs throughout Nabokov's work but only in his autobiography does it assume such a sharply delineated meaning. The significance of the rainbow-based chromesthetic Russian and English acronyms is clear. The primary rainbow word, ВЕЁПС КЗ, represents Nabokov's literary creation in his native Russian and the secondary rainbow word, KZSPYGV his English language writing. Though most readers think of Nabokov primarily as an English-language writer, recall that when the first English and Russian versions of the autobiography were being written he had published only two English novels, but nine in Russian. Neither *The Real Life of Sebastian Knight* (1941) nor *Bend Sinister* (1947) display the verbal artistry of the last Russian novels such as *Dar (The Gift, 1937)* nor the subsequent stylistic virtuosity of the later English works starting from *Lolita* (1955). In the forties and early fifties Nabokov was very much concerned with this problem of attempting to bring the level of his English prose style to that of his Russian. The latter part of this period was that of the writing of *Lolita* and in his postscript to the novel Nabokov touches on this problem.[18] After sum-

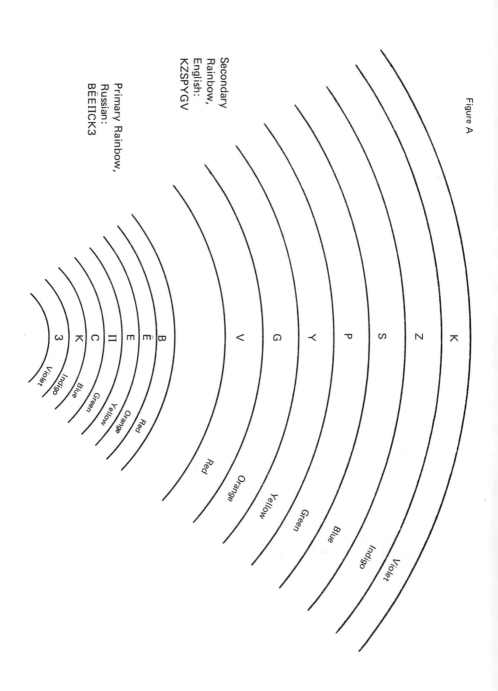

Figure A

Secondary
Rainbow,
English:
KZSPYGV

Primary Rainbow,
Russian:
BЁЕПCКЗ

K

Z

S

P Blue

Y Green

G Yellow

V Orange

Red

В Red

Ё Orange

Е Yellow

П Green

С Blue

К Indigo

З Violet

Indigo

Violet

marizing *Lolita* as the record of his love affair with the English language, Nabokov goes on to say

> My private tragedy...is that I had to abandon my natural idiom, my untrammeled, rich and infinitely docile Russian tongue for a second-rate brand of English, devoid of any of those apparatuses—the baffling mirror, the black velvet backdrop, the implied associations and traditions—which the native illusionists, frac-tails flying, can magically use to transcend the heritage in his own way.

The English reader cannot agree that Nabokov's change of language was a tragedy. Indeed, Nabokov suggests in the postscript to his own Russian translation of *Lolita* that the confrontation of the two texts at last disabused him of the notion that his Russian style is vastly superior to that of his English (296). Perhaps if now rewriting his memoirs Nabokov would reverse the assignment of his primary rainbow to Russian and its secondary reflection to English—in any other than a purely chronological sense. The identification of Nabokov's mirror image rainbows as an emblematic analogue to the two languages of his literary creation brings us back to the source of the double rainbows—their chromesthetic origin in the Russian and English sound systems.

The chromesthesia-rooted rainbows are beyond any reasonable doubt consciously elaborated symbols of Nabokov's creative process. It is, however, quite possible to argue that the basis of this symbolic imagery is literary rather than psychological synesthesia. That is, Nabokov may indeed possess psychological synesthesia and use it as the basis for a metaphor describing his art. The use of synesthesia as the basis of the art metaphor does not, however, necessarily mean that synesthesia is an active agency in Nabokov's creative process. It could simply be a convenient, if very apt, vehicle for the metaphor symbolizing his creative processes. The question being raised here is whether or not the relationship between Nabokov's synesthesia and his art is purely metaphorical (i. e., literary) or is it psychological (i.e., inherent). It is not to be excluded that the answer lies somewhere between these polarities.[19]

The material examined up to this point has been largely from *Speak, Memory* and to its autobiographical predecessors where the author speaks in his own name. It is, however, in one of Nabokov's novels, *The Gift,* that we find the most explicit statement of a theory concerning the relationship of chromesthesia and literary creativity. This occurs in an imaginary dialogue between the protagonist Fyodor Godunov-Cherdyntsev, a young writer, and the poet and critic Koncheyev. Their talk ranges over much of Russian literature. In passing, Godunov-Cherdyntsev observes that Leskov, although a second-rank writer, "has a Latin feeling for blueness: *lividus.* Lyov Tolstoy, on the other hand, preferred violet shades..." (84). Finally Koncheyev asks Fyodor:

How did it begin with you?

When my eyes opened to the alphabet. Sorry, that sounds pretentious, but the fact is, since childhood I have been afflicted with the most intense elaborate *audition colorée.*

So that you too, like Rimbaud, could have—

Written not a mere sonnet but a fat opus, with auditive hues he never dreamt of. For instance, the various numerous 'a's of the four languages which I speak differ for me in tinge, going from lacquered-black to splintery-gray—like different sorts of wood. I recommend to you my pink flannel 'm'. I don't know if you remember the insulating cotton wool which was removed with the storm windows in spring? Well, that is my Russian 'y', or rather 'ugh', so grubby and dull that words are ashamed to begin with it. If I had some paints handy I would mix burnt-sienna and sepia for you so as to match the color of a gutta-percha 'ch' sound; and you would appreciate my radiant 's' if I could pour into your cupped hands some of those luminous sapphires that I touched as a child...when my mother allowed her perfectly celestial treasures to flow out of their abyss into her palm, out of their cases onto black velvet...and if one turned the curtain slightly..., one could see, along the receding riverfront, facades in the blue-blackness of the night, the motionless magic of an imperial illumination, the ominous blaze of diamond monograms, colored bulbs in coronal designs....

Buchstaben von Feuer, in short.[20]

Although in the foreword to the English translation of *The Gift,* Nabokov specifically warns the reader against identifying Fyodor with the book's author, this particular passage undeniably seems to be drawn from Nabokov's own psychological landscape. In almost every detail the passage corresponds to the autobiographical information in *Drugie berega* when Nabokov is discussing his own synesthetic gift (27-28). Thus the genesis of literary creativity which is "the gift" referred to in the book's title is assigned to colored hearing or chromesthesia.

The foregoing facts, taken together, constitute a strong case for positing a central role for chromesthesia in Nabokov's creative processes. We have noted, however, that synesthetic images are comparatively rare in his work. If in fact synesthesia is so important in Nabokov's creative psychology, we must raise the question of why it is used so sparingly—at least in its most explicit form, the metaphor. A part of the answer may be quite simple. The effectiveness of an artistic device may tend to vary inversely with the frequency of its use. A further factor may be that the expression of the psychological trait has been partially sublimated into the more general tendency toward chromatism which we have noted. Indeed, it seems likely that at least in some measure ,Nabokov's aesthetic chromatism is an outgrowth of his psychological chromesthesia. Finally it is quite clear that Nabokov does not draw directly on some subconscious source but has a wide knowledge of both psychological and literary synesthesia. Consequently it seems likely that Nabokov's use of literary synesthesia is carefully tempered by a more or less explicit theory about its literary uses and limitations. None of these speculations, however, are wholly convincing explanations for the relative infrequency of synesthetic images in Nabokov's work considering that we have posited a critical role for synesthetic mechanisms in his creative process. This raises a further question. Might not psychological synesthesia be manifested in some other way?

It is not without significance that Nabokov's memoirs are entitled *Speak, Memory.* Memory with its adjunct time is a (and perhaps the) dominant theme in Nabokov's writing. Memory, for Nabokov, is man's line of defense against oblivion and death. This theme is quite explicit in Nabokov's newest novel *Ada* as well as in *Speak, Memory.* Van, the hero of *Ada,* is the author of a philosophical treatise, *The Texture of Time,* and counts his life span not from his day of birth but from his first memory 195 days later (535-536). It is of great interest in this regard that Nabokov's account of his earliest recollections is cast in the form of a synesthetic image. "In probing my childhood.... I see the awakening of consciousness as a series of spaced flashes, with the intervals between them gradually diminishing until bright blocks of perception are formed, affording memory a slippery hold" (20). It is of no less interest that in those passages where the mechanism of memory is being examined scenes are often invoked in the full panoply of the sense modalities. This process is well illustrated in the following passage:

> I witness with pleasure the supreme achievement of
> memory, which is the masterly use it makes of innate
> harmonies when gathering to its fold the suspended
> and wandering tonalities of the past. I like to imagine,
> in consummation and resolution of those jangling
> chords, something as enduring in retrospect, as the
> long table that on summer birthdays and namedays
> used to be laid for afternoon chocolate out of doors, in
> an alley of birches, limes and maples at its debouch-
> ment on the smooth-sanded space of the garden pro-
> per that separated the park and the house. I see the
> tablecloth and the faces of seated people sharing in the
> animation of light and shade beneath a moving, a fabu-
> lous foliage, exaggerated, no doubt, by the same fac-
> ulty of impassioned commemoration, of ceaseless re-
> turn, that makes me always approach that banquet
> table from the outside, from the depth of the park—
> not from the house—as if the mind in order to go back
> thither, had to do so with the silent steps of a prodigal,
> faint with excitement. Through a tremulous prism, I
> distinguish the features of relatives and familiars, mute
> lips serenely moving in forgotten speech. I see the
> steam of chocolate and the plates of blueberry
> tarts. I note the small helicopter of a revolving samara
> that gently descends upon the tablecloth, and, lying
> across the table, an adolescent girl's bare arm indo-
> lently extended as far as it will go, with its turquoise-
> veined underside turned up to the flaky sunlight, the
> palm open in lazy expectancy of something—perhaps
> the nutcracker. . . And then, suddenly, just when the
> colors and outlines settle at last to their various duties
> —smiling, frivolous duties—some knob is touched and
> a torrent of sounds comes to life: voices speaking all-
> together, a walnut cracked . . . . (170-71).

*Mechanism
of memory*

Sight

*Angle of
vision*

*Colors via
a prism*

Sound

This long passage has been given in full as an example and as a description of the mechanism and power of Nabokov's memory. The
reader cannot but be amazed by the writer's almost magical power
of conjuring up the minutia of the past and Nabokov himself believes that his "almost pathological keenness of the retrospective
faculty is a hereditary trait" (75).

What is the connection between Nabokov's prodigious powers of recall, his thematic preoccupation with memory, and his synesthesia? We would suggest that Nabokov's psychological synesthesia is one of the central mechanisms in the functioning of his memory. This conjecture is, of course, based on the psychological hypothesis that synesthesia can and does play a role in the memory processes (as well as the direct perceptual processes) of some individuals. There is at least one precedent for this assumption. The eminent Soviet psychologist A. R. Luria worked with a subject who had well-nigh total recall.[21] In the course of investigations which extended over a period of nearly thirty years it was learned that the subject also displayed a very highly developed form of synesthesia. All five of the sense modalities were cross-blended in his perception. Luria ultimately concluded that "the meaning of these synesthetic responses for the process of recall lay in the fact that the synesthetic components created, as it were, the background of each recollection by providing redundant information and thus assuring the exactness of the recollection" (19). If some part of a recollection was incorrect "the supplementary synesthetic cues failed to coincide with each other and thus let the subject know that "something was not correct in his recollection. This forced him to correct the inaccuracy" (19).[22] The passage bears a remarkable resemblance to Nabokov's description of memory's use of innate harmonies in resolving the jangling chords of the mislaid past.[23]

It does not seem unreasonable to posit a similar connection between synesthesia and memory in the case of Nabokov. The synesthetically intermixed sensory cues seem to reinforce each other and to resonate thus fixating scenes of memory and imagination far more vividly than is possible through discrete modes of perception.

NOTES

1. Quoted in "The Chemistry of Madness," *Life* (Nov. 26, 1971), 67-68.

2. Gladys A. Reichard, Roman Jakobson, and Elizabeth Werth, "Language and Synesthesia," *Word,* 5, No. 1, 224.

3. Roman Jakobson, "Kindersprache, Aphasie und allgemeine Lautgesetze," *Selected Writings,* I, 387-88.

4. The earliest attested examination of synesthesia is the Latin medical dissertation by Dr. G. T. L. Sachs in Erlangen in 1812. *Historia Naturalis Duorum Leucaethopium Auctoris Ipsius et Sororis eius [The Natural History of Two Albinos: the Author Himself and His Sister],* cited in Friedrich Mahling, "Das Problem der 'Audition Colorée,'" *Archiv für die gesamte Psychologie, 57 (1926), 165-301.*

5. See the article "Synesthesia" in the *Princeton Encyclopaedia of Poetry and Poetics,* ed. Alex Preminger (Princeton, 1965).

6. See Enid Starkie's biographical and critical study *Arthur Rimbaud* (New York, 1947), 132-35, for a balanced view of Rimbaud's aesthetic doctrine.

7. Max Nordau, *Degeneration* (New York, 1895), 142. Quoted by Alfred Engstrom in his "In Defense of Synesthesia in Literature," *Philological Quarterly,* XXV, 1 (1946), 1-2.

8. Engstrom, 10-11.

9. *Words and Things* (Glencoe, 1958), 154. This point is also made by Stephen Ullmann, *The Principles of Semantics,* 2nd ed. (Oxford, 1957), 268. Ullmann is one of the few scholars who has devoted extensive study to literary synesthesia. See particularly the section "Panchronistic Tendencies in Synaesthesia," 266-88. The only other recent major study of the topic is Glenn O'Malley, "Literary Synesthesia," *Journal of Aesthetics and Art Criticism,* XV (1957), 391-411.

10. The history and interrelations of the three versions of Nabokov's highly stylized autobiography are complex. Most of the segments were initially written as vignettes for the *New Yorker* in the late forties and in early 1950. These and several other parts published elsewhere were reworked and published in book form as *Conclusive Evidence* (New York, 1951). An expanded and revised Russian version was published as *Drugie berega [Other Shores]* (New York, 1954). Finally, a considerably revised and augmented English version was published in 1966 as *Speak, Memory: An Autobiography Revisited.* Each subsequent variant has to some degree expanded its treatment of Nabokov's alphabetic chromesthesia. Quotes in this essay are from the 1966 *Speak, Memory* unless otherwise specified. Quotes from the Russian version are indicated thus: (DB——).

11. V. Nabokov, *The Eye* (New York, 1966), 79.

12. Republished in Nabokov's *Poems and Problems* (New York, 1970), 166.

13. *Poems and Problems,* 158-59.

14. This poem is apparently "Dozhd' proletel" ("The Rain Has Flown"), which has been reprinted with Nabokov's English version in *Poems and Problems,* 18-19.

15. The letters enclosed in brackets indicate the phonetic and phonemic value of the preceding Cyrillic characters.

16. This mirror image device is but one of Nabokov's "doubles." As Peter Lubin has put it, "Vladimir Nabokov ingeminates." For examples, see Lubin's "Kickshaws and Motley," *TriQuarterly,* 17 (Winter, 1970),187. A number of examples dealing specifically with the mirror theme are in W. W. Rowe, *Nabokov's Deceptive World* (New York, 1971), 63-65.

102

17. This and the following definition are from *Webster's Third New International Dictionary* (Springfield, 1961).

18. V. Nabokov, *Lolita* (New York, 1956), 318-19. The author's Russian translation appeared in 1967 (New York: Phaedra Publishers).

19. The meaningfulness of this opposition is based on another thus far tacit assumption, i.e., that Nabokov's assertion that he possesses psychological synesthesia is true. On the positive side we offer only the ingenuous proof that Nabokov says it is so. On the other side we must face the fact that Nabokov's statements about the general phenomenon of synesthesia reflect a great deal of secondary information about the subject. As an example of his knowledge of the field, we can point to his passing reference to "an albino physician in 1812, in Erlangen" as the first author to discuss *audition coloree* (35). See footnote 4. This case has been mentioned only rarely in the literature. Further, overtly synesthetic motifs, both literary and psychological, seem to have been most prevalent in Nabokov's writing in the second half of the thirties—chiefly in *The Gift* (1935-37) and "Mademoiselle O" which was written in French in 1936. The only other explicit references, to my knowledge, are those in the second chapter of his autobiography, and a brief episode in *Ada* describing a case in which a blind madman identifies different colored pencils by touch (468-469). Although Nabokov's assertion is ultimately unverifiable, we see no reason to question the presence of the psychological syndrome at least in some measure.

20. The phrase *Buchstaben von Feuer* is in German both in the original Russian text and in the English translation. It is apparently drawn from Heinrich Heine's early poem *Belsazar* and refers to the biblical "handwriting on the wall." It is of interest that Heine made much use of synesthetic metaphors in his writing. The author is indebted to Professor Harry Steinhauer for this information.

21. A. R. Luria, *The Mind of a Mnemonist, A Little Book about a Vast Memory,* trans. Jerome Bruner (New York, 1968). The quotations here are my own from the Russian text, *Mal'enkaja knizhka o bol'shoj pamjati:Um mnemonista* (Moscow, 1968).

22. Psychologists have done little recent work on synesthesia—much less its possible connection with hypernormal recall. Apart from Luria's work, I have encountered only Gerald S. Blum, *A Model of the Mind* (New York, 1961), which reports the case of a hypnotherapy subject who displayed both synesthesia and eidetic imagery. No connection between the two is posited however. In a personal communication with the author, Professor Blum remarks that Luria's hypothesis seems a plausible one.

23. A fictionalized version of a hypothesized connection between color and memory is advanced in *Ada* by Van who theorizes that color associations (innate harmonies? DBJ) play an essential role in recall of the past (546-549).

Anthony Olcott

THE AUTHOR'S SPECIAL INTENTION:
A STUDY OF *THE REAL LIFE OF SEBASTIAN KNIGHT*

The Real Life of Sebastian Knight (1941—hereafter RLSK) is
a book little treated by Nabokov's critics, perhaps because in
relation to his later, larger works it seems simple, or perhaps
because it is Nabokov's first novel in English. Whatever the reason,
the neglect is unjustified, for Nabokov used in RLSK all of his
now-famous devices to create beneath a simple appearance a
marvelously contrived and complicated book.

Chess images, for example, abound in the novel.[1] A most
obvious image is Knight's name and his self-identification with the
chess piece (which also suggest his Anglophilism) (p. 17).[2] Also
important are the two Bishops, Clare and her husband. A third
bishop appears when V., the narrator of the novel and his brother's
biographer, lodges the rival biography written by Mr. Goodman,
Knight's one-time secretary, on a hypothetical shelf next to *Fall of
Man,* by Godfrey Goodman, who until his death in 1656 was the
Bishop of Gloucester (p. 61). The fourth bishop was still-born
(p. 101). In a sense, the novel begins and ends on a chessboard,
for Knight's death in St. Damier motivates V. to begin the biography and in his last bit of research he goes to the country home of
Nina Rechnoy, on the way to which he passes through the town a
second time (p. 164). *Damier* is the French word for the chess
board, which V. remembers only when he sees a chessboard
scrawled on the wall of a telephone booth (p. 198). Knight is
described as knowing "that his slightest thought or sensation had
always at least one more dimension than those of his neighbors"
(p. 66), just as the knight's move has always one more dimension
than those of the other pieces, a theme which also appears in the
L-shape of the Bishop's living room (p. 77).

Another method through which Nabokov patterns his novels
is the recurrence of details in apparently unrelated contexts, used
in most of his works. In RLSK, for example, Sebastian dies at age
36, in 1936. His street address in London is 36 Oak Park Gardens,

and the room which V. thinks contains the dying Knight at St. Damier is numbered 36. The telephone number of Dr. Starov, Knight's doctor, is Jasmin 61-93, which unscrambles to Knight's date of death. Similarly, Virginia Knight gives her son a bag of sugared violets, which V. later finds in Sebastian's drawer (p. 17). She dies in Roquebrune, at a *pensione* named "Les Violettes" (p. 19). Knight finds a "Les Violettes" to visit in a Roquebrune, but it is the wrong *pensione* in the wrong town (p. 20). The only remaining inhabitant of the dead Knight's bathroom is an empty talc-tin "with violets figured between its shoulders" (p. 37). Also, Helene von Graun has a black bull-dog (p. 154), as does Knight (p. 103),[3] and Clare Bishop by chance marries a man with the same surname (p. 77).

Related to Nabokov's games and his use of apparent coincidence are the seemingly superfluous details, mentioned in passing and never returned to, which actually allude to many other parts of a book. An example of this device is the class list which appears in *Lolita* (annotated edition, pp. 53-54) and which is exhaustively explained by Alfred Appel in his annotations (pp. 359-361). Another example, perhaps a better one, appears too in V.'s book. This is the "sequence which for a moment seemed to form a vague musical phrase" (p. 41) upon Knight's bookcase, which V. lists thusly:

> *Hamlet, La Morte D'Arthur, The Bridge of San Luis Rey, Doctor Jekyll and Mr. Hyde, South Wind, The Lady With the Dog, Madame Bovary, The Invisible Man, Le Temps Retrouvé, Anglo-Persian Dictionary, The Author of Trixie, Alice in Wonderland, Ulysses, About Buying a Horse, King Lear . . .*(p. 41)

This "phrase" is "musical" apparently because each of its parts touches upon either Knight's life, his work, or upon V.'s task. The Anglo-Persian dictionary, for instance, belonged to Clare, who studied Eastern languages (p. 82). *Hamlet* and *King Lear* remind the reader of Knight's Cambridge degree in English literature, as well as of his Anglophilism. Moreover, what Goodman mistakenly believes to be and reports as the plot of Knight's very first, destroyed novel (p. 64) is in fact the plot of *Hamlet*. The author of *The Bridge of San Luis Rey* attempts to research backwards from an event to find its cause in a way that is very like Knight's method in his second novel, *Success,* and *South Wind* is one of those novels

Knight parodies in *The Prismatic Bezel* for "the fashionable trick of grouping a medley of people in a limited space (a hotel, an island, a street)" (p. 92). Norman Douglas also represents a minor strain of this musical phrase, that of homosexuality, which he shares with Marcel Proust, author of *Le Temps Retrouvé*. Later the two authors are to share a wall in the garret of Gaston Godin *(Lolita,* p. 116). Proust is alluded to by Goodman as "the author M. Proust, whom Knight consciously or subconsciously copied" (p. 116), as well as by Knight himself (p. 54).

La Morte D'Arthur has a certain application to V.'s story, since it is not only about the lives of knights but also culminates in the death of the title character. *Doctor Jekyll and Mr. Hyde* seems to have a reverse application, since, at least in V.'s opinion, he and his brother merge into one personality that might be both, either, or neither of them (p. 205). Nabokov has expressed admiration for Stevenson, as well as for H. G. Wells, the author of *The Invisible Man,* a work which shares with V.'s book both supposedly invisible narrators and subjects about which the reader knows increasingly little.

Strictly speaking, *The Lady With the Dog* is only a short story, but the third volume of the Constance Garnett translation of Chekhov's works (MacMillan Co., 1917-1927) is entitled *The Lady With the Dog and Other Stories* and includes the short story "The Black Monk," the plot of which the gullible Mr. Goodman mistakes as a real event in Knight's life (p. 65).

Other of the books seem to be present only because they are Nabokov's favorites and represent a kind of "seal of approval." Besides the Shakespeare, the Proust, and the Stevenson, *Madame Bovary* and *Ulysses* have received Nabokov's praise, while he admired *Alice in Wonderland* enough to translate it. Perhaps the last represents slightly more than approval, for V. too knew the work, to judge from his exchange with the Blauberg hotel keeper, who spoke "in the elenctic tones of Lewis Carroll's caterpillar" (p. 123).

About Buying a Horse was written by Sir Francis Cowley Burnand; its chess application is obvious. Caine's *The Author of Trixie* is about an arch*bishop* who secretly writes a frivolous novel (thanks, Professor Boldino).

In either case, these books in particular and all of the games and allusions in general serve as an excellent illustration of one of the major pitfalls Nabokov creates in his works. Because he composes on index cards,[4] which enables him to write a book in any sequence he pleases, the seemingly unrelated details of a work can in fact be connected, to take on a collective significance greater than the sum of their parts, because of the author's art. Thus here the list gives a kind of portrait of Knight and his life. However, it is more important to note just how artful, how deceptive, this portrait is, for it only *seems* to impart meaning, while in fact conveying only very little. All of the information contained in the allusions noted above are stated openly elsewhere in the book, and the natural desire of the alert reader, once he has discovered some of them, to search for other, perhaps "deeper" references gradually leads one further and further from the subject at hand, so that the list conveys ultimately only Knight's reading habits, information easily obtained in a cursory look at the list. It is a masterful Nabokovian trick, since the pursuit of the seemingly natural clue actually leads one nowhere, while ignoring or never noticing the clue proves ultimately more productive.[5]

Of course, the textual games, while helpful, are not vital aspects of the book. The chess game between Pahl and Uncle Black no more explains RLSK than Word-Golf explains *Pale Fire;* such details serve a different purpose. Although they impart very little real meaning to the reader, they do make him acutely aware of the author, functioning behind his narrator to fashion a more complete story than that of which the narrator, and the careless reader, is aware. This is particularly true in RLSK; on the surface the story is singularly puzzling. No reasons are ever given for actions; it is never clear why Sebastian left Clare, nor is Nina's attraction for Knight explicit. Not even V.'s burning desire to write his brother's biography is completely understandable, and yet a reader generally finishes the book feeling as though something definite, albeit inexplicable, has happened.

One of the oddities of the book is that the characters, particularly Sebastian Knight, are never clearly described. V. attempts to delineate his brother, but fails, largely due ot his own vague and imprecise descriptions. At one point V., like Tolstoy in *Anna Karenin,* tries to show his brother by describing a portrait painted by a friend:

The painter had wonderfully rendered the moist dark greenish-gray of their iris, with a still darker rim and a suggestion of gold dust constellating round the pupil. The lids are heavy and perhaps a little inflamed, and a vein or two seems to have burst on the glossy eye-ball. These eyes and the face itself are painted in such a manner as to convey the impression that they are mirrored Narcissus-like in clear water—with a very slight ripple on the hollow cheek, owing to the presence of a water-spider which has just stopped and is floating backward. A withered leaf has settled on the reflected brow, which is creased as that of a man peering intently. The crumpled dark hair over it is partly suffused by another ripple, but one strand on the temple has caught a glint of humid sunshine. There is a deep furrow between the straight eyebrows, and another down from the nose to the tightly shut dusky lips. There is nothing much more than this head. (p. 119)

We thus know Sebastian's eyes, the withered leaf, and later, that the water-spider has a club-foot shadow. Of Sebastian's face, we know almost nothing.

V. assumes in describing the portrait that Sebastian is looking at himself in a pool of water. As described, the painting would in fact be of a man staring outwards from a kind of watery veil, so that the viewer would take the part of Narcissus, or Knight. Thus as V. looks at the picture, the scene is a physical representation of the relationship between his brother and himself; they peer at one another through the "veil" of death, mirroring vague but related facial features. This image of water as a separating barrier, as death, recurs frequently in the book. Knight separates himself from V. by living in England, beyond the English Channel. Until he meets Nina, Knight shows very little ability to stay on the Continent (pp. 72 and 88). After they meet he cannot stay in England, and trails her all over Europe, finally dying in a small French town. His life is disrupted and his death predestined not only by his crossing of the Channel, but also by meeting Nina Rechnoy, whose name means, in Russian, "of the river." This water theme also appears in Knight's last book, titled *The Doubtful Asphodel;* the asphodel is a kind of narcissus, supposed to stand on the "other shore" of death (p. 180), as well as to presage it. Seeing one's own reflection in water is also considered an ill omen, so that Knight's portrait, as well as his last book, in fact becomes a kind of mirror of death.

Having resolved to write his brother's biography, V. begins to duplicate his brother's life. At first the parallel is vague and conventional; most biographies begin with the subject's early years and research from there, and though he disclaims the method (p. 20), so does V. Then, however, he begins to feel propelled, led on by some other force, which he begins to suspect is his brother's ghost (p. 101). The result is that the chronology of Knight's life becomes tangled. V. recognizes that in part, noting:

> My quest had developed its own magic and logic and though I some-
> times cannot help believing that it had   gradually grown into a dream,
> that quest, using the pattern of reality for the weaving of its own
> fancies, I am forced to recognize that I was being led right, and that in
> striving to render Sebastian's life I must follow the same rhythmical
> interlacements. (p. 137)

These "rhythmical interlacements" are of course the chronology of V.'s research. As the research continues, his book, as well as his life, falls more and more into the pattern of Knight's life and as such begins to move toward Knight, beyond the water, toward the other side of the mirror.

This mirroring is amplified by other doublings throughout the book. Some of them are mere games, such as Dr. Starov's name, which in Knight's phrase "old Dr. Starov" (p. 185) could be roughly translated as "old Dr. Old." In the same way Knight's secretary, through an obsolete meaning of "goodman" becomes Mr. Mister. Other mirrors are, however, more important. Virginia Knight's visit to her son after an absence of almost five years is described in this way:

> She had raised her veil above her lips to kiss the boy, and no sooner had
> she touched him than she burst into tears, as if Sebastian's warm tender
> temple was the very source and satiety of her sorrow. Immediately
> afterwards she put on her gloves and started to tell my mother in bad
> French a pointless and quite irrelevant story about a Polish woman who
> had attempted to steal her vanity-bag in the dining-car. (p. 10)

V.'s disapproval is so clearly evident that it is odd he remarks nothing when reporting that his brother did a very similar thing upon meeting Helen Pratt, Clare Bishop's friend. The meeting was uncomfortable because Helen had just parted from Clare a moment before and neither of them had seen Knight for six years. V. describes the meeting in this way:

He colored slightly as he shook hands with Miss Pratt, and then accompanied her to the underground station. She was thankful he had not appeared a minute earlier, and still more thankful when he did not trouble to allude to the past. He told her instead an elaborate story about a couple of men who had attempted to swindle him at a game of poker the night before. (p. 184)

Nor does V. notice a similar pettiness in Nina when Pahl Rechnoy describes his first wife as the type who loved, among other things, "raising hell in hotels when she thought the maid had stolen her small change which she afterwards found in the bathroom" (p. 146), even though the events mirror one another very closely, tying the three people together. Knight also mirrors his mother in succumbing to Lehmann's disease, and all three share a fondness for rapid and erratic travel. That V. misses these similarities reflects serious doubt upon his ability to narrate impartially and reliably his brother's life.

In the beginning of his book, V. has very good control; he is witty, ironic, and parodistic. As the story evolves, he changes, and begins to lose that control. Part of this loss is the result of V.'s inability, even while tracing the outline of his brother's life, to recognize that the pattern of his own life begins to reproduce that outline. Near the middle of the book, the reproduction becomes very clear, although V., characteristically fails to notice. He has exhausted all sources of information except the mysterious Russian woman whose letters he had found in Knight's study (p. 38) and leaves for Blauberg, the resort at which Knight had met her, with vague hopes of finding the woman's name in a hotel register. He is completely rebuffed by the hotel keeper and must withdraw in defeat. At this point, without further information, the biography would have to end, a possibility which disturbs V. He wonders whether to "leave it thus and write the book all the same? A book with a blind spot. An unfinished picture,—uncolored limbs of the martyr with the arrows in his side" (p. 125). It is at this crucial moment that V. meets the amazing Mr. Silbermann, who supplies him with the addresses necessary to continue his "hagiography." What V. fails to notice is that he has encountered Mr. Silbermann before, in Knight's story "The Back of the Moon," where he is called Mr. Siller. Even though Mr. Silbermann obligingly names the story in which he appeared, V. fails to recognize that his traveling companion and "the meek little man waiting for a train who helped three miserable travelers in three different ways" (pp. 103-104) are the same person. This encounter is important in several ways. The first is of course that Silbermann gives V. a notebook in which he begins to write RLSK (p. 33) and which, at the time of V.'s present tense, apparently still contains the manuscript (pp. 133-134). He also gives V. the best advice in the book, realizing that it is both dangerous and futile to search for Nina, futile because the past has no meaning for women of her type and dangerous because of her powers over men. Most important, Mr. Silbermann's backwards arithmetic and cartoon-character manner signal V.'s arrival on the far side of his brother's looking glass.

After getting the addresses, V., like his brother, travels around Europe in search of the mysterious woman. He finds her, though he fails to realize it until her chance error (p. 171), and succumbs to her powers as mysteriously as did his brother. V.'s control gets progressively weaker as the book continues and here is near its worst. Nabokov shows how V., although he seems to despise them, disregards the woman's radio, tea, and love of scandal, all the things about her which show her smallness, and falls strangely under her thrall. As he says:

> Let me repeat that I am loathe to trouble these pages with any kind of matter relating personally to me; but I think it may amuse the reader (and who knows, Sebastian's ghost too) if I say that for a moment I thought of making love to that woman. It was really very odd,—at the same time she got rather on my nerves,—I mean the things she said. I was losing my grip somehow. (p. 168)

This is very nearly the same reaction Knight had. As Nina explained it to V. (in the third person she was affecting):

> he, well, he was anything but nice—he got positively wicked when he found out that he was falling in love with Helene. Oh no, *he* did not turn into a sentimental pup, as she had expected. He told her bitterly that she was cheap and vain, and then he kissed her to make sure that she was not a porcelain figure. (p. 159)

Not only has V., upon meeting Silbermann, entered directly into his brother's footsteps, even to the extent of falling under the powers of the same woman, but he also has entered into his brother's books. He describes *The Doubtful Asphodel* in this way:

111

> We follow the gentle old chess player Schwarz, who sits down on a chair in a room in a house, to teach an orphan boy the moves of the knight; we meet the fat Bohemian woman with that gray streak showing in the fast color of her cheaply dyed hair; we listen to a pale wretch noisily denouncing the policy of oppression to an attentive plainclothesman in an ill-famed public-house. The lovely tall primadonna steps in her haste into a puddle, and her silver shoes are ruined. An old man sobs and is soothed by a soft-lipped girl in mourning. Professor Nussbaum, a Swiss scientist, shoots his young mistress and himself in a hotel-room at half past three in the morning. (p. 175)

It must be remembered that V. had read his brother's last novel before Knight's death and that he loved it a great deal (p. 182), so it is strange that he should not recognize in Uncle Black the gentle old chess player Schwarz (*schwarz* is German for black), nor in the boy his pupil. The fat Bohemian lady has been substantivised; her nationality becomes her name in Lydia Bohemsky (p. 153). The pale wretch has been punned upon; he becomes Pahl Rechnoy, noisily describing his oppressive former wife to the attentive biographer-detective, V. The primadonna is the real Helene von Graun, who steps into the puddle alighting from her car (p. 170), although her shoes seem to have belonged to Clare (p. 103). The old man and the girl comforting him are seen in the Berlin apartment of Helene Grinstein (p. 135), while unfortunate Professor Nussbaum and his mistress are alluded to by the hotel keeper in Blauberg (p. 124). Only once does V. seem to take notice of this, in an aside to his description of Nina:

> She looked away. Her small hard bosom heaved (Sebastian once wrote that it happened only in books but here was proof that he was mistaken). (p. 168)

He fails however to realize that Knight might well have been correct, and that he himself has been drawn into a book.

At the end of the novel V. dashes to the dying Knight's side, hoping to learn the simple answer to some huge and complex puzzle, as in *The Doubtful Asphodel*. Throughout V.'s book, like Knight's, a man, Knight, "is dying. . .and drawing up a ghostly knee" (p. 175). In V.'s book, as in Knight's, we meet characters and themes "like the swell and fall of uneven breathing, now rolling up this image, now that, letting it ride in the wind, or even tossing it out on the shore, where it seems to move and live for a minute on its own and presently is drawn back again by gray seas where it sinks or is strangely transfigured" (p. 175). And it is here that the final references to the Narcissus theme appear, for it is here that the reader realizes that V. has been drawn into his brother's life, into his imaginative world, to share the same visions and thoughts. Perhaps what best underscores V.'s submergence into his brother's imagination is the realization that the book the reader holds was written in a notebook given to V. by Mr. Silbermann, a fictitious character created by his brother.

V. emphasizes throughout the book that his brother, unlike himself, had repudiated his Russian background, wishing to become English. V. considers himself quite Russian, even wanting to translate *The Doubtful Asphodel* (p. 182). Nonetheless, he is taken for English by Nina (p. 155), while Sebastian is completely unable to keep his Russianness out of his poems (p. 49). Thus it is significant that Sebastian's last letter is in Russian and that in death his name, according to Dr. Starov's telegram, becomes again the Russian *Sevastian* (p. 190). Appropriately too, V. is led mistakenly to the bed-side of an Englishman, Mr. Kegan, while the nurse refers to Knight as "the Russian gentleman" (p. 204). In a sense, the brothers have exchanged places, as Knight becomes in death a Russian, and V. becomes an English author. It is, as V. concludes, as though he had become Sebastian.

> So I did not see Sebastian after all, or at least I did not see him alive. But those few minutes I spent listening to what I thought was his breathing changed my life as completely as it would have been changed, had Sebastian spoken to me before dying. Whatever his secret was, I have learnt one secret too, and namely: that the soul is but a manner of being—not a constant state—that any soul may be yours, if you find and follow its undulations. The hereafter may be the full ability of consciously living in any chosen soul, in any number of souls, all of them unconscious of their interchangeable burden. Thus—I am Sebastian Knight. . . Sebastian's mask clings to my face, the likeness will not be washed off. I am Sebastian, or Sebastian is I, or perhaps we both are someone whom neither of us knows. (pp. 204-205)

Is this then the conclusion, that V., by following his adored brother's footsteps, has become him? That he has begun to see his own face in Knight's biography, to unite with the life he had previously so acutely envied (p. 180)? The conclusion, as well as the movement of the Narcissus theme and V.'s sense of being manipulated from the hereafter by his brother's shade seem to justify that conclusion. There are, however, certain difficulties.

The greatest of these is chronological. Exactly when does V. reach his conclusion, at the end of the book, immediately after his brother's death, or at some indeterminate point between? V. is normally careful with tense, using the present only synchronously with the actual writing of his book, but in the account of his nightmarish journey to St. Damier, he slips briefly from the correct narrative past into a direct present (p. 195). Thus, with this precedent, the changes in tense in his conclusion are ambiguous.

V.'s biography is for the most part in chronological order, moving from Knight's birth toward his death, paralleled at the same time by the chronology of V.'s search, which means that as the biography and V.'s research move nearer to Knight's death, they are also moving farther from it, as each moment of V.'s investigation succeeds the one before. Since Knight's death is the impetus for beginning the biography, as the book moves onward toward Knight's end, it also moves towards its own conception, in effect enclosing the two-dimensional time scheme within a circular pattern of cause and effect. Thus confusion easily arises. For example, the ambiguous use of the present tense just mentioned seems even more pronounced when the reader realizes that the immediacy of such usage is employed at the end of the novel, though the event itself occurred just before V. resolved to write his book; in other words, events at polar ends of the novel are united in the present tense. Yet this circularity seems virtually to disappear when it is remembered that the two events, in comparison to the complete scope of the book, Knight's life, occurred very close together, only three or four months apart.

Thus the intricate construction of the novel, in raising and not answering questions which seem crucial to understanding it, create a curious tension between the various chronologies. In another instance, quite early in the book, V. describes the contents of his brother's desk drawer, which he had opened when they were both young (p. 17), and one of the objects he mentions is a portrait of a classmate's sister. This clearly is Natasha Rosanov, the existence of whom later so much surprises V. (pp. 136-137), yet at her first appearance he says nothing, just as he says nothing when Nina's letters to Knight are first discovered (p. 38). This indicates that V. found out about Natasha and Nina only later,

114

after he had begun to write. This necessarily implies that he began his book not knowing its outcome, with no clear idea of his subject, which would in turn suggest that the book is as much about V., his vagaries and moods, as about his brother. This would imply that V.'s increasing lack of control has serious, if obscured, consequence for the book. Curiously, what functions in the novel as the crisis or climax of that debilitation, V.'s nightmare (pp. 187-190), in fact precedes its apparent cause, thus implying that V.'s control is poor throughout the book, which throws into ambiguity literally everything which V. writes.

At one point V. cautions the reader, saying:

> Beware of the most honest broker. Remember that what you are told is really threefold: shaped by the teller, reshaped by the listener, concealed from both by the dead man of the tale. (p. 52)

If, however the teller is attempting to find in his "dead man" a portrait of himself, then it is the teller who must conceal his real person from the listener, by disguising himself behind specious comparisons and incorrect conclusions. The irony is that any such attempt only makes the teller's presence more apparent, because by making clearly improbable or unlikely assertions, the narrator reveals his own biases, the sum of which eventually produce a kind of self-portrait. RLSK is not, however, an obvious exercise with an unreliable narrator, as is, for example, *Pale Fire.* While it is a simple matter to find absurdities in Kinbote's commentary, it is much more difficult to catch V. making obvious errors. Often V. is clearly imprecise, but whether or not he is inaccurate, mistaken, or lying is never certain, because there is in the center of the novel the intricate chronological structure which reduces any question to ultimate ambiguity.

There is, for instance, the problem of judging just how good an author Sebastian Knight really was. He seems never to have received adequate reviews, but Nabokov himself is no stranger to hostile, uncomprehending criticism. Certain of Nabokov's literary methods are shared as well by Knight. However, other factors tend to suggest that Knight was not the marvelous author V. supposed him to be. There is for instance the quip made by an old critic: "Poor Knight! he really had two periods, the first—a dull man writing broken English, the second—a broken man writing dull English!" (p. 7). There is also the matter of Knight's books, of which we see only excerpts. It is impossible to judge from plot summaries, but all of Knight's books sound a little bit dull. *The Prismatic Bezel* bears certain resemblances to Nabokov's books *Mary* (1925) and *King, Queen, Knave* (1928) in its use of the boarding house device, but somehow it all sounds in V.'s words too ethereal and somewhat forced. *Success* is similar to Nabokov's *The Gift* in which fate continually attempts to push together Zina and Fyodor, which they repeatedly resist. Yet in *The Gift* this thread is only one of an enormous number, and it seems scant for *Success* to concentrate upon that as its single theme. *The Doubtful Asphodel* does sound the most interesting of Knight's books, but that may be because it is a partial description of V.'s book. Certain other aspects of Nabokov's art, such as word play and neologizing, are noticeably absent from the sections of Knight's work which V. quotes. Knight does pun occasionally (p. 55), but for that matter so does V. (p. 34), who is also, unlike his brother, a word-coiner (p. 82).

Nabokov expects readers to make moral judgments about his characters,[6] although he has never outlined any particular morality or philosophy which he believes his novels illustrate or which he is trying to promulgate. Certain of his particular hatreds however, most noticeably aggressive philistinism and physical cruelty, have become apparent through his books. Thus the two photographs in Knight's study may have special significance. One is a picture of a curly child playing with an equally curly puppy, and the second a picture of a Chinese about to be beheaded (p. 41), a combination which V. finds in questionable taste. It is possible that Knight has hung them together as a morbid illustration of some kind of vulgar similarity between the two, so that they are not necessarily meant as a signal by Nabokov that Knight has a repulsive side. Knight's love of practical jokes, however, also indicates a streak of perversity and cruelty which V. simply doesn't perceive. This in turn reflects poorly upon V.'s abilities to judge his brother, and hence himself.

Nabokov sometimes makes his repellent characters grossly ignorant of the physical world. To judge from the notebook V. finds in Knight's office, upon which was "an impossible butterfly" (p. 39), it is possible Knight possessed such ignorance. Knight also, in describing his reverie at the *pensione* in which he supposed his mother to have died, makes a passing reference to a "bed of purple pansies" (p. 19). A reader is of course forced to accept the statement, but considering that the *pensione* is named Les

Violettes, it seems logical to presume that Knight is mistaken, that he is gazing at a bed of violets.

V.'s capabilities, however, are no more certain than his brother's. As noted, he values his brother's books perhaps more highly than they deserve. The brothers are placed into direct competition as writers only once, in V.'s remarks about their walk through Paris. They encounter flocks of pigeons, which V. describes thus:

> They settled among the pearl-gray and black frieze of the Arc de Triomphe and when some of them fluttered off again it seemed as if bits of the carved entablature were turned into flaky life. (p. 74)

Sebastian uses the same moment in his third book, *Lost Property,* as "that stone melting into wing" (p. 74). It is difficult to say ultimately which is better, but V.'s description is more vivid, evocative, and truer to the incident, while Knight's seems imprecise and perhaps too lyrical, although a reader can never know if Knight's context could justify such lyricism. Nevertheless, the comparison makes it clear that their powers of expression are not, as V. supposes, different as a Bechstein piano and a baby's rattle are different (p. 34).

V.'s character is much more difficult to grasp, since he really does allow very little of himself into the book. Certain features do stand out, however. For instance, his parody of a mystery novel shows V. to be a truly miserable detective. Not only is he unable to get information from the hotel-keeper, but his one Sherlock Holmes stratagem is a complete failure (p. 153), he burns all clues to his brother's study (p. 38), and he refuses to interrogate the two first-hand witnesses, Clare and Nina. The intent is more than humor, for it shows a concern for the privacy of the past which people like Mr. Goodman do not share. It is significant as well that V. is reluctant to attack Goodman, even when the agent so clearly deserves it. Nevertheless, it must also be remembered that this concern for privacy does not extend to Olga Olegovna Orlova, the diarist whose identity V. so lightly reveals on the first page of his book.

Other facts tend to suggest that V. is an unreliable reporter and perhaps a bit of a failure. He does poorly and unenthusiastically in his work and his slap-dash journey to his brother's side underscores his lack of control and suggest an innate mediocrity. He admits he is prone to take the cheapest opportunity in life

(p. 191), and he lives easily for many years on checks from his brother (p. 31). His judgement about his brother's sexual habits and life is also questionable. His vehement denial that the reason for Clare and Sebastian's break-up was even in part sexual suggests poor judgement, as well as fastidiousness which Nabokov, for one, has never shared. Although a reader can never know for sure, Clare's death in pregnancy, in which she "bled to death next to an empty cradle" (p. 101), suggests a certain sterility which could in fact have prompted Knight to leave her, tempted away by Nina. This is aided by Nina's strong sexual powers, which are shown by V.'s sudden and inexplicable temptation to make love to her. The reasons V. gives are physical, almost Tolstoyan. V. remarks upon Nina's flimsy frock (p. 169), their accidental collision (p. 166), their proximity on a bench (p. 171), all details which suggest Nina possesses an enormous sexual energy.

No final judgement seems possible, since there are always the little facts which contradict the seemingly natural conclusions. We never really know Knight, but then perhaps that is the point. As Clare said, "A title must convey the color of the book, not its subject" (p. 72). What then is the book's color? Nabokov answers that in V.'s summary of *The Doubtful Asphodel:*

> Sebastian Knight had always liked juggling with themes, making them clash or blending them cunningly, making *them* express the hidden meaning, which could only be expressed in a succession of waves, as the music of a Chinese buoy can be made to sound only by undulation. . . It is not the parts that matter, it is their combinations. (p. 176)

This is the method of RLSK and the final assessment of the book. Nabokov allows the character to describe the world around him, a world which he must describe without knowing its pattern. There is hidden at the center of V.'s life a chaos which continually pokes its way out, destroying seemingly logical paragraphs, undermining apparently sound conclusions. The character describes the random phenomena he can see, not realizing that he has described their pattern; he is describing the back side of a quilt. But an alert reader can see the patterns, and thus their maker, the master mind, Vladimir Nabokov. It is he, functioning behind V., who infuses Knight's biography with the sense not only that a reader does not know Knight, but that no man can know another's life. Perhaps it is precisely that mystery which is one's "real" life, or perhaps instead it is the pattern, the random but extraordinarily linked details of a life, which to another must constitute reality. Perhaps indeed it is only the artful intricacy of that pattern, crafted by a known or unknown hand, which can ultimately be called real. Once again, what was true of *The Doubtful Asphodel* is true of RLSK:

> We hold a dead book in our hands. Or are we mistaken? I sometimes feel when I turn the pages of Sebastian's masterpiece that the "absolute solution" is there, somewhere, concealed in some passage I have read too hastily, or that it is intertwined with other words whose familiar guise deceived me. I don't know any other book that gives one this special sensation, and perhaps this was the author's special intention.   (p. 180)

APPENDIX

A Chronology of Events in *The Real Life of Sebastian Knight*

1899, December 31	Sebastian Knight is born
1904	Virginia Knight leaves her husband
1905, autumn	Knight's father remarries, to V.'s mother
1906	V. is born
1908, winter	Virginia Knight reappears to visit Sebastian
1909	Virginia dies in Roquebrune
1913, early January	the father is wounded in a duel
1913, early February	the father dies
1916, summer	Knight is in love with Natasha Rosanov
1917, summer	Knight goes with the Pans to Simbirsk, V. is in the Crimea
1918, November	the family flees to Finland
1920	Knight enters Cambridge
1921	Knight visits the family in Paris
1923, spring	V.'s mother dies. Knight finishes school and comes to the funeral. After it, he goes to Monaco to see Roquebrune but visits the wrong town.

1923	V. enters the Sorbonne
1924, spring	Knight meets Clare Bishop
1924, April-October	Knight is at work on *The Prismatic Bezel*
1924, November or December	V. meets Clare and Knight in Paris
1925	*The Prismatic Bezel* appears
1925, July-1927, April	Knight is at work on *Success*
1926, summer	Knight discovers he has Lehmann's disease
1927, autumn-1929, summer	Knight is at work on his three short stories, written in this order: "The Funny Mountain," "Albinos in Black," "The Back of the Moon."
1929, June	Knight goes to Blauberg, where he meets Nina
1929, June or July	Knight meets V. in Paris and they dine at a Russian restaurant
1929, July or August	Nina and Pahl Rechnoy are divorced
1929, September	Knight leaves Clare for Nina
1930, January	Knight begins *Lost Property*
1932	His stories appear collected under the title *The Funny Mountain*
1933	Roy Carswell is painting Sebastian's portrait
1934	Knight fires Goodman
1935, spring	*The Doubtful Asphodel* appears
1935	Knight makes final attempt to see Nina
1935, August	Knight is seriously ill
1936, mid-January	Knight writes, in Russian, to V., asking him to burn Nina's letters
1936, mid-January	Starov wires V. to come—Knight dies in St. Damier
1936, end of January	V. visits Knight's London apartment, burns the letters
1936, February	V. visits Cambridge
1936, March 1	V. visits Goodman
1936, March	V. talks with Helen Pratt and P. G. Sheldon, attempts to talk with Clare
1936, late March	V. visits Roy Carswell, sees the portrait
1936, March or April	V. meets Mr. Silbermann
1936, April	V. begins *The Real Life of Sebastian Knight*
1936, April	V. goes to Berlin to meet Helene Grinstein
1936, April	V. goes to Paris and talks with Pahl Rechnoy, M. Lecerf, and M. Bohemsky

1936, April   V. goes to the Lecerf country home, discovers Nina's identity—on the way he passes St. Damier for the second time.

NOTES

1. Strother B. Purdy, *"Solus Rex:* Nabokov and the Chess Novel," *Modern Fiction Studies* (Winter 1968-69), 386-87.

2. Vladimir Nabokov, *The Real Life of Sebastian Knight* (Norfolk, Conn., New Directions, 1959). This edition is used for all quotations.

3. Knight's dog is called a bull-terrier but the description is of a bull-dog.

4. Alfred Appel, Jr., "An Interview with Vladimir Nabokov," *Nabokov: The Man and His Work,* L. S. Dembo, ed. (Madison, 1967), 24.

5. Such a trick is common in Nabokov's work. A particularly clear discussion appears in his remarks on chess problems in *Speak, Memory* (New York, 1966), 291-92.

6. Vladimir Nabokov, *Despair* (New York: Capricorn, 1966), 9.

Our Gang's Miss Jean Darling in a 1929 publicity still

Alfred Appel, Jr.

TRISTRAM IN MOVIELOVE:
LOLITA AT THE MOVIES

Because Vladimir Nabokov the literary anatomist is often be-
mused by culturally representative if not campy trivia—ads, songs,
poor novels, terrible films—the wide-ranging inclusiveness of his
fiction (and *Onegin* Commentary) has sometimes been misunder-
stood. "No, I loathe popular pulp," he told interviewer Nicholas
Granham, author of a book on the not always artful films of Samuel
Fuller. "I loathe go-go gangs, I loathe jungle music...I especially
loathe vulgar movies—cripples raping nuns under tables, or naked-
girl breasts squeezing against the tanned torsoes of repulsive young
males. And, really, I don't think I mock popular trash more often
than do other authors who believe with me that a good laugh is
the best pesticide."[1] Drawing upon his sense of Gogol's delinea-
tion of *poshlost'* in *Dead Souls* and realizing Flaubert's dream of
an expansive *Dictionary of Accepted Ideas,* Nabokov *does* mock
"popular trash" more frequently than any other contemporary
author, and some of the best, darkest, and most "moral" laughter
in *Lolita* is achieved at the expense of the movies, expressed in
terms uniform with the vision of Nabokov's *émigré* fiction, where
the commercial cinema is continually mocked and eviscerated.[2]
Nabokov's vision is consistent too with his generation's view of
movies, the Marxist line (!) on "popular culture" as an opiate, a
sop for the masses.

Early in *Lolita,* our narrator recalls how young Humbert
Humbert had learned the so-called facts of life from "an American
kid, the son of a then celebrated motion-picture actress whom he
seldom saw in the three-dimensional world"[3] and the two dimensions
of reel life, to use an old pun, are a most pervasive reality in *Lolita's*
America. Humbert's unfailingly dim view of Hollywood is consistent with his characterization as a displaced European intellectual,
a teacher and journeyman scholar whose touchstones are literary
and artistic. Having unsuccessfully searched Europe for his lost
Riviera love, "Annabel Leigh," Humbert finds her in America, but
it is Lolita, not Humbert, who completes the seduction at The Enchanted Hunters hotel—a Lolita to whom "sex" is a mechanical,
matter-of-fact charade. "Lambert Lambert," Humbert tells us, was

one of the pseudonyms he considered for his memoirs (p. 310), thus invoking the first name of Henry James' innocent ambassador to Europe, seduced by the charms of France. "You talk like a book, *Dad,*" says Lolita, playing her role in an inversion of James' *Daisy Miller* (1878), and their journey through America—in Jamesian terms a vast Schenectady—ironically reverses yet another nineteenth-century pilgrimage. In *The Innocents Abroad* (1869), Mark Twain tested European cultural artifacts and attractions against his own democratic ideals, and found Rome's Colosseum to be a pile of old rocks. Humbert's is a latter-day mock-grand tour, viewed through the dark prism of obsession and loss. Although he discovers "enormous Chateaubriandesque trees" (p. 147) and "Claude Lorrain clouds" (p. 154) and an "El Greco horizon in Kansas" (p. 155), these landscapes are peopled by creatures foreign to him in more ways than one. "You mean...you never did it when you were a kid?" asks Humbert's avatar of Poe's child-bride, kneeling above him at the fateful moment before their first intimacy. "Never," answers the hapless enchanted hunter (p. 135), and throughout *Lolita* his love for her, perversity notwithstanding, is contrasted with an ethic drawn from the two-dimensional realm of "Movie-love" (p. 256).

Introduced on the novel's third page by that informative "American kid" and concluded only by Clare Quilty's death almost three hundred pages later, the movie motif functions as an elaborate, extended metaphor, a negative image, or what used to be termed an ironic correlative, held in apposition to a veritable avalanche of allusions to the love poets of ancient and modern Europe. By having Lolita examined by a "Dr. Ilse Tristramson" (p. 200), Nabokov punningly compresses the novel's major network of literary allusions. Tristram's lovestruck "sons" are everywhere in *Lolita:* Dante, Petrarch, Ronsard, Belleau, Shakespeare, Goethe, Byron, Keats, Baudelaire, Browning, Verlaine, and Belloc, to name but a few. The principal sources for Humbert's allusive and least elusive quotations, paraphrases, and interpolations are Poe, Mérimée's *Carmen* (1845), and the Latin poets of Rome. Every time he intones "My Lolita" (and he does so on some thirty occasions), he is succinctly evoking Propertius, Horace, or Catalus, writing of his faithless Lesbia; *"That* Lolita, *my* Lolita," elegizes a more expansive Humbert (p. 67), echoing a donnish translation of Catulus' *"Lesbia nostra, Lesbia illa"* ("my Lesbia, that Lesbia"). Humbert has earned the right to identify himself with the Old

World's poets of love. In the process of writing his American memoir and confession, Humbert the self-styled *"manqué* talent" (p. 17) has become an artist, and joined their company. His allusions are, in T. S. Eliot's famous phrase, "fragments shored" against the ruin of a love ethic having nothing to do with pedophilia, Humbert's clinical malady.

Lolita's movie metaphor anticipates one of the signal chapters of Richard Brautigan's *Trout Fishing in America* (1967). Contemplating Hemingway's recent suicide and the vanished Indians and fur traders of Lewis and Clark's virgin land, the narrator remembers a winter he had spent as a child in Great Falls, Montana, during World War II, when he had seen a Deanna Durbin movie seven times ("Whatever it was about, she sang! and sang!"). Afterwards he had sustained a fantasy that he would one day walk down to the frozen Missouri River and find it looking just like a Deanna Durbin movie, something that Meriwether Lewis would never have recognized.[4] Although not always as innocent and blandly wholesome as a Deanna Durbin opus, and surely no virgin land, Lolita's world *is* in many ways a movie, as Humbert is quick to realize. When he first sees Lolita, he parades before her, he says, in "my adult disguise (a great big handsome hunk of movieland manhood)" (p. 41). Shortly afterwards he notices that Lo has clipped an ad from a slick magazine, picturing a "haggard lover," jocosely designated by her as "H. H.," and has "affixed [it] —to the wall above the bed, between a crooner's mug and the lashes of a movie actress" (p. 71). But, alas, once they get to know each other better, Humbert must admit that, "To the wonderland I had to offer, my fool preferred the corniest movies, the most cloying fudge" (p. 168). "You see," says Charlotte Haze, "*she* sees herself as a starlet; *I* see her as a sturdy, healthy, but decidedly homely kid" (p. 67). Humbert's dream incarnate is of course Lolita; hers is Hollywood. That she will eventually prefer Clare Quilty to Humbert Humbert is the result of her "veritable passion" for Hollywood (p. 172), though no one would suggest that, from her point-of view, a distinctive moral choice is offered her. When Humbert calls Lolita "Carmencita," he is alluding to both Mérimée's enchantress and filmdom's first vamp, the "Spanish dancer" of the Gay Nineties who dazzled Kinetoscope viewers.

The highlight of Lolita's year-long cross-country tour with Humbert is a visit to Hollywood, where they see "the ugly villas of handsome actresses" (p. 159); observe "the roan back of a screen actress" at an expensive restaurant (p. 157); have a major row "on Third Street, Los Angeles, because the tickets to some studio or or other were sold out" (p. 160); and visit Schwab's, the drugstore which, legend has it, many stars were discovered. Lolita saves Humbert's bribe-money for a trip to Broadway or Hollywood (p. 187), and, in the poem Humbert writes after her disappearance, he lists "Profession: none, or 'starlet'" (p. 257). Ada's teen-age "dramatic career" (p. 425) is clearly an abortive realization of Lolita's unfulfilled ambition. "Who is your hero, Dolores Haze? / Still one of those blue-caped star-men?" Humbert wonders (p. 258). She is steeped in Hollywood cosmology, and "yearn[s] to climb Red Rock [in Elphinstone] from which a mature screen star had recently jumped to her death after a drunken row with her gigolo" (p. 212); it is in Elphinstone that Lolita will depart with *her* drunken gigolo, Clare Quilty (p. 249). "The Joe-Roe marital enigma is making yaps flap," notes Humbert, burlesquing a Walter Winchell-type gossip column in a movie magazine (p. 256). Lolita consumes vast quantities of such magazines, reading with "celestial trust" the articles, advertisements, and advice columns in *Movie Love* or *Screen Land* (p. 150), from the tale of "Jill, an energetic starlet who made her own clothes and was a student of serious literature" (p. 141), to the ads that ask her to "Invite Romance by wearing the Exciting New Tummy Flattener. Trims tums, nips hips" (p. 256). Sustaining the satire, a photograph of Ada and Marina on a California patio appears in *Belladonna,* the Antiterran edition of one of Lo's celestial journals (p. 428), and saccharine movie mag Happy Family celebrations circa 1950 ("The immortal Raphael never painted lovelier mother-and-child pictures than those caught by *Modern Screen's* camera in these exclusive shots of Elizabeth Taylor and her son"— *Modern Screen,* December 1953) are submitted to Nabokov's black humor: the agents of Lemorio (=*l'amour),* a flamboyant old film comedian, are "an elderly couple, unwed, [who have] lived as man and man for a sufficiently long period to warrant a silver-screen anniversary" (p. 513). After Lolita's departure, Humbert destroys a great accumulation of teen trash. "You know the sort," he states confidently. "Stone Age at heart; up to date, or at least Mycenaean, as to hygiene. A handsome, very ripe actress with huge lashes and a pulpy red underlip, endorsing a shampoo...Tristram in Movielove. Yessir!" declares Humbert, summarizing his and Nabokov's attitude toward a vision of love distorted and coarsened in the crooked glass of Hollywood (p. 256).

It was "an innocent game on her part...in imitation of some simulacrum of fake romance," says Humbert of their first kiss at the hotel (p. 115), but it is a game that encapsules a certain aspect of some forty "innocent" years of American culture, beginning with the child stars of the nineteen-thirties. While there were many such performers in the twenties—Jackie Coogan in Chaplin's *The Kid* (1921), Hal Roach's *Our Gang* comedies, and Mary Pickford, a perennial child star—this curious and very American phenomenon reached its zenith of popularity during the nineteen-thirties, concurrent with the Great Depression, the first major inroads of progressive education, and the dissemination of Freud's remarks on infant sexuality. Shirley Temple, as everyone knows, was the Number One Box-Office Attraction in 1935, displaced a few years later not by Clark Gable but by Mickey Rooney. Few moviegoers under the age of forty have any sense of the pervasiveness of those child performers. Nor would they recognize many of the names of the thirty-five or so famous child stars of the time, featured in film upon film, or the faces of the hundreds of rapidly-aging children who poured through the casts of *Our Gang*—not without charm under Hal Roach's supervision (reissued on TV as *The Little Rascals)*, less so at M-G-M—but all part of an open-ended family of tyrannizing tots that, for better or worse, enthralled audiences of all ages until the early nineteen forties.

Where film critics and historians have generally ignored the child stars, a certain kind of comic anthopologist has made the most (and least) of them. Nathanael West reduces their collective image in the person of Adore, a hopeful child actor in *The Day of the Locust* (1939). "If it weren't for favoritism," says Adore's mother bitterly, "he'd be a star. It ain't talent. It's pull. What's Shirley Temple got that he ain't got?"[5] Adore appears, " dragging behind him a small sailboat on wheels. He was about eight years old, with a pale, peaked face and a large, troubled forehead. He had great staring eyes. His eyebrows had been plucked and shaped carefully. Except for his Buster Brown collar, he was dressed like a man, in long trousers, vest and jacket" (p. 139), a sad imitation of Freddie Bartholomew's sartorial splendor in *Little Lord Fauntleroy* (1936). The toy is an affecting touch, like Lolita reaching for a comic book from Humbert's wretched conjugal bed, or escaping his claws to go roller-skating. When Adore rolls his eyes back in his head and snarls, his grotesqueries fully communicate the pathos of his situation. "He thinks he's the Frankenstein monster," says his

"There is flirtation in the air. It is Harry Speak, all dressed up and making eyes at Mary Ann Jackson," stated the original caption for this 1928 *Our Gang* publicity still. "Greta Garbo and John Gilbert have nothing on Mary Ann . . . and Harry," reads the caption for a still that shows them kissing.

mother, correctly, and she is the manipulative Gothic Doctor's stand-in. Urged by her to perform, he renders "Mama Doan Wan No Peas," imitating a blues singer expertly (Jimmy Rushing's recording with Count Basie?). *"Mama doan wan' no glass of gin, / Because it boun' to make her sin,/An' keep her hot and bothered all the day,"* he sings, and "The gestures he made with his hands were extremely suggestive" (p. 140), his voice carrying "a top-heavy load of sexual pain" (p. 141). After the guests applaud, "Adore grabbed the string of his sailboat and circled the yard. He was imitating a tugboat. He tooted several times, then ran off" (p. 141).

Adore is a central detail in West's Goyaesque Dark Painting, an important bit player in a Brueghel-like panorama of grotesques, a landscape of creatures crippled by their dreams of success in the cinema or a paradise in California. At the movie premiere which concludes *The Day of the Locust,* Adore indeed *becomes* a little monster; he hits pathetic Homer Simpson in the face with a stone, and the maddened man, now in his own right a Frankenstein monster, punches and then stamps on the fallen child actor, precipitating a riot ("A pervert attacked a child," exclaims a woman with "snaky gray hair" [p. 183].)The ensuing chaos provides West's surrogate in the novel, Tod Hackett, with a completion for his blocked-out painting, "The Burning of Los Angeles," if not a solution to his blocked sexuality. At once a cinematic vision and a Boschian plague of locusts, Tod's painting is the ultimate cleansing apocalypse, an artist's moral attack on the cancer of mass culture. The novel ends with Tod carried off in a police car, "imitat(ing) the siren as loud as he could," paralleling the way Adore had imitated a tugboat after performing his song. Tod Hackett has perished too, engulfed by the flames in his painting, his regressive sexuality and impotency ironically counterpointed by the boy's precociously "sexy" delivery and more appropriate childish noises.

Although she is poor, Adore's mother has managed to send him to one of Hollywood's many "talent schools." Less avaricious mothers all across America also squandered their hard-earned savings in behalf of tap-dance lessons for daughters they had cast in Shirley Temple's image. The illegitimate, supposedly mute child named Shirley T. in Eudora Welty's story "Why I Live at the P.O." (1941) yells her first words in "the loudest Yankee voice" the narrator has ever heard: "OE'm Pop-OE the Sailor-r-r-r Ma-a-an!" Leaden feet pound on the upstairs hall. " 'Not only talks, she can tap-

Boys will be boys: "Chubby" Chaney kisses a Greta Garbo cutout in the 1931 *Our Gang*
two-reeler, *Love Business,* and compresses the "Dream Factory" ethic. The film lovers on
the left are Thelma Todd and Charley Chase, another Hal Roach comedy team. Pete the
dog patiently waits, and little Dorothy DeBora endures, in the spirit of the pop song of
the time, "Don't Fall Asleep" ("Don't fall asleep and dream you're Gable/ Don't fall
asleep, I'm young and able . . . Forget the charm of Greta Garbo/ And keep your mind
on me . . ."). Although *Our Gang* helped to set the pattern for such charades, the
sequence is uncharacteristic of Hal Roach's Gang productions, given their number (eighty
talkies), which sometimes cleverly mocked the "cuteness" of the standard child-star fare.
At M-G-M, however (post-1938), the gang continually mimed the manner and content of
their plastic Metro parents; *The Big Premiere* (1940), *Ye Olde Minstrels* (1941), *Doin'
their Bit* (1942), and *Melodies Old and New* (1942) are typical. Even the titles sound
"adult."

*(Photo courtesy Richard W. Bann and Leonard Maltin from their forthcoming book on
the Our Gang comedies.)*

Graham Greene seems to have been the first critic to discuss the eroticism of a (chaste) child performer, just as almost twenty years later he would be the first litterateur to recommend an unknown novel entitled *Lolita,* published in Paris by the infamous Olympia Press. Reviewing *Captain January* in *The Spectator* (August 7, 1936), Greene wrote that "the latest Shirley Temple picture is sentimental, a little depraved, with an appeal interestingly decadent. Shirley Temple acts and dances with immense vigour and assurance [above], but some of her popularity seems to rest on a coquetry quite as mature as Miss Colbert's [in *Under Two Flags]* and on an oddly precocious body as voluptuous in grey flannel trousers as Miss Dietrich's" (from *Graham Greene on Film* [New York, 1972], p. 92). Greene extended this line of discussion in a review of *Wee Willie Winkie,* remarking on her appeal to the "antique audience" within the film itself and the audience of "middle-aged men and clergymen" without. Published in *Night and Day* (I, October 28, 1937, 31), that review is omitted from the above volume, for certain legal reasons. As a "highbrow," Greene avoided most of the child-star features; *Wee Willie Winkie* may have been worth a viewing only because it was directed by John Ford, who had recently been acclaimed for *The Informer.* If Greene had seen more of these films he would have realized that such performances adhered to a convention, and he might have tempered his remarks about perverse intentions and audience response. In any event, lawyers for 20th Century-Fox and Shirley Temple sued for criminal libel (for the court's ruling, see the Appendix to *Graham Greene on Film),* the short-lived magazine folded, and guilty Greene fled England for Mexico, where—thanks to Miss Shirley Temple—he wrote *The Power and The Glory* (1940).

dance!' calls [her mother]. 'Which is more than some people I won't name can do.' " The aggressive vulgarity of Shirley T. reflects the mean and empty lives of the adults in the story, the Milky Way bars, casual *amours,* and mindless games (Casino and Old Maid) which sustain them.

Our own unstated figurative response to a lengthy parlor performance by a professional child—*I'd like to kill that kid!*—is fulfilled by Flannery O'Connor, a West disciple, who literally attacks nineteen-thirties-like "cuteness" in the title story of *A Good Man Is Hard to Find* (1955). Its title, of course, refers ironically to the song (Bessie Smith's is the best version), though this escapes younger readers and many university teachers, since one generation's popular culture is another's esoterica. When the family stops at Red Sammy's lunchroom, the mother puts a coin in the nickelodeon, and little June Star goes out onto the dance floor and does *her* Shirley T. tap routine. " 'Aint' she cute?' Red Sam's wife said, leaning over the counter. 'Would you like to come be my little girl?' 'No, I certainly wouldn't,' June Star said. 'I wouldn't live in a broken-down place like this for a million bucks!' and she ran back to the table." Readers as cold-blooded as the author may well feel that June Star meets her just reward at the hands of Bobby Lee and The Misfit, who later murder the entire family. An interesting book could be written about the child star phenomenon; the subject clearly deserves something better than the nostalgia-gossip pastiche it naturally invites. As an interlude in cultural history, it is anything but a sweet story.

Because West was, among other things, an accurate reporter, Adore's mother is a typical figure. Tens of thousands of ambitious mothers besieged the Hollywood studios throughout the thirties, their untalented young properties in tow; few succeeded in placing them—in legitimate pictures, that is. Most of these disappointed stage-mothers (and fathers) returned home, but others stayed on and doubtless helped to feed various furtive needs: the pornographic film market and the white slave traffic that flourished in Southern California during the nineteen-thirties. In *The Day of the Locust* the elegant and cultured Mrs. Jenning, formerly a prominent silent screen star and now a high-priced procuress, shows *Le Predicament de Marie* to her party guests. It is an "utterly charming" film farce in which all the male members of the household in question pursue buxom Marie, a servant; she in turn has Lesbian designs on the little girl of the family (pp. 74-76)—perhaps an

Top: C. Aubrey Smith and Shirley Temple in *Wee Willie Winkie*
Bottom: Shirley and friends in *Wee Willie Winkie*

Demonic Rockwell, or Tom Sawyer and Becky Thatcher go Hollywood:
Mickey Rooney and Shirley Jean Rickert as Gable and Garbo.

"actress" who failed to make the grade in *Our Gang?* Visiting California in 1941, his second year in America, Nabokov heard rumors of nympholeptic house parties hosted by outwardly solid citizens, the girleens supplied by "an agency" in Los Angeles, and surely these tawdry, darkly resonant tales were not lost on the creator of Humbert Humbert, whose eye for the significantly monstrous is as keen as Nathanael West's. After completing his Hollywood screenplay of *Lolita* (1960), Nabokov was asked to adapt *The Day of the Locust.* It would have been a fitting union: American Black Humor of the nineteen-sixties, in fiction and film, owes much to *Lolita, Miss Lonelyhearts* and *The Day of the Locust.* Confronting as it does the Gothic past and present of a former child performer, *Whatever Happened to Baby Jane?* (1962) utilizes pop culture in the requisite Westian (or Nabokovian) manner.

Hollywood's grotesque and pitiful underground activities had their chaste equivalent in the very movies which had failed to employ those children, had indeed failed them in every way. The basic pattern for the most bizarre convention of these films was first suggested by a few *Our Gang* skits in the late twenties and then developed by Educational (!) Studios's "Baby Burlesks," a shoddy series of cheaply made one-reelers that presented very young children in burlesques of the most famous adult stars of that era; the spactacle of child stars acting "grown-up" would be a predictable, staple ingredient of many subsequent feature films, and West's Adore is a transcribed observation rather than a fantastic creation. Shirley Temple's first roles were in the "Baby Burlesks"; the producer, according to his former sub-starlet, would punish naughty performers by putting them in a darkened, primitive ice box (he later served a prison term, but for other crimes). In *The Incomparable More Legs Sweetrick* (1931), Shirley, age three, does a Marlene Dietrich routine; shortly afterwards, in leopard-skin diapers, she played Jane to another toddler's Tarzan; but in *Captain January* (1936), she is out of the freezer forever: a mature star at eight, or a "l'il' de-icer," to borrow *Smilin' Jack's* comic strip description of appealing, petite females. Cast as Starr, the adopted orphan daughter of bachelor lighthouse keeper Guy Kibbee, and wearing bell-bottomed pants after Ginger Rogers's example in *Follow the Fleet* (1936), Shirley does a whirling, tapping Astaire-Rogers song and dance number with Buddy Ebsen before a gang of his enchanted bachelor chums at The Sailor's Rest. "You can

Can-Can At the Codfish Ball" sings Shirley, accentuating each "can" with a vulgar shake of her own. Applauding wildly, the nautical celibates would seem to measure her performance against their memories of pants-wearing Dietrich in *Morocco* (1930), Fred and Ginger's "Let Yourself Go" number in *Follow the Fleet,* or Ginger's "I'll be Hard to Handle" routine in *Roberta* (1935), *her* trousered debut. In a subsequent scene aproned Kibbee bakes her a birthday cake while comfy Shirley reads smugly, less a daughter than a wifely image in a latter-day Women's Lib fantasy. C. Aubrey Smith, his troops and Sikhs are in her sway in *Wee Willie Winkie* (1937), the zenith of Shirley's powers, or so thought movie reviewer Graham Greene in England, much to his and his editors' regrets. Jane Withers, age nine, impersonates Garbo in *Ginger* (1935), and in *This is the Life* (1935), Jane's jaunty take-off on Dietrich's *Blonde Venus* (1932), her white tails and top hat, achieves a high (or perhaps low) level of mimetic perfection. Playing Garbo and Gable in one of the many *Mickey McGuire* comedies from the early thirties, Shirley Jean Rickert (on loan from *Our Gang)* and

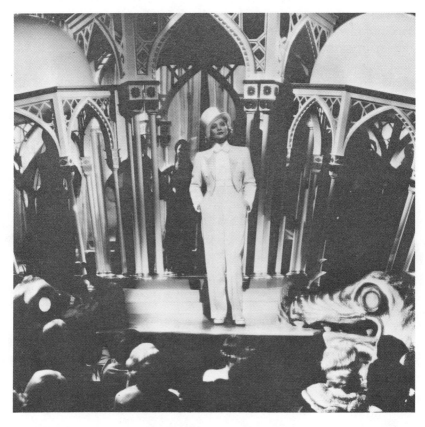

Marlene Dietrich in *Blonde Venus.*

Jane Withers as Dietrich in *This is the Life.*

Top: The "child" lifts the curtain on the girls in *The Gold Diggers of 1933.*
Bottom: "Get out in the California sunshine": Leslie Howard in *Stand-In.*

Mickey Rooney are two wan and world-weary enough ten-year-olds, quite distant from *The Adventures of Tom Sawyer* (1876) and the innocent Booth Tarkington and Norman Rockwell children who exist only in our poor memory as the sole models for images of screen mischief. Rooney later played Huckleberry Finn (1939), but anti-climactically, since Twain's famous territory ahead would seem to have already absorbed the young actor, leaving few questions unanswered; like Jay Gatsby, who gathers rather than loses illusions (Balzac reversed), Mickey's movie *persona* grew more innocent with age. Throughout most of *Strike Up the Band* (1940, directed by Busby Berkeley), Mickey only has eyes for swing music. "How would you feel, losing out to a snare drum?" complains lovestruck Judy Garland to a girl friend. Although Mickey and Judy are cheek-to-cheek by the film's finale, their lips never touch (the full extent of Gatsby's dream of Daisy); they remain sibling pals to the end. The willful asexuality of screen adolescents seems even more curious in view of the sexual charades indulged by the same stars when they resembled children. Shirley Temple's first marriage in 1945 was much publicized, but her fans had been prepared for such trauma earlier that year by *The Bachelor and the Bobby Soxer,* when Shirley downed her initial screen drink, eliciting newspaper headlines based on the assumption that *Bright Eyes, Captain January,* and *Wee Willie Winkie* had been all lollipops and animal crackers.

What seems implicit in even the sunniest of these screen satires is made explicit by the leering, demonic midget, dressed as a child, who lifts the curtain on a chorus line of disrobing girls and winks lasciviously at the audience during Busby Berkeley's famous "Pettin' in the Park" number in *The Gold Diggers of 1933,* and who later that year, in *Footlight Parade's* "Honeymoon Hotel" number, is discovered by Ruby Keeler and Dick Powell under the covers of their nuptial bed.[6] Wearing a baby bonnet and nightie, the midget is a mock-ardent bridegroom; forced from the bed, he crawls around the room. Finally ejected, he peers through the keyhole—a lucky witness to the primal scene?—then turns around, and once again winks at the voyeurs seated below him; what they don't see on the screen may be analogous to the rigid censorship of dreams, a sterner entity than the Production Codes of that era (even today one rarely remembers any dream beyond a "PG" rating—grant us more "Rs"!). Equally salacious is a scene in *Stand-In* (1937), which featured Leslie Howard as Atterbury Dodd, a stuffy young banker and efficiency expert, ignorant about films, dispatched to Hollywood by the studio's financial bosses in New York City. An aggressive stage-mother, daughter in hand, forces her way into Howard's hotel room. The seven-year-old girl does a seductive song-and-dance routine, much to the embarrassment of Howard, who throws them out; a little girl, he says, should be outdoors, playing in the California sunshine. And when *Our Gang*, having joined M-G-M's star-studded lot, stages a variety show to raise money for a needy neighbor *(ca.* 1939) or, a few years later, do so in behalf of the Red Cross, the female members of the cast vamp a la Harlow in an uncomfortably convincing manner, the realism heightened by the fact that theirs is an encapsulated world, a microcosm dominated by little people, if not children—as in the comic strip *The Teenie Weenies,* rather than the *Tiny Tim* strip. After W. C. Fields had accepted an assignment in a movie that would also feature the precocious, scene-stealing Baby LeRoy—a star after nine months on this earth, a has-been at age three—a reporter asked Fields who his co-star would be. "Fellow named LeRoy, says he's a baby," answered Fields, demonstrating his greatness and prescience, since we have recently endured men named Abbie Hoffman and Charles Reich, who say they are boys and ask us to behave like babies.

Whatever the intentions of the filmmakers may have been, these "Movielove" charades assume a distinctive life of their own. The performers are too expert, too talented; little Shirley, her lines and lyrics always memorized perfectly, was known as "one take Temple." When West's tiny Adore sings *his* song, "He seemed to know what the words meant, or at least his body and his voice seemed to know. When he came to the final chorus, his buttocks writhed and his voice carried a top-heavy load of sexual pain... Then he grabbed the string of his sailboat and circled the yard... 'He's just a baby,' Mrs. Loomis said proudly, 'but he's got loads of talent' " (p. 141). Except for the crudest low-budget films, the charades of the child stars seem to complement rather than burlesque adult behavior, as though the performers were adults alchemically reduced in size, as in Tod Browning's sci-fi horror film of the time, *The Devil Doll* (1936). The amorous midgets in the same director's *Freaks* (1932) were also an edifying spectacle to many moviegoers, despite the higher intentions of Browning, if not M-G-M producers and publicists: "THE STORY OF THE LOVE LIFE OF THE SIDESHOW," declared their ads, when *Freaks* was re-released

The apotheosis of the child, ca. 1929: *Our Gang's* Joe Frank Cobb as king.

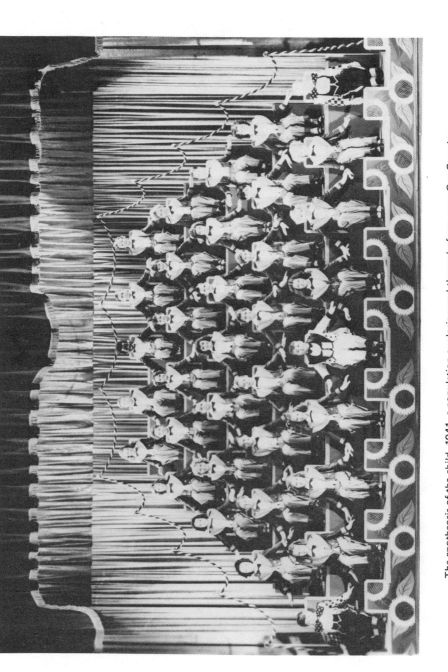

The apotheosis of the child, 1941, a population explosion and the end of one era: *Our Gang* in a production number from their M-G-M short, *Ye Olde Minstrels*. (Photo courtesy Richard W. Bann and Leonard Maltin from their forthcoming book on *Our Gang*.)

as *Nature's Mistakes.* The midget's marriage to a "normal" woman (Olga Baclanova) who covets his money also had a certain crowd appeal ("Can a Full Grown Woman Love a Midget?" asked the ads).[7] Audiences may or may not have had a perverse taste for miniatures; such generalizations are risky, and certain "miniatures" were obviously innocent enough: Laurel and Hardy as child stars, scaled down against huge sets, playing their own sons in *Brats* (1930)—and more than one babysitting graduate student father, slumped next to a playpen with a medieval Latin text in his lap, has found himself enjoying an innocuous old *Our Gang* short on TV. Along with the Busby Berkeley dance extravaganzas, the child-star feature films were the quintessential escapist entertainment of the Depression era, and that context is of course important.[8] Moreover, what is "cute" to one generation of audiences is often laughable to another. But viewed today, those movies possess none of the campy charms of Busby Berkeley; their vulgarity is eerie and disquieting because it extends beyond the screen into our own time, and our own child-centered culture of the moment. Humbert's terrible demands notwithstanding, Lolita is as insensitive as children are to their actual parents; sexuality aside, she demands anxious parental placation in a too typically American way, and affords Nabokov an ideal opportunity to comment on the Teen and Sub-Teen Tyranny. It is poetic justice that Lolita should seduce Humbert at The Enchanted Hunters hotel; the irony is obvious, but telling. Nabokov underscores his point with a resonant pun, characteristic of both himself and Joyce. The seduction takes place in the invented town of Briceland (note the *i* rather than *y*). Anyone over thirty-five should recall the popular weekly radio program of the forties, *Baby Snooks,* starring the late Fanny Brice. A satire rather than a residium of the cinema's child stars of the thirties, the show featured only Baby Snooks, a sappy but demanding little girl of indeterminate age, who spoke a patois of baby talk and teen jargon, and her helpless, ineffectual Daddums (twice Humbert calls himself this). Year after year the program explored all but one of the various ways the tyrannical Baby Snooks could victimize her poor daddy. The town of Briceland is well named. Nabokov's book is Baby Snooks and Daddums in apotheosis. Lolita is a Baby Snooks who, icon-like, dominates our scene, recalling the kingly image of *Our Gang's* Joe Frank Cobb; Shirley Temple's reign in the thirties (Sikhs at her feet in *Wee Willie Winkie);* and the film *Waterloo* in

143

The Day of the Locust, where "The colors of the Lunenberg battalion, borne by a prince of the family of Deux-Ponts, were captured by a famous child star in the uniform of a Parisian drummer boy" (pp. 133-34), an ironic forecast of Adore's demise in the subsequent, less triumphant mob scene, an entire culture's Waterloo. Born too soon to partake of Woodstock, not to mention Dick Clark's TV *American Bandstand* of the fifties, Lolita looks back to Baby LeRoy, and her cold joyless copulations with indefatigable Charlie Holmes in the bushes at "Camp Q" (=Quilty), by Lake Climax, connect the child-star charades of the thirties with the "Movielove" shams of the forties.

To have each cabin at Camp Q "dedicated to a Disney creature" (p. 112) is a far more telling attack on calculated innocence and child-tyranny than, say, Pynchon's similar assault in *Gravity's Rainbow*. His "Zwölfkinder," a little country run by children, is a kind of German Disneyland, with a child mayor, a child city council, and child police [Thomas Pynchon, *Gravity's Rainbow* (New York, 1973), pp. 419-20]. No parent is admitted unless accompanied by a child, and at least one father indulges an incest fantasy at the kiddie-controlled hotel. The entire sequence owes not a little to *The Day of the Locust* and *Lolita*, obviously, and is even more indebted to John Wyndham's sci-fi novel *The Midwich Cuckoos* (filmed as *Village of the Damned* [1960]), in which a strange race of children threatens to take over the town and, by implication, the world. Because Pynchon, unlike West or Nabokov, savors prolixity, the comic point of Zwölfkinder, however derivative, is later dulled by a little girl's imitation of Shirley Temple, a grunted rendition of "On the Good Ship Lollipop" that echoes West's Adore. When the girl fails to respond to the obscene requests of the drunken crowd, her "stage-mother" gives her a public spanking drawn from the pages of Sacher-Masoch. The erotic exhibitionistic punishment inspires a wild mob orgy (pp. 465-68). As happens so often in *Gravity's Rainbow*, the ensuing, rampant sadism confuses the issue, and the scene degenerates in every sense of the word, dissipating the satire of Hollywood and Nazi Germany, too. A tedious catalogue of wanton acts sacrifices art to pathology.

Lolita stands alone among post-war novels in its uncompromising yet controlled dramatization of the manner in which the iconography of popular culture forms or twists its consumers. Where *Gravity's Rainbow* frequently waxes nostalgic over the very

144

pop materials it would seem to be eviscerating, *Lolita* is consistently lucid and unambiguous, authoritative but never strident. Pynchon's gentler moments are jarring because they contradict his principal metaphor, which offers pop as the circumscribing mythology of a hateful technological culture. No one should argue that a writer must be negative on the subject. Manuel Puig's fine novel *Betrayed by Rita Hayworth* (1968) is as tender as it is moving, and Albert J. Guerard's brilliant autobiographical essay "Was Lia de Putti Dead at 22?" (1971), eloquently explores a psyche's survival, the man and writer's creative evolution from the boy's indelible, far from unhealthy infatuation with a young screen star in the nineteen-twenties.[9] Most modern fiction, however, treats such phenomena in a less sanguine manner. Nathanael West, James M. Cain, and Horace McCoy, among others, have etched in acid nightmarish images of people lost to pop culture.

The iconography of popular culture is not simply a matter of cosmetics and good or willfully bad counter-culture grooming; it can be psychically crippling, a literally fatal "existential choice." As a young hoodlum Joey ("Crazy Joe") Gallo fashioned himself after Richard Widmark's giggling, black shirt-white tie image in *Kiss of Death* (1947); twenty-five years later he died violently in public at his pre-wedding dinner while enjoying a Show-Biz celebrity inspired by *The Godfather's* success, shot in Technicolor by rival Mafiosi who, among other things, resented Gallo's media-created glamour (a book contract, actor friends, TV interviews). Musical comedy star Jerry Orbach delivered the eulogy at Crazy Joe's funeral. Lecturing on *Madame Bovary* at Cornell in 1953 *(Lolita* was nearing completion), Nabokov would emphasize Emma's reading material and dwell on each cliché. *"Stale romanticism!* Memorize those titles," he would warn in mock-donnish tones, "for they describe her sense of 'reality' (quotes, please, around that word)." ("Describe and evaluate the importance of Emma's reading preferences in *Madame Bovary.* Be specific," read one of the final exam questions.) The Emma Bovary who is poisoned by romantic prose and verse figures throughout Nabokov's *King, Queen, Knave* (1928), whose celluloid characters, Franz and Martha, also live outside of themselves, as it were, conceiving their love story in the terms of a movie or pulp fiction plot. Their plan to toss cuckolded Dreyer from a rowboat parallels the central scenes in Dreiser's *An American Tragedy* (1925) and F. W. Murnau's film *Sunrise* (1927). "A coincidental resemblance," says Nabokov, "but a good one." Martha dies suddenly, *too* suddenly, infected by the cold and corny nature of their pop murder plot rather than by any medically feasible chill. Her quick demise is also a judgment on the expectations of the old-fashioned reader. The pervasive, debilitating aura of popular culture is examined even more closely in *Lolita.*

The women in *Lolita,* the large and the small, are a product of the movies they have viewed. "First time I've seen a man wearing a smoking jacket, sir—except in movies, of course," says one of Lo's schoolmates (p. 191). Charlotte Haze, belonging to an earlier era and aspiring to a more European image, has a "shiny forehead, plucked eyebrows and quite simple but not unattractive features of a type that may be defined as a weak solution of Marlene Dietrich" (p. 39).[10] Furtively holding Lolita's hand while Charlotte drives the car, Humbert notices how "The wings of the driver's Marlenesque nose shone, having shed or burned up their ration of powder, and she kept up an elegant monologue. . and smiled in profile, and pouted in profile, and beat her painted lashes in profile" (p. 53), her version of a stylized performance on the silver screen. "When you wanted me to spend my afternoons sunbathing on the Lake instead of doing my work, I gladly gave in and became a bronzed glamor boy for your sake, instead of remaining a scholar," says Humbert, whose heated verbal attack leaves Charlotte on her knees, shaking her head, clawing at his trousers. "She said I was her ruler and her god" (p. 93), a bit of "sexist" hyperbole drawn, no doubt, from a popular novel or film. After Charlotte's accidental death beneath the wheels of a car, someone tells Humbert that Lolita's mother "was a celebrated actress killed in an airplane crash" (p. 191), an ironic tribute to her sundry histrionics and a blending of her death, her pale re-creation of Dietrich, and the actual fate of Carole Lombard, their contemporary.

Lolita and her friends, however, naturally draw upon the typical films of the nineteen-forties and early fifties, and their unnatural vision of "corporate desire" *(Pale Fire,* l. 454)—a drab vision of sexuality divorced and dissociated from love, quite different from the very human eroticism communicated in the thirties by a Dietrich or a Harlow, or funned by Mae West. Although the stellar names are not given in the text, Lolita and her friends would have had as their female exempla the icy narcissistic perfection of a Lana Turner, the porcelain features of a Hedy Lamarr, the vacuous glamour of a Linda Darnell or a Rhonda Fleming, the plastic gambols of a Betty Grable or a Virginia Mayo, the grotesque "sexy" posturings of a Jane Russell *(The Outlaw* [1943]) or a Jennifer Jones *(Duel in the Sun* [1947]).[11] There are exceptions, of course: Ingrid Bergman, too ladylike to enter this discussion, and Rita Hayworth, beauty redeemed by talent, both of them *hors de concours;* Bette Davis and Joan Crawford, "emasculators" who inevitably paid for their indomitable willfulness; Katherine Hepburn, a liberated Sister who escaped such punishments; and Joan Bennett, Ida Lupino, Gloria Grahame, and Lauren Bacall, whose cool, tough, and sardonic acting styles look back to the thirties, to Lombard, Hepburn, Jean Arthur, Ginger Rogers, Barbara Stanwyck, Rosalind Russell, Irene Dunne, and Myrna Loy—all clearly women as opposed to objects, their performances often enlivened by wit, even when the films were not comedies. But Lolita and her friends derive their inspiration, such as it is, from the waxen mannequins of the subsequent decade (an outgrowth of World War II's inert, pin-up needs?), and their sexuality, whether innocently mimed or mechancially performed, represents yet another charade; to grow up too quickly is perhaps never to grow up at all, and it is an old American story. A summary emblem for this aspect of *Lolita* is a *trompe l'oeil* painting by the American surrealist, Man Ray, titled *Observation Time—The Lovers* (1932-1934), picturing a huge pair of female lips, filling the cloud-stippled sky as they float miraculously above a landscape.[12] Although the lips suggest two lovers coupling, their disembodied state simultaneously charts the distance separating love from lovemaking. Current college audiences admire Bogart in *The Maltese Falcon* (1941) because he doesn't seem to confuse the two and can turn in Mary Astor to the police. "That's cool, man," murmured at least one student, unaware that scenarist-director John Huston had shrewdly omitted Hammett's last scene, which reveals Sam Spade as a desperate, shoddy man, spurned by Effie and seated at his desk, shivering. A week after seeing *The Maltese Falcon,* the same audience laughed derisively at Dana Andrews' unabashedly romantic, unconsummated love for Giene Tierney in *Laura* (1944). "You never did *it* when you were a kid?" asks Lolita (my emphasis), sounding a very contemporary note.

In his diary Humbert remarks his realization that he could kiss Lolita with impunity. "I knew she would . . even close her eyes as Hollywood teaches" (p. 50). As a "modern child, an avid reader of movie magazines, an expert in dream-slow close-ups,

[she] might not think it too strange" if "the glamorous lodger" were to take a few liberties, reasons Humbert (p. 51), quite correctly, as he learns shortly in the most prolonged and explicitly sexual passage of *Lolita* (pp. 59-63). Their sprawling tom-foolery on the couch soon sends an unconcerned Lolita onto his active lap, and culminates three pages later with "the last throb of the longest ecstasy man or monster had ever known" (p. 63).

Unique to *Lolita,* this interlude perversely promises the common reader something Humbert, unlike Quilty, will never again produce; the shaping of Humbert's pain, the bliss of eroticism and the burden of obsession, in no way depend upon sexual exhibitionism. "And nothing prevented me from repeating a performance that affected her as little as if she were a photographic image rippling upon a screen and I am humble hunchback abusing myself in the dark," says Humbert (p. 64), anticipating the kinds of pleasures available to any audience of one of Clare Quilty's "underground" pornographic films. But Humbert doesn't repeat the performance. Lolita has gone out with a friend—to a movie.

What kind of movies do Humbert and Lolita view? They form a veritable survey course in the popular American product. In his diary, Humbert notes how, on the previous evening, as "Warm dusk had deepened into amorous darkness [,] The old girl [Charlotte] had finished relating in great detail the plot of a movie she and L. had seen sometime in the winter. The boxer had fallen extremely low when he met the good old priest (who had been a boxer himself in his robust youth and could still slug a sinner)"—a paraphrase which conjures up images of John Garfield and a priestly Pat O'Brien or Spencer Tracy (p. 47). Amorous Humbert is not above taking advantage of a movies aura, but at a "matinee in a small airless theater crammed with children and reeking with the hot breath of popcorn," Gene Autry arouses but cannot assist an anxious Humbert:

> The moon was yellow above the neckerchiefed crooner, and his finger was on his strumstring, and his foot was on a pine log, and I had innocently encircled Lo's shoulder and approached my jawbone to her temple, when two harpies behind us started muttering the queerest things—I do not know if I understood aright, but what I

thought I did, made me withdraw my gentle hand, and of course the rest of the show was fog to me (p. 173).

American sites become movie sets: Humbert and Lolita visit "Antebellum homes with iron-trellis balconies and hand-worked stairs, the kind down which movie ladies with sun-kissed shoulders run in rich Technicolor, holding up the fronts of their flounced skirts with both little hands in that special way, and the devoted Negress shaking her head on the upper landing" (p. 158), Hattie McDaniel or Butterfly McQueen fluttering after Vivian Leigh in *Gone With the Wind* (1939). Sometimes a trite turn in the unfolding of Humbert's own story suggests to him the hack scenarist's easy solution: "With people in movies I seem to share the services of the machina telephonica and its sudden god," laments Humbert, in regard to the manner in which an irate neighbor's phone call interrupts "a strident and hateful" argument with Lo, allowing her to run out of the house and escape for the nonce (p. 207). Yet given the number of movies inflicted upon Humbert, it is remarkable that he isn't plagued by a myriad of movie specters:

> We took in, voluptuously and indiscriminately, oh, I don't know, one hundred and fifty or two hundred programs during that one year, and during some of the denser periods of movie-going we saw many of the newsreels up to half-a-dozen times since the same weekly one went with different main pictures and pursued us from town to town. Her favorite kinds were, in this order: musicals, underworlders, westerners. In the first, real singers and dancers had unreal stage careers in an essentially grief-proof sphere of existence wherefrom death and truth were banned, and where, at the end, white-haired, dewy-eyed, technically deathless, the initially reluctant father of a show-crazy girl always finished by applauding her apotheosis on fabulous Broadway. The underworld was a world apart; there, heroic newspapermen were tortured, telephone bills ran to billions, and, in a robust atmosphere of incompetent marksmanship, villains were chased through sewers and storehouses by pathologically fearless cops (I was to give them less exercise). Finally there was the mahogany landscape, the florid-faced, blue-eyed roughriders, the prim pretty schoolteacher arriving in Roaring Gulch, the rearing horse, the spectacular stampede, the pistol thrust through the shivered windowpane, the stupendous fist fight, the crashing mountain of dusty old-fashioned furniture, the table used as a weapon, the timely somersault, the pinned hand still groping for the dropped bowie knife, the grunt, the sweet crash of

"The black trains roared past, shaking the windows of the house; with a movement like ghostly shoulders shaking off a load, heaving mountains of smoke swept upward, blotting out the night sky. The roofs burned with a smooth metallic blaze in the moonlight; and a sonorous black shadow under the iron bridge awoke as a black train rumbled across it, sending a chain of light flickering down its length. The clattering roar and mass of smoke seemed to pass right through the house as it quivered between the chasm where the rail tracks lay like lines drawn by a moonlit fingernail and the street where it was crossed by the flat bridge waiting for the next regular thunder of railway carriages. The house was like a spectre you could put your hand through and wriggle your fingers.

"Standing at the window of the dancers' room, Ganin looked out onto the street: the asphalt gleamed dully, black foreshortened people walked hither and thither, disappearing into shadows and re-emerging in the slanting light," write Nabokov in *Mary* (p. 95), employing the Max Reinhardt lighting effects one associates with countless German films of the period, the chiaroscuro and awesome machines of *Metropolis* (1926), the well-named *Asphalt* (1928), and *The Hands of Orlac,* whose train wreck (above) Nabokov still vividly remembers. Thirty years later, describing his tormented first conjugal night with Lolita, Humbert recalls how the "residential, dignified alley of huge trees" beyond his window "degenerated into the despicable haunt of gigantic trucks roaring through the wet and windy night" (p. 132), a very Germanic *Stimmung* akin too to the visuals of *Thieves' Highway* (1949), a *film noir* directed by the very "Germanic" American Jules Dassin, whose *Brute Force* is alluded to by Humbert (p. 264).

> fist against chin, the kick in the belly, the flying tackle; and immed-
> iately after a plethora of pain that would have hospitalized a
> Hercules (I should know by now), nothing to show but the rather
> becoming bruise on the bronzed cheek of the warmed-up hero
> embracing his gorgeous frontier bride (pp. 173-73).

If Humbert has viewed typical naturalistic "story" musicals of
the forties and fifties (daughter Kathryn Grayson or Jane Powell
versus papa Lewis Stone, as opposed to reruns of the best lyric
dance fantasies of the thirties), then he is correct, though it
doesn't matter: his remarks are in character and are not always
consistently those of Nabokov, who admits to having actually enjoyed a few Technicolor Westerns ("for their limpid landscapes")
and at least one gangster movie, genus *film noir—The Killers* (1946),
from Hemingway's story. The dark *mise-en-scène* of *The Killers,*
as detailed by German refugee director Robert Siodmak, recalls
émigré Nabokov's subsequent recreation of the same period's
America, its bleak rented rooms and uninviting roadside diners,
its vagabond cars which serve as home and haven, death chamber or
prison cell—all set against the lonely, neon-lit nightscapes of urban
and rural America depicted so tellingly, so movingly in countless
films noirs of 1943-1958 *(Double Indemnity* through *Touch of
Evil),* amazingly subversive Hollywood works which delineate
crises of self and society. By definition hostile, Humbert's film
criticism is not altogether unfair: the chase through underworld
sewers mocks a convention abused by first-class directors (Fritz
Lang's *While the City Sleeps* [1956]), as well as grade-C hacks (the
acrid *Gang Busters* serial [1942], and *The Falcon* series, which
Nabokov viewed regularly with his young son Dmitri [ca. 1943-
44]). Most important, that spectacular frontier-fist fight looks
forward to Humbert's considerably less acrobatic Western-style
tussle with his cornered shadow, Clare Quilty (p. 301), while the
staging of Quilty's death—a grand vaudevillian version of the movie
gunplay of *King, Queen, Knave* and *Laughter in the Dark*—easily
outdoes the "robust atmosphere of incompetent marksmanship"
of any previous "underworlder." It is fitting and thematically consistent that Humbert's nemesis, the novel's most sinister presence,
is in fact a specter from the movie world, who indeed "pursues
[Humbert and Lolita] from town to town" with a tenacity far
greater than those newsreels.

"My dear sir," Quilty tells Humbert, who is bent on destroying him, "stop trifling with life and death. I am a playwright. I

have written tragedies, comedies, fantasies. I have made private movies out of [Sade's] *Justine* and other eighteenth-century sex-capades. I'm the author of fifty-two successful scenarios. I know all the ropes" (p. 300). Prior to their checking-out of The Enchanted Hunters hotel, Humbert had observed "A fellow of my age in tweeds" (Quilty) staring at Lolita as she sat in the lobby, "deep in a lurid movie magazine" (p. 140), and Humbert, will later learn that Quilty's enticements, akin to Valentinov's overtures to Luzhin, included an offer to take her to "Hollywood and arrange a tryout for her, a bit part in the tennis-match scene of a movie picture based on a play of his—*Golden Guts*—and perhaps even have her double one of its sensational starlets on the klieg-struck tennis court. Alas, it never came to that" (p. 278). Quilty's unkept promise and its pornographic alternate at once represent a debasement of the novel's most wondrous scene, Humbert's own unrealized movie of it, and the enchantments of art cherished by Nabokov,who makes foul Quilty the victim of his irony, his scorn, and, in Part Two, Chapter Thirty-Five, something even more lethal.

Shortly before she departs with Quilty, Lolita and Humbert play a tennis game which, to Humbert, is "the highest point to which I can imagine a young creature bringing the art of make-believe, although I daresay, for her it was the very geometry of basic reality" (p. 233). Admittedly "susceptible to the magic of games" (p. 235), Humbert and his creator in this scene (pp. 233-36) come as close as they ever will to depicting Lolita's ineffable charms, from her "gaspingly young and adorable apricot shoulder blades [and] lovely gentle bones, and [her] smooth, downward-tapering back" (p. 233), to the infinite grace of her game:

> The exquisite clarity of all her movements had its auditory counterpart in the pure ringing sound of her every stroke. The ball when it entered her aura of control became somehow whiter, its resilience somehow richer, and the instrument of precision she used upon it seemed inordinately prehensile and deliberate at the moment of clinging contact. Her form was, indeed, an absolutely perfect imitation of absolutely top-notch tennis—without any utilitarian results. . . I remember at the very first game I watched being drenched with an almost painful convulsion of beauty of assimilation. My Lolita had a way of raising her bent left knee at the ample and springy start of the service cycle when there would develop and hang in the sun for a second a vital web of balance between toed foot, pristine

armpit, burnished arm and far back-flung racket, as she smiled up with gleaming teeth at the small globe suspended so high in the zenith of the powerful and graceful cosmos she had created for the express purpose of falling upon it with a clean resounding crack of her golden whip.

It had, that serve of hers, beauty, directness, youth, a classical purity of trajectory, and was, despite its spanking pace, fairly easy to return, having as it did no twist or sting to its long elegant hop (pp. 233-34).

Humbert savors all the qualities of her game which produce in him the "delirious feeling of teetering on the very brink of unearthly order and splendor" (p. 232): "the polished gem of her dropshot" (p. 235); the ease with which, "Despite her small stature, she covered the one thousand and fifty-three square feet of her half of the court" and "entered into the rhythm of a rally"; the way "Her overhead volley was related to her service as the envoy is to the ballade"—that is, as the concluding, summary postscript is to the stanza of the poem (p. 234).

By explicitly employing the vocabularies of poetics and music to describe the poetry of her play, Nabokov brings to mind Johan Huizinga's remarks on the "Nature and Significance of Play." "Inside the play-ground an absolute and peculiar order reigns," writes Huizinga in *Homo Ludens* (1944). Play "creates order, *is* order. Into an imperfect world and into the confusion of life it brings a temporary, a limited perfection. Play demands order absolute and supreme. . . The profound affinity between play and order is perhaps the reason why play. . . seems to lie to such a large extent in the field of aesthetics. . . The words we use to denote the elements of play belong for the most part to esthetics, terms with which we try to describe the effects of beauty"—and Humbert's key words and phrases complement Huizinga's statement: "elegan [ce] "; "balance"; "instrument of precision"; "rhythm"; "classical purity"; "unearthly order." Play, concludes Huizinga "is invested with the noblest qualities we are capable of perceiving in things: rhythm and harmony."[13] On the tennis court, Lolita occupies a sphere whose innate harmonies are artistic, musical, timeless. "She would wait and relax for a bar or two of white-lined time before going into the act of serving," writes Nabokov in the sentence which opens the description of her game (p. 233). "At match point, her second serve, which . . . was even stronger and more stylish than her first, would strike vibrantly the harp-cord of the net" (p. 235). Humbert now realizes how, among other things, his own discordant coaching had failed Lolita,

> not only because she had been so hopelessly and irritatingly irritated by every suggestion of mine—but because the precious symmetry of the court instead of reflecting the harmonies latent in her was utterly jumbled by the clumsiness and lassitude of the resentful child I mistaught. Now things were different, and on that particular day, in the pure air of Champion, Colorado, on that admirable court at the foot of steep stone stairs leading up to Champion Hotel where we had spent the night, I felt I could rest from the nightmare of unknown betrayals within the innocence of her style, of her soul, of her essential grace (p. 235).

Their game is interrupted, however, by two new tennis players (Quilty's friends), Bill Mead and Fay Page ("Maffy on Say"), who is, inevitably, an actress (p. 236). For Humbert the game is in several senses over; Quilty will soon spirit Lolita away. When Humbert is called to the telephone, Quilty himself appears, and forms a new game: "From the . . . terrace I saw, far below, on the tennis court which seemed the size of a school child's ill-wiped slate, golden Lolita playing in a double. She moved like a fair angel among three horrible Boschian cripples" (p. 237).

Early in the novel, Humbert says, "If I close my eyes I see but an immobilized fraction of her, a cinematographic still, a sudden smooth nether loveliness, as with one knee up under her tartan skirt she sits tying her shoe" (p. 46),* and as he describes her tennis, he can only mourn his failure to preserve that Champion scene: "Idiot, triple idiot! I could have filmed her! I would have had her now with me, before my eyes, in the projection room of my pain and despair!" (p. 233). ". . . That I could have had all her strokes, all her enchantments, immortalized in segments of celluloid, makes me moan with frustration. They would have been so much more than the snapshots I burned!" (p. 234). Like Valentinov's filmic re-creation of Luzhin and Turati's extraordinary chess game, Quilty's "movie picture" *Golden Guts* would clearly have been something less splendid, at best a trivialized version of Humbert's magical vision, and at worst—the lurid reality of Quilty's cinematic plans, which ironically underscores the corruptness of at least one scenarist. Instead of Hollywood, Lolita experienced Quilty's Duk Duk Ranch where, she says,

---

*Lolita's pose recalls any of several paintings of nymphets by Balthus. See James Thrall Soby, *Balthus* (New York, 1956), especially pp. 19 and 23.

"his friends were his slaves" and "weird, filthy things" were done. "I mean, he had two girls and two boys, and three or four men, and the idea was for all of us to tangle in the nude while an old woman took movie pictures," she explains. Lolita "refused to take part because she loved him, and he threw her out" (p. 278). Although some readers may miss them, we are spared too close a paraphrase of the groupings and gropings at Nabokov's Duk Duk, where the action, so to speak, is mainly linguistic, as it is throughout the novel.*

The two contrasting movies "double" one another, as do Humbert and Quilty ("That absurd intruder had butted in [to the game] to make up a double, hadn't he, Dolly?" says Humbert, punning unintentionally [p. 238]), but whereas the Humbert-Quilty relationship finally parodies the neatly divisible Good and Evil selves of a Poe or Dostoevsky *Dopplegänger* fiction,[14] the doubling of their films is singularly unambiguous. Moral and aesthetic perspectives cohere, as ideally they should: the scenarist's sexuality, dissociated from love and naked in every way, degrades its objects, while the artist's obsession, transformed by love and humanized by language, redeems its subject, and, one would hope, the readers who had anticipated in *Lolita* "the copulation of cliches" (p. 315). Nabokov is for once didactic, and Humbert's "movie," preserved only in prose, is a sensuous recording of visual and aural delights.

Tennis has replaced copulation in Humbert's pages, tracing the course of *his* transcendence, at least. No wonder Nabokov made public his horrified reaction to William Woodin Rowe's enthusiastic dissection of the sexual "symbolism" in Nabokov's work, Lolita's wondrous tennis in particular: " 'Wickedly folded moth' suggests 'wick' to Mr. Rowe, and 'wick,' as we Freudians know, is the Male Organ. 'I' stands for 'eye,' and 'eye' stands for the Female Organ. Pencil licking is always a reference to you know what. A soccer goal hints at the vulval orifice (which Mr. Rowe evidently sees as square). . . . No less ludicrous is his examination of Lolita's tennis and his claim that the tennis balls represent testicles (those of a giant albino, no doubt)," writes Nabokov, an enraged Humbert firing point blank at an academic Quilty *(New York Review,* October 7, 1971).

Movie-maker Quilty also doubles the desires of those

Duk is an obscene Oriental word for copulation, sometimes transliterated in English as *dak* or *dok.*

Top: A heavy-handed Gothic *Doppelgänger* about to strike Conrad Veidt in the second of three versions of *The Student of Prague* (1926). *Bottom:* That uplifting moment is repeated by Claude Rains fifteen years later in *The Wolf Man,* the Germanic setting moved to "Wales." Lon Chaney, Jr., is the werewolf ("lanky, big-boned, wooly-chested, with thick black eyebrows . . . talons still tingling"), and Evelyn Ankers is his victim (a "purplish spot on her naked neck"?). *(Photos courtesy National Film Archive)*

disappointed "learned readers" (p. 59) who, ignoring Humbert's sorrowful warning ("I have only words to play with!" [p. 34]), had nevertheless hoped for the replaying of a good many "sexy" scenes. Teasingly located at the start of the affair, but never repeated, these explicit scenes formulate the reader-viewer's voyeuristic prurience.* On *Lolita's* last page, his fictive life ebbing, Humbert's voice becomes strangely distant and authorial: "And do not pity C. Q. [=Quilty]. One had to choose between him and H. H., and one wanted H. H. to exist at least a couple of months longer, so as to have him make you [Lolita] live in the minds of later generations" (p. 311). Quilty, then, might have been the putative author, and one wonders how many readers have unconsciously wished that Quilty *had* narrated *Lolita,* and that his movie had formed the body of the narrative.

Reunited at last with a pregnant, far from nymphic Lolita, Humbert realizes that "I loved her more than anything I had ever seen or imagined on earth, or hoped for anywhere else" (p. 279). After interpolating "Little Carmen's" lyrics, Humbert had parenthetically added: "Drew his .32 automatic, I guess, and put a bullet through his moll's eye" (p. 64). When Lolita conclusively refuses to return to Humbert, "I pulled out my automatic—I mean this is the kind of fool thing a reader might suppose I did" (p. 282). Only the literal-minded reader who has in mind Humbert's hints and the denouement of *Carmen,* or, more likely, the reader nurtured on a life time of "Little Carmens"— of pulp fiction, pop songs, and "Movielove" melodramas—would believe, in spite of everything Humbert has said, that he would nonetheless kill *this* Lolita, *his* Lolita. Humbert's biting rhetorical trap has dispatched that reader to Quilty's party, Lolita's Purgatory. "It never even occurred to me to [shoot her]," adds Humbert. " 'Good by-aye!' she chanted, my American sweet immortal dead love," elegizes Humbert, no longer a Horatian poet *manqué.* Experiencing a pain and despair far removed from the "grief-proof sphere of existence" of his Hollywood, he drives away "through the drizzle of the dying day, with the windshield wipers in full action but unable to cope with my tears" (p. 282).

Quilty's is obviously a prophetic hobby, since his "private movies" at the Duk Duk Ranch limn yet another genre, one that

---

*See my article "The Eyehole of Knowledge: Voyeuristic Games in Film and Literature," *Film Comment* (May, 1973), a discussion of Nabokov, Robbe-Grillet, Hitchcock, Rohmer, Chabrol, and others.

became public enough a decade after *Lolita's* American publication. Had Quilty survived, he might easily have become an *auteur* such as the director of the recent X-rated *Homo on the Range* ("All-Male Ranch Movie" read the marquee at Chicago's Bijou [1972]), or *Ada's* "brilliant" Victor Vitry, or Russ Meyer—or, worse yet, one of those directors who pretentiously couple their imaginative combinations of characters in the soft-focus, slow-motion name of art. Asked for his opinion of director Tony Richardson's 1969 film version of *Laughter in the Dark*, Nabokov addressed himself to this subject:

> I was appalled by the commonplace quality of the sexual passages. I would like to say something about that. Clichés and conventions breed remarkably fast. They occur as readily in the primitive jollities of the jungle as in the civilized obligatory scenes of our theater.In former times Greek masks have set many a Greek dentition on edge. In recent films, including *Laughter in the Dark*, the pornograpple has already become a cliché though the device is but half-a-dozen years old. I would have been sorry that Tony Richardson should have followed that trite trend, had it not given me the opportunity to form and formulate the following important notion: theatrical acting, in the course of the last centuries, has led to incredible refinements of stylized pantomime in the presentation of, say, a person eating, or getting deliciously drunk, or looking for his spectacles, or making a proposal of marriage. Not so in regard to the imitation of the sexual act which on the stage has absolutely no tradition behind it. The Swedes and we have had to start from scratch, and what I have witnessed up to now on the screen—the blotchy male shoulder, the false howls of bliss, the four or five mingled feet—all of it is primitive, commonplace, conventional, and therefore disgusting. . . The lack of art and style in those paltry copulations is particularly brought into evidence by their clashing with the marvelously high level of acting in virtually all other imitations of natural gestures on our stage and screen. This is an attractive topic to ponder further and directors should take notice of it.[15]

Nabokov might also have said that the new freedom on the no-longer silver screen is rampant *poshlost'*, or posh lust, as Humbert might say, and in *Ada,* published shortly after the release of Richardson's film, Nabokov mocks both literary adaptations and the screen's nude freedoms. Ada appears in *Don Juan's Last Fling* as the gypsy girl whom the dashing Don rescues, somewhat anticlimactically:

The Don rides past three windmills, whirling black against an ominous sunset, and saves her from the miller who accuses her of stealing a fistful of flour and tears her thin dress. Wheezy but still game, Juan carries her across a brook (her bare toe acrobatically tickling his face) and sets her down, top up, on the turf of an olive grove. Now they stand facing each other. She fingers voluptuously the jewelled pommel of his sword, she rubs her firm girl belly against his embroidered thighs, and all at once the grimace of a premature spasm writhes across the poor Don's expressive face. He angrily disentangles himself and staggers back to his steed (p. 489).

Ubiquitous, versatile Quilty—lecturer, pornographer, and playwright ("I have been called the American Maeterlinck" [p. 303])—clearly anticipates a wide rage of current types, from highbrow aestheticians of trash to starlets on TV talk shows ("I'd only undress if the story called for it and it was, like, dignified, you know?"). Clare Quilty is clearly expendable.

In addition to concluding the novel's main parodic theme,[16] the killing of Quilty (Part Two, Chapter Thirty-Five) also lays to rest the movie motif. Searching for Quilty's "ancestral home [on] Grimm Road" (p. 293) the night before the execution (Chapter Thirty-Four), Humbert drives along "a narrow winding highway," past a "series of short posts, ghostly white." In front of him, "like derelict snowflakes, moths drifted out of the darkness into my probing aura. At the twelfth mile, as foretold, a curiously hooded bridge sheathed me for a moment and, beyond it, a whitewashed rock loomed on the right. . . I turned off the highway up gravelly Grimm Road. For a couple of minutes all was dank, dark, dense forest. Then, Pavor Manor, a wooden house with a turret, arose in a circular clearing. Its windows glowed yellow and red" (p. 294), and Nabokov's description clearly cries out for an illustration by Gustaves Dore or Moreau, or, even better, Charles Addams. At the end of the brief chapter, after "casing" Quilty's manor, Humbert passes a drive-in cinema: "In a selenian glow, truly mystical in its contrast with the moonless and massive night, on a gigantic screen slanting away among dark drowsy fields, a thin phantom raised a gun, both he and his arm reduced to tremulous dishwater by the oblique angle of that receding world,—and the next moment a row of trees shut off the gesticulation" (p. 295). The raised gun foreshadows Quilty's death and looks back twenty-three years to a like moment in *Laughter in the Dark* (p. 20), while the gigantic screen serves as a

"That's a swell little gun you've got there": *Top,* Franklin Pangborn and Bea Lillie as
"the villain" in *Exit Smiling*'s play-within-the-film, a mock melodrama. *Below,* erratic
Pangborn is calmly disarmed. "This was the end of the ingenious play staged for me
by Quilty," says Humbert when Quilty has finally expired.

summary image, a kind of tombstone for Quilty, who dies, as it were, as he has lived, receding into the world he has created, reduced by parody. "I could not help seeing the inside of that festive and ramshackle castle in terms of 'Troubled Teens,' a story in one of her magazines, vague 'orgies,' a sinister adult with penele cigar, drugs, bodyguards," says Humbert (pp. 294-95).

Your Home is You is one of Charlotte Haze's essential volumes, and Pavor [= Latin: "fear" or "panic"] Manor is the mock-Symbolic obverse of her Good Housekeeping Syndrome. House-wrecker Nabokov funs many of the familiar, staple Gothic ingredients first recommended by Walpole's *The Castle of Otranto* (1764). A thunderstorm accompanies Humbert on the way back to Grimm Road, but when he reaches Pavor Manor, "the sun was visible again, burning like a man, and the birds screamed in the drenched and steaming trees," like the horror-film cockatooes in *Mad Love* (a 1935 remake of *The Hands of Orlac,* with Peter Lorre) and *Citizen Kane's* imported "Gothic" jungle (1941). "The elaborate and decrepit house seemed to stand in a kind of daze, reflecting as it were my own state," says Humbert, invoking Poe's crumbling House of Usher (p. 295). Miasmic Pavor Manor's portentous ambience and disarrayed innards burlesque a number of other structures: a "symbolic" medieval setting in Maeterlinck, or one of Quilty's own Maeterlinck—or Lenormand-influenced plays; Hollywood's prefabricated, *poshlyaki* houses of horror, or their source, German Expressionist melodrama as produced at the famous UFA studio. "I detested the heavy-handed German Gothic cinema," says Nabokov, a Berlin resident for fifteen years (1922-1937). "We saw many of those films in the twenties—all trash except for the one about the downfall of a very grand doorman [Jannings in *Der letze Mann (The Last Laugh,* 1924)]—and *The Hands of Orlac* [1925]. That was wonderful, with Veidt and Kortner, whom I met in London after he had bought an option on my *Camera Obscura.* Kortner was a gifted artist and a very homely man—ideal for those films!—whose homeliness disappeared when you were with him, dissolved by the delightfulness of his person. I remember perfectly scenes in *Orlac:* the nocturnal train crash in which the concert artist [Veidt] loses his hands (steam, smoke, infernal confusion), and the 'executed' murderer's unexpected return, his broken neck bolstered by a terrible brace, his face masked, mechanical claws in place of the hands that have been grafted onto Orlac's maimed limbs. That was wonderfully macabre

161

and bizarre. But most of those films were awful, and imitations of them are even worse," says Nabokov, whose forthcoming book of interviews and articles will be titled *Strong Opinions*. The Germanic *Stimmung* ["mood"] of *The Last Laugh, The Hands of Orlac,* and other German films distinguished by their chiaroscuro (if not their plots and performances) is visually evident in many of Nabokov's novels, from *Mary* (1926) through *Lolita;* Humbert frequently employs horror-film effects that would be blatant or ridiculous on the screen: "And less than six inches from me and my burning life, was nebulous Lolita! After a long stirless vigil, my tentacles moved towards her again, and this time the creak of the mattress did not awake her. I managed to bring my ravenous bulk so close to her that I felt the aura of her bare shoulder like a warm breath upon my cheek. And then, she sat up, gasped, muttered with insane rapidity something about boats, tugged at the sheets and lapsed back in her rich, dark, young unconsciousness," reminisces Humbert of his first night with Lolita at The Enchanted Hunters hotel (p. 132), a scene that brings to mind the restless Sleeping Beauties of *Mad Love* and *The Cat and the Canary* (1939), laboratory examples of the ways in which the macabre can quickly grade into absurdity; the best American horror films of the nineteen-forties—*The Seventh Victim* (1943) and *The Curse of the Cat People* (1944)—produced by Russian-born Val Lewton (Nazimova's nephew), allowed audiences to *imagine* their phantasms, the product of poetic suggestion rather than gross make-up and / or Gothic trappings. Pavor Manor broadly mocks the latter genre: Quilty's "steaming trees" recall the unsubtle atmosphere provided by Universal Pictures' busy fog machines in their Sherlock Holmes series of the forties (see *The Scarlet Claw,* 1945) and horrid horror films such as *The Wolf Man* (1941), direct descendants of the Gothic films abhorred by Nabokov *(The Student of Prague* [1926], for example, a pastiche of E. T. A. Hoffmann and Poe's "William Wilson," whose *doppelganger* conventions are parodied in Quilty's person and, earlier, in *Despair).*

Humbert's self-loathing is often visualized in the metamorphic man-into-monster images of the popular cinema—"And a metamorphosis is a thing always exciting to watch," writes Nabokov in *Gogol,* referring to etymological phenomena (p. 43)* "I am lanky, big-boned, wooly-chested Humbert Humbert, with thick

---

*Everything in *Lolita* is constantly in the process of metamorphosis, including the novel and reader; see Note 18/6, *The Annotated Lolita* (pp. 340-41).

black eyebrows and a queer accent, and a cesspoolful of rotting monsters behind his slow boyish smile," says Humbert (p. 46), who also characterizes both himself and Quilty as "apelike"; describes himself rushing along a suburban street like R. L. Stevenson's evil "Mr. Hyde" ("My talons still tingling, I flew on" [p. 208]); and who assumes (wrongly) that a photographer at The Enchanted Hunters has immortalized "the bared teeth of Humbert Humbert sidling between the bridelike lassie and the enchanted cleric" (p. 129). "Nothing could have been more childish than. . . the purplish spot on her naked neck where a fairy tale vampire had feasted," notes Humbert at their honeymoon hotel on the night that he first possesses Lolita (p. 141). Although Nabokov's cosmetic effects are more subdued, "werewolf" Humbert is kin to hirsute Lon Chaney, Jr., in *The Wolf Man*, a Beauty and the Beast saga somewhat less artful than Nabokov's version of that fairy tale,[17] or Jean Cocteau's more faithful re-recreation, *La Belle et la Bete* (1946, with Jean Marais as The Beast). It is fitting that the two enchanted hunters in Nabokov's Grimm tale should finally confront one another in the mock-Gothic Manor, where the novel's principal parodies are united. More specifically, the manner in which Quilty is executed, in both senses of the word, parodies the hack scenarist's stock-in-trade, so loved by Lolita, her friends, and her mother.

"The archetypal American is a killer," asserts D. H. Lawrence in his *Classic Studies in American Literature* (1922), and refugee Humbert tries to play the role as Quilty, among others, might have written it. Hastily outfitted for the scene by George Raft or Humphrey Bogart's haberdasher at Warner Brothers (raincoat, black suit, black shirt, but, alas, no tie [p. 297]), Humbert has carefully readied his .32 caliber automatic. "I had inherited it from the late Harold Haze [Humbert explains earlier], with a 1938 catalog which cheerily said in part: 'Particularly well adapted for use in the home and car as well as on the person'" (p. 218), a blurb worthy of a National Rifle Association newsletter. Naturalist Nabokov abhors hunting, and its equation with a "masculine" ethic. "I read [Hemingway] for the first time in the early forties," says Nabokov, "something about bells, balls and bulls, and loathed it. Later I read his admirable 'The Killers' . . ."[18] Acting like a full-blooded American, Humbert had roamed the woods with John Farlow, "an admirable marksman, [who] with his .38 actually managed to hit a humming bird, though I must say not much of it could be retrieved for proof—only a little iridescent fluff. A burley ex-policeman called Krestovski, who in the twenties had shot and killed two escaped convicts, joined us and bagged a tiny woodpecker—completely out of season, incidentally. Between these two sportsmen I of course was a novice and kept missing everything, though I did wound a squirrel. . ." (p. 218). Humbert has kept Haze's weapon in a box, "loaded and fully cocked with the slide lock in safety position, thus precluding any accidental discharge. We must remember," he adds, "that a pistol is the Freudian symbol of the Ur-father's central forelimb" (p. 218). Nabokov's parody of "phallic symbolism" is aimed at the American mystique about guns. " 'You lie here,' I whispered to my light-weight compact little chum [his gun], and then toasted it with a dram of gin" (p. 218), and Humbert joins the company of those earlier American heroes who anthropomorphized their weapons, from Fenimore Cooper's Natty Bumppo talking to his rifle in *The Pioneers* (1823) to Hemingway's Santiago engaged in a one-sided conversation with his fishing gear in *The Old Man and the Sea* (1952).

Humbert heads for Pavor Manor, Chum—as he now calls his gun—"Aching to be discharged" (p. 294). He has treated him all too lovingly. "Such a thorough oil bath did I give Chum that now I could not get rid of the stuff. I bandaged him up with a rag, like a maimed limb, and used another to wrap up a handful of spare bullets" (p. 295). Following Quilty upstairs and striving for the efficiency of, say, Lee Marvin, killer Humbert "gingerly unwrapped dirty Chum, taking care not to leave any oil stains on the chrome—I think I got the wrong product, it was black and awfully messy. In my usually meticulous way, I transferred naked Chum to a clean recess about me and made for the little boudoir" (p. 297). Humbert had imagined Quilty as wielding that familiar gangster icon, a cigar—a "penele" (p. 295), which is very masculine, inasmuch as the coined adjective means "penis-like" [from *penes,* a plural form]. Quilty, however, soon reveals "the melancholy truth" about himself—impotency (p. 300)—and, says Humbert, "His condition infected me, the weapon felt limp and clumsy in my hand" (p. 299). Pathetic Chum performs poorly at first, clicking helplessly, then sending, "with a ridiculously feeble and juvenile sound," a bullet into "the thick pink rug, and I had the paralyzing impression that it had merely trickled in and might come out again" (p. 299). Humbert had earlier hoped to achieve the perfect crime that had eluded wife-murderer "G. Edward Grammar" (pp. 289-90), an actual crime based on a newspaper story, but an invented name that reverses Edward G. Robinson. The chapter's initial pages similarly toy with a well-established grammar, upending the cliched American conjunction of manhood, sexuality, and guns that is celebrated in our literature and lore, and in countless Westerns and thrillers such as *Gun Crazy* (1949), an early salute to Bonnie and Clyde; *The Gunfighter* (1950), with its "virginal," ingenue killer (Skip Homeier); and *The Fastest Gun Alive* (1949), an epic of failed and compensatory masculinity in which shopkeeper Glenn Ford, the son of a famous marshal, is a fancy marksman but no killer, pretending to be a "fast gun" now in retirement (with six spurious notches on his gun butt). Ford sneaks away from his childless wife to shoot by himself, caresses his firearm in a most tender way, gazes at it diffidently, has it admired by a young boy (an obligatory moment in many Westerns of the period), exhibits it proudly to disbelievers in a saloon, and finally tests it against grizzled old Broderick Crawford, who has become a fast gun because his wife ran away with a gambler (or so Crawford's sidekick explains, an Orthodox Freudian diagnostician in 1885). "No matter how fast you are there's always somebody faster" (the cuckold's perception), intones a blindman at the outset of the film, cast as tragedy's chorus or seer, an all-seeing Tiresias (myth meets *poshlost'* on the frontier). The policeman's wife in *On Dangerous Ground* (1951) languorously straps on his revolver for him, with a kiss, and says how much she'll miss him while he's out on night patrol. Recent films do not bother with innuendo. In *Hit Man* (1972), hoodlums surprise the hero in bed, naked save for an outsized shotgun, which he fires from the loin at an improper angle, the ultimate in "symbolism" until some X-rated trick photography (or phenomenal post-Bondian virility) can produce a literally blazing phallus, prefigured years ago by the roman candles of *Fireworks* (1947), Kenneth Anger's one-reel Fourth of July homosexual revery, funned in turn by the Riveria fireworks which remark Grace Kelly's and Cary Grant's embrace in Hitchcock's *To Catch a Thief* (1955). "That's all I got between me and them, between me and the whole world," says Rico (Edward G. Robinson) of his gun in *Little Caesar* (1930), the archetypal gangster film whose "little" is operative; Robinson, like tough guys Raft, Cagney, and Bogart, is a short man, as good Freudians *and* Jungians should note. (In

Symbols of Transformation [1927] , Jung discusses the "smaller than small and bigger than big" shape-shifting of the libidinal hero.) " 'Say! [Quilty] drawled (now imitating the underworld numbskull of movies), 'that's a swell little gun you've got there. What d'you want for her?' " (p. 299).[19] Chum is a male, as Humbert has said, and envious Quilty's pronoun, prefiguring the "feminine 'ahs!' " of his death struggle (p. 305), is an apt choice, a carefully planted "Freudian slip." The slangy sense of that cliché, lending itself to a jejune pun (picked-up by The Freudian Slips, a female rock group), quite literally describes *Johnny Guitar* (1954), which starred Joan Crawford as a saloon owner named Vienna (appropriate city) in a baroque testing of the Western's mythology, a good-natured send up of *Belle Star* (The Bandit Queen, 1941) and Dietrich's role as the outlaw den mother in *Rancho Notorious* (1952, possibly Fritz Lang's worst American mistake). "I've never seen a woman who was more like a man," one of her bartenders says of Vienna, who, in an extension of the Diettrich-Una Merkel brawl in *Destry Rides Again* (1939), symbolically completes that most enviable "Freudian" transformation by shooting it out with Mercedes McCambridge at the end of the film, in what one hopes is intended as a parody akin to the way in which Quilty will bite the dust.

After Quilty cheerfully tries out his bad French, Humbert asks him whether he wants to be executed sitting or standing. "Ah, let me think. . .It is not an easy question," answers Quilty, (p. 300), as "feminine" and nonplussed as the debonair, Thespian "heavy" (Beatrice Lillie!) in a fine, little-known Hollywood silent comedy, *Exit Smiling* (1926), a good subtitle for Quilty's entire death scene. Fitfully awakened to the peril, Quilty lurches and sends Chum "hurtling under a chest of drawers" (p. 300). They wrestle for the weapon in the style of "the obligatory scene in the Westerns of [the reader's] childhood":

> Our tussle, however, lacked the ox-stunning fisticuffs, the flying furniture. He and I were two large dummies, stuffed with dirty cotton and rags. It was a silent, soft, formless tussle on the part of tow literati, one of whom was utterly disorganized by a drug while the other was handicapped by a heart condition and too much gin. When at last I had possessed myself of my precious weapon, and the scenario writer had been reinstalled in his low chair, both of us were panting as the cowman and the sheepman never do after their battle (p. 301).

After pausing to read aloud his own death sentence in the form of Humbert's poem ("poetical justice," Humbert calls it [p. 301]), Quilty is variously impatient ("This pistol-packing farce is becoming a frightful nuisance" [p. 303] , conciliatory, and remarkably athletic. Although an "underworlder" denouement is more within the reach of handicapped Humbert, his diligent target practice serves him poorly. Shooting bullets rather than blanks, revived Chum only manages to send Quilty's black rocking-chair into a fast, zestful, panic-striken "rocking act," its owner flashing into the music room to play several vigorous chords on the piano, "his nostrils emitting the soundtrack snorts which had been absent from our fight." But Humbert's next bullet propels Quilty "from his chair higher and higher, like old, gray, mad Nijinski, like Old Faithful, like some old nightmare of mine, to a phenomenal altitude, or so it seemed, as he rent the air" with a velocity and comic trajectory that easily outdistance all the hurtling and caterwauling figures in the "obligatory scenes" of Hollywood thrillers (p. 304). With one hand "pressed to his brow" and the other "clutching his armpit as if stung by a hornet, down he came on his heels and, again a normal robed man, scurried out into the hall" (p. 305). More bullets find their mark, yet "bloated" Quilty manages to "trudg[e] from room to room, bleeding majestically," the bravura comedy burlesquing, among many things, the river of rhetoric and gore that runs from the Elizabethans to Mickey Spillane (p. 305). One of the most comical scenes in modern literature, it is as deeply serious as it is funny: Humbert's guilt is not to be exorcised so easily; "false" *Doppelgänger* Quilty, and all that he represents, *is* slow to die. He finally expires "in a purple heap" (p. 307), the color of his prose, as evidenced by his play, *The Enchanted Hunters* (pp. 202-03). "This...was the end of the ingenious play staged for me by Quilty," declares Humbert as he departs the Horror House and walks "with a heavy heart" through "the spotted blaze of the sun" (p. 307), lighting effects by UFA or RKO Pictures, where many German refugee technicians were employed in the forties.

Watching Lolita's stylish game in Champion, Colorado, Humbert had imagined her a "real girl champion," "acting a girl champion in a movie" (p. 234), a remarkable forecast of Quilty's plans for her, as yet unknown to Humbert. Quilty has in turn anticipated *Humbert,* since the stage version of Quilty's *Golden Guts* (p. 278), however trashy it may be, would seem to predate the tennis scene and Humbert's own "movie" of "golden Lolita" (p. 237) and "the clean resounding crack of her golden whip" (p. 233). These coincidences extend far beyond Nabokov's conception of Quilty as Humbert's horrific alter ego and mock-Double. When Quilty first appears in person, on the darkened, pillared porch of The Enchanted Hunters hotel, and is about to engage Humbert in the verbal sparring that prefigures their eventual fight (p. 129), Humbert recalls how he "could not really see him but what gave him away was the rasp of a screwing off, then a discreet gurgle, then the final note of a placid screwing on" (p. 128), as though a doll or puppet were being assembled in the wings, a homunculus was coming to life in the artist-alchemist's workshop (a foreground reality in *King, Queen, Knave,* where the Inventor's auto-mannequins fail to work but the author's moral dummies run all too smoothly). Nabokov's are the sounds of an antic Dr. Frankenstein at work in Pavor Manor's horror-movie attic Laboratory.

Trailing his "fiend's spoor" (p. 249) across the "crazy quilt" landscapes of America (pp. 154 and 309), Humbert notices how the license plates of four of Quilty's rented cars had "formed interrelated combinations (such as 'WS 1564' and 'SH 1616,' and 'Q32888' or 'CU 88322') which, however, were so cunningly contrived as to never reveal a common denominator" (p. 253). The letters and numerals on Quilty's first two plates offer Shakespeare's monograms and dates of birth and death, an ironic emblem, while the letters on the second set of licenses refer to Quilty and his nickname "Cue." Their numerals include "32," a mirrored allusion to the April 23rd birthday Nabokov shares with Shakespeare and Shirley Temple, and add up to a quietly telling fifty-two. Humbert and Lolita spent fifty-two weeks together on the road, there are that many lines in Humbert's poem to her (pp. 257-59), and Quilty is the author of fifty-two successful scenarios. In his Foreword to *Lolita,* John Ray, Jr. Ph.D., states that Lolita, Quilty, and Humbert, our putative and extraordinarily perceptive author, have all died in '52 (p. 6). There are fifty-two cards in a deck, and the author of *King, Queen, Knave* draws several more from his sleeve.

Akin to hundreds of such involuted inlays and patterned elements scattered throughout the novel, the "coincidences" serve to reveal "the common denominator," the manipulative hand of cardsharp, conjurer, puppeteer Nabokov, who somehow manages to stage the tennis scene in "Champion," and who pulls the strings most blatantly in fantastic Pavor Manor, where all of the novel's carefully achieved realism is suspended, and "the two literati" are sent against each other in a fight between "two large dummies, stuffed with dirty cotton and rags" (p. 301), ruled over by Nabokov the artist and judge, who passes sentence on a bad writer, "Movielove's" champion. The killing of Quilty thus serves poetical justice, if no other, and murder, along with parody, becomes an act of criticism, more suited to art than life.

NOTES

1. "The Strong Opinions of Vladimir Nabokov—as imparted to Nicholas Garnham," *The Listener* (October 10, 1968), 463.

2. See the first part of my article, "Nabokov's Dark Cinema: A Diptych," *TriQuarterly*, No. 27 (Spring 1973).

3. Vladimir Nabokov, *Lolita* (New York, 1958), p. 13. Parenthetical textual references are to this edition and my own edition, *The Annotated Lolita* (New York, 1970), which share the same pagination. The textual references to other Nabokov books are to the hardcover American first editions.

4. Richard Brautigan, *Trout Fishing in America* (San Francisco, 1967), 88-91.

5. Nathanael West, *Miss Lonelyhearts & The Day of the Locust* (New York, 1962), p. 138. Subsequent page references to this edition, a current New Directions paperback volume, will be in the text.

6. "Cupid is the night clerk / 'Neath the stars above / He just loves his night work / And we just love to love," and so forth.

7. In retrospect, however, *Freaks* would seem to have been shocking not so much for its subject matter as for the way it attacked the corrupt (and abnormal) "big people's" manipulation and humiliation of the deformed members of the circus sideshow, particularly its women. "Go ahead and laugh! Women are funny, ain't they?" says a hermaphrodite named Venus to a clown who is grinning at her.

8. Contemporary comic strips, after all, also featured children: *Wash Tubbs; Dickie Dare; Tim Tyler's Luck; Little Orphan Annie;* Junior in *Dick Tracy;* and Terry, only ten when *Terry and the Pirates* began. These comics, however, variants of earlier child strips, were basically adventure stories, and, except for the right-wing proselytizing of Annie's Daddy Warbucks, they do not belie their genre. And in the late thirties, when an adolescent Terry has a series of "crushes"—on a very experienced older woman, Burma, or his contemporary, April Kane—they are rendered most innocently, as opposed to the adult sexuality of his sidekick Pat Ryan and the Dragon Lady. Comic books, a development of the late thirties, are another matter entirely. Unlike the newspaper strips and the movies in question, they were created exclusively for children.

9. Albert Guerard's memoir/essay appears in *TriQuarterly*, No. 20 (Winter 1971), 255-83.

10. Lolita is "Dolores on the dotted line" (p. 11), but an evolving diminutive to others: Dolly, Lola, Lolita, Lo. By describing her on the novel's first page as "Lola in slacks" (p. 11), Humbert would seem to be aptly connecting mother and daughter through an allusion to Marlene's "scandalous" wearing of slacks and her famous role as Lola Lola (a double name, too), the young cabaret entertainer who ruinously enchants an aging professor in Sternberg's classic German film, *The Blue Angel* (1930). But Nabokov says that this is "probably a happy coincidence. I doubt I had the association in

mind," especially since he has never seen that film. "The first-run cinema palaces in Berlin were quite expensive, you know," he says, recalling that period of emigre life. "In Europe we usually went to the neighborhood cinema," though they did see Dietrich in *Shanghai Express.* Yet Nabokov *has* seen still photos of *The Blue Angel;* so...this very minor matter is interesting for what it suggests about a major matter, conscious intention in art.

11. Marilyn Monroe's pre-eminence is post-Lolita, since Humbert dies in 1952. But even Marilyn, alas, often appears ludicrous today, especially in some of her earlier melodramas, or in those comedies which quickly degenerate into caricature *(The Seven Year Itch* [1955] as opposed to *Some Like it Hot* [1959]).

12. The most readily available illustration of the painting is in William S. Rubin, *Dada and Surrealist Art* (New York, n.d.), 65.

13. Johan Huizinga, *Homo Ludens: a Study of the Play Element in Culture* (Boston, 1955), 10.

14. See my article, *"Lolita:* The Springboard of Parody," *Wisconsin Studies in Contemporary Literature,* VIII (Spring 1967), reprinted in L. S. Dembo, ed., *Nabokov: The Man and his Work* (Madison, 1967), or my Introduction to *The Annotated Lolita,* pp. lxiii-lxviii.

15. "Conversations With Nabokov," *op. cit.,* 212.

16. See *"Lolita:* The Springboard of Parody," *op. cit.,* for a more succinct discussion, the Introduction to *The Annotated Lolita.*

17. For more on the "fairy tale" in Nabokov, see Note 33/3 in *The Annotated Lolita* (pp. 346-47).

18. Alfred Appel, Jr., "An Interview with Vladimir Nabokov," in *Wisconsin Studies, op. cit.,* 142.

19. Some of Nabokov's fun recalls films which he has never seen: *Baby Face Harrington* (1935), Raoul Walsh's wonderful satire on the gangster genre, and the black-garbed hoodlums' dance number in Vincente Minnelli's *The Band Wagon* (1953). The entire chapter, in tone and conception, shares many qualities with the John Huston-Truman Capote collaboration, *Beat the Devil* (1954), the shaggy-dog thriller that casts Bogart, Peter Lorre, Jennifer Jones, Gina Lollobrigida, *et al,* in comic inversions of their standard roles. Lorre as a German named O'Hara is particularly delightful, an Ur-Quilty. As an undergraduate at Cornell, I sat behind Nabokov at a downtown showing of the film in the spring of 1954 (an Ur-Kinbote?), and vividly remember his loud laughter, especially at the moment when Lorre pauses before a character who is having his portrait painted and says, in his inimitable nasal whine, "That doesn't look like him! It has only one ear!" The film did not influence Nabokov, however; *Lolita* had just been completed, and the killing of Quilty had been written several years before, out-of-sequence, as Nabokov often works. It might be claimed, however, that Lorre's performance, here and elsewhere, influenced Peter Sellers' Quilty in the film version of *Lolita.*

Photo credits:

> *MOMA = The Museum of Modern Art/Film Stills Archive*
> *NFA = National Film Archive*

MOMA for pages 342, 348, 356, 361, 378 (bottom).
NFA for pages 351, 353, 358, 368, 374.
Films, Inc. courtesy Doug Lemza for page 378 (top).

This article, which first appeared in *Russian Literature Triquarterly,* appears in different form in Mr. Appel's book, *Nabokov's Dark Cinema* (1974). [Editor's note.]

William W. Rowe

THE HONESTY OF NABOKOVIAN DECEPTION

As a creative artist, Vladimir Nabokov frequently leads the reader to subtly unjustified conclusions. This effect derives, to a considerable degree, from the disarming honesty of Mr. Nabokov's highly deceptive writing. The present essay seeks to specify and illustrate three techniques which promote what may be termed Nabokovian honest deception.

In *Ada,* Lucette is tied to a tree in a game devised by Ada and Van to enable them to make love unobserved. As they return, we read: "Writhing Lucette had somehow torn off one of the red knobbed grips of the rope and seemed to have almost disentangled herself when dragon and knight, prancing, returned."[1] Elsewhere I have suggested (on the basis of later clues) that Lucette was very probably tying herself back up after viewing the lovers in full action.[2] The words "seemed to have almost disentangled herself" (rather than "had almost...") may thus be seen to promote an almost fastidiously honest deception. Few authors, one feels, are so scrupulous about deceiving, yet this instance of what may be termed "easily unnoticed precision" is quite typical of Nabokov's writing.

In *Speak, Memory* Mr. Nabokov describes how, as a boy, he was shown a trick with matches by General Kuropatkin. They are interrupted, and as the General rises from the sofa, loose matches jump into the air. Fifteen years later Nabokov's father, fleeing from the Bolsheviks, was accosted "by an old man who looked like a gray-bearded peasant in his sheepskin coat. He asked my father for a light. The next moment each recognized the other. I hope old Kuropatkin, in his rustic disguise, managed to evade Soviet imprisonment..."[3] The characteristic phrase is "an old man who looked like." Once again, it seems, few writers would abstain from less scrupulous deception—from writing, simply: "by a gray-bearded peasant..." Two factors may be noted: the strict integrity that regulates Nabokovian deception, and the vivid detail (gray beard, sheepskin coat) that promotes the reader's false impression. It is almost as if the author uses his reader's own perceptiveness against him.

In the poem "Pale Fire," John Shade makes much ado (more than 100 lines) about his mystical vision of a white fountain and his quest to track it down in the experience of a Mrs. Z. The quest finally reveals, however, that a misprint had turned Mrs. Z's experience of "mountain" into "fountain." Introducing the episode, Nabokov has Shade pen: "I came across what seemed a twin display" (line 746). And he does so even though Shade could justly have claimed he had found the printed account of a duplicate experience. Here then, Mr. Nabokov seems especially careful to provide the reader with the truth ("what seemed") even while misleading him. As in the above examples, the effect seems aptly suggested by Mr. Nabokov's characterization, in *Speak, Memory,* of his own Russian writing: "clear, but weirdly misleading sentences" (p. 288). Or, one is tempted to suggest the modification: "deceptive, but weirdly honest."

In *King, Queen, Knave* Franz's eerie landlord Pharsin promises to return a couch to Franz's room as soon as his, Pharsin's, wife returns.[4] Later, Pharsin announces that his wife has returned. He opens his door, and: "...over the back of the chair Franz glimpsed a gray head with something white pinned to its crown" (p. 120). Leaving, Franz calls back through the door: "How about that couch?" In answer, "a hoarse, strained, old-womanish voice" replies: "The couch is already in your room. I gave you my own couch." Only much later (p. 227-8) does the reader definitely learn that Pharsin's "wife" was really a dummy rigged up to fool Franz. But though the demented Pharsin may lie about this wife, Nabokov the narrator does not: the voice that Franz hears is "old womanish," not "an old woman's." As usual, few authors would deceive us so scrupulously.

Early in *Despair,* Hermann returns to his hotel room: "...I found there, amid mercurial shadows and framed in frizzly bronze, Felix awaiting me. Palefaced and solemn he drew near. He was now well shaven..."[5] Since this is not "Felix" (whom Hermann believes to be his twin), the reader may feel unfairly deceived when he discovers that Hermann is consulting a mirror. Yet the mirror is clearly suggested, prior to the word "Felix," by the phrase "framed in frizzly bronze." "Mercurial" also serves as an easily unnoticed hint at the truth.

In a second type of Nabokovian honest deception, the reader is given information which proves crucial only much later. Deep in *Lolita,* for example, we are invited to believe that Humbert will kill his nymphet (when he learns that she will never again be his): "Then I pulled out my automatic—I mean, this is the kind of

172

a fool thing a reader might suppose I did."[6] But the Foreword had informed us that Mrs. Schiller would die in childbirth (p. 6), even though Lolita only becomes Mrs. Schiller not long before Humbert seems about to kill her.

Similarly, the reader of *Ada* is momentarily invited to believe that Van Veen remains almost superhumanly athletic in his old age: "At ninety, he still danced on his hands—in a recurrent dream" (p. 571). Long before, however, Van had apparently suffered "an irretrievable loss of the rare art" (p. 323).

We meet the hero of *Pnin* on a train, and near the bottom of the second page, our narrator remarks: "Now a secret must be imparted. Professor Pnin was on the wrong train." The opening sentence of the novel, however, was: "The elderly passenger sitting on the north-window side of that inexorably moving railway coach, next to an empty seat and facing two empty ones, was none other than Professor Timofey Pnin." In retrospect, the word "inexorably" seems to hint at the ominous conspiracy far more clearly. But as we first encounter it, this word tends only to suggest the motion of a railway coach steadily jogging forward into the distance.

After numerous trials and tribulations, Pnin arrives at the Cremona Women's Club. "Some people," remarks the narrator, "—and I am one of them—hate happy ends. We feel cheated. Harm is the norm. Doom should not jam."[7] As he goes on to relate, however, Pnin "not only arrived safely but was in time for dinner" (though he might have discovered "that his lecture was not this Friday but the next"). Yet as we learn only from the last two words of the book, poor Pnin had presumably arrived in time, but bringing the wrong lecture. Thus, as the careful reader might well have suspected, "doom" did not jam after all.

In Part Two of *Lolita,* a single sentence combines the two types of honest deception noted thus far. Humbert is accosted by a janitor, who complains that a man was sick on the front steps while bringing Rita home: "In the process of listening to him and tipping him, and then listening to a revised and politer version of the incident, I had the impression that one of the two letters which that blessed mail brought was from Rita's mother, a crazy little woman, whom we had once visited on Cape Cod and who kept writing me to my various addresses, saying how wonderfully well matched her daughter and I were, and how wonderful it would be if we married; the other letter which I opened and scanned

173

rapidly in the elevator was from John Farlow" (p. 267). Nearly two full pages later, after various digressions and a discussion of John Farlow's letter, tthe reader may well be surprised to learn that the first letter was from Lolita. Distracted by Humbert's (appropriately bothersome) account of the janitor's complaining and by his (appropriately confusing) description of a typical letter from Rita's "crazy" mother, one can easily fail to notice the phrase: "I had the impression." But note also the words "blessed mail," which only two pages later may be seen to have anticipated the letter from Lolita.

Yet another combination of "easily unnoticed precision" and "premature key information" may be seen in the highly complex "dissociation" episode in *Despair*. Most readers will believe that Hermann projects himself as a spectator of his own love-making, imagining himself ever further away from the bed, until: "Alas, one April night, with the harps of rain aphrodisiacally burbling in the orchestra, as I was sitting at my maximum distance of fifteen rows of seats and looking forward to an especially good show—which, indeed, had already started, with my acting self in colossal form and most inventive—from the distant bed, where I thought I was, came Lydia's yawn and voice stupidly saying that if I were not yet coming to bed, I might bring her the red book she had left in the parlor" (p. 38). This request reveals to Hermann (and to most readers) the fact that his spectator self is real, and his performing self, imaginary. Easily unnoticed, the words "where I thought I was" reveal this slightly earlier. But note also that what seems in context to be imagined proves, ironically, quite true: "as *I was sitting...* an especially good *show...* my acting self in colossal form and *most inventive... distant* bed." For, once Mr. Nabokov has misled the reader into believing that Hermann is on his bed, numerous hints at the truth actually serve to sustain the vivid deception.[8]

As Carl Proffer has observed, Hermann's fatal stick mistake when he murders Felix is foreshadowed by Lydia's vague notion (p. 33) that the word "mystic" somehow connects "mistake" and "stick."[9] Somewhat similarly, the words "conquering hero" above Lolita's picture of Quilty (p. 71) aptly predict his victory, as Alfred Appel, Jr. has noted.[10] Early in *Laughter in The Dark*, Albinus watches a movie which prefigures his automobile accident and his attempt to kill Margot, as Dabney Stuart has shown.[11] Here, Mr. Nabokov has added a rather sinister touch of prophetic irony. As Albinus watches the movie scene predicting his attempt to murder Margot, we are told that such "happenings" did not interest him "since he had not yet seen their beginning" (p. 12). The words "not yet seen" are of course true in two frames of reference, but when Albinus finally experiences this scene, he is entirely blind.[12] Another hidden prediction is Albinus' statement, "Catch me calling on him again!" (p. 120). As I have noted elsewhere, these words ironically anticipate Albinus' desperate return to "call on" Udo Conrad, from whom he painfully learns that Margot and Rex are lovers.[13]

Mr. Nabokov takes particular pleasure in offering the reader premature key information which makes explicit reference to the future, such as "Catch me calling on him again!"[14] Presenting Pnin to the Cremona Women's Club (p. 26-7), Judith Clyde unwittingly sustains a protracted prediction that he has brought "the wrong lecture" (p. 191). To appreciate the full ironic humor, one must keep in mind that since Pnin "was utterly helpless without the prepared text" (p. 15), there was presumably no lecture whatsoever. "He hardly needs any introduction... We have a long evening before us... and I am sure you would all like to have time to ask him questions afterwards... Therefore I will not take up your precious time any longer and will only add... I am sure you will all be delighted to know that there is a grand surprise in store for all of us. Our next lecturer is the distinguished poet and prose writer, Miss Linda Lacefield." Poor Pnin, as a non-lecturer, does indeed "hardly need any introduction." And the three references to time become, in retrospect only, quite obviously ironic. Note also that Judith Clyde is "sure" that everyone will want "to ask him questions afterwards." Even the words "our next lecturer" are more fitting than Judith realizes, as is her coy reference to the "surprise in store for all of us."

Even in italics, Nabokovian predictions can be effectively disguised in a different context. When questioned about service and cleaning in *King, Queen, Knave,* Pharsin had answered: "I do everything... I *make* everything. I alone" (p. 54). Only much later, of course, can Pharsin's words be seen to apply to his artificial wife as well. In *Ada,* a single letter effects the disguise. About to "put a wet finger on the hole in her swimsuit," Pedro tells Ada: "Your leetle aperture must be raccommodated" (p. 200). Considerably later (p. 293), Van will learn that Phillip Rack has been one of Ada's lovers. As Carl Proffer has noted, the name "Rack"

175

suggests a *Kama Sutra* position,[15] so the prophetic play of meaning in *"rac*commodated" is rich indeed.

In a third type of Nabokovian honest deception, the solution to a mystery is hidden within its presentation. For instance, Kinbote's note to line 962 of the poem "Pale Fire" suggests that the title is taken from Shakespeare. "My readers," he adds, "must make their own search. All I have with me is a tiny vest pocket edition of *Timon of Athens*—in Zemblan! It certainly contains nothing that could be regarded as an equivalent of 'pale fire' (if it had, my luck would have been a statistical monster)."[16] While these words do not say so, they give one the erroneous impression that the title does not come from *Timon.* And the ridicule of loose translations, "monstrously" distorting the originals, helps to sustain the deception. Mr. Nabokov thus offers the reader a crucial clue while apparently withholding it.

In Chapter Three of *Pnin,* the hero fails to recognize a movie actor who remains nameless: "...that cane, that bowler, that white face, those black, arched eyebrows, those twitchy nostrils meant nothing to him. Whether the incomparable comedian danced in the sun with chapleted nymphs near a waiting cactus, or was a prehistoric man... humorless Pnin remained indifferent" (p. 80). The key word is "chapleted," which signals Charlie Chaplin, yet many readers will fail to notice this.

An extremely subtle such clue may be seen as Lolita reveals to Humbert the identity of her mysterious lover: "And softly, confidentially, arching her thin eyebrows and puckering her parched lips, she emitted, a little mockingly, somewhat fastidiously, not untenderly, in a kind of muted whistle, the name that the astute reader has guessed long ago" (p. 273-4). The average reader, who has probably not guessed, will no doubt feel cheated as Humbert continues: "I, too, had known it, without knowing it, all along. There was no shock, no surprise. Quietly the fusion took place, and everything fell into order..." But note that just as Humbert ponders his long awaited information, we read: "Quietly the fusion took place..." By slightly altering the spelling, the reader may also effect a "fusion"—Quilty. The word is even capitalized, yet few readers will detect its hidden information. For Humbert has convincingly implied ("the astute reader has guessed long ago") that the identity of Lolita's lover is being completely withheld.

Timofey Pnin's wife has numerous lovers, but she finally

deserts him for Dr. Eric Wind. Early in the novel, Pnin recalls his childhood attempts to discover the key of recurrence in a wallpaper pattern of rhododendron and oak. At this point, he is seated on a bench in a park containing rhododendron and oak: "During one melting moment, he had the sensation of holding at last the key he had sought; but, coming from very far, a rustling wind, its soft volume increasing as it ruffled the rhododendrons—now blossomless, blind—confused whatever rational pattern Timofey Pnin's surroundings had once had" (p. 24). Only later does the reader learn that Dr. Eric Wind, "coming from very far" (p. 46), has "confused whatever rational pattern Pnin's surroundings had once had," for despite his wife's numerous affairs, Pnin remains unenlightened until he is told of Dr. Wind. Note that in the park description the word "but" implies, yet does not state, that the key will be withheld from the reader as well as from Pnin. The effect thus closely resembles Humbert's seeming refusal to reveal Quilty's name, as well as Kinbote's mention of his apparently useless translation of *Timon of Athens.*

In *Speak, Memory* Mr. Nabokov recalls looking at the evening sky: "...the eye found a vista that only a fool could mistake for the spare parts of this or any other sunset... There it lay in wait... an accumulation of brilliant convolutions, anachronistic in their creaminess and extremely remote... my marvelous tomorrow ready to be delivered to me" (p. 213). So ends Chapter Ten. Chapter Twelve opens with his meeting "Tamara," the girl with whom he has an affair, thus decoding, after all, the cryptographic sky through its pun, "marvelous tomorrow." This example, like the next one, can be considered a combination of types two and three ("tomorrow" comes early, yet it is hidden in the sky that "only a fool" could see as a mere sunset).

As revealed in the author's Foreword to *Nabokov's Quartet,* the narrator of "The Vane Sisters" is "supposed to be unaware that his last paragraph has been used acrostically by two dead girls to assert their mysterious participation in the story."[17] Taking in order the first letter of each word in the last paragraph, one can form this sentence: "Icicles by Cynthia; meter from me—Sybil" (p. 90). (As the story opened, the narrator had stopped to watch the dripping of some "brilliant icicles." He noticed "a rhythm, an alternation in the dropping... as teasing as a coin trick.")

Actually, the narrator himself mentions earlier a work "in which, unknown to its author, the first letters of the words in its

177

last paragraph formed... a message from his dead mother" (p. 85).[18] Moreover, the last paragraph of "The Vane Sisters" describes a dream previously said to be "somehow full of Cynthia." The narrator even tells us that he tried to "re-read" this "dream—backward, diagonally, up, down—trying hard to unravel something Cynthia-like in it, something strange and suggestive that must be there." In addition, the dream description refers to "her inept acrostics." Given the extensive, even emphatic ("must be there") honesty of this deception (there is even more ado about acrostics, p. 88), Mr. Nabokov's explanation in the Foreword seems *almost* unnecessary.

In what could be considered a fourth type of honest deception, Mr. Nabokov employs a strategically inadequate specification to inveigle the reader into jumping to erroneous conclusions. In *Lolita,* for instance, Humbert examines Charlotte and her house and concludes: "But there was no question of my settling there" (p. 39). One glimpse of Lolita, however, and Humbert's ambiguous words prove true in a sense exactly opposite to their apparent meaning in context.

En route to the Cremona Women's Club, Pnin struggles at length to avoid losing his precious lecture. At one point, he suddenly clutches "...his right side. *It* was there, *slava Bogu* (thank God)!" (p. 19). Presumably, the reader concludes that Pnin's lecture is now safely inside his coat pocket. Pnin soon grows suspicious, however, and yanks "it" out: "It was Betty's paper." Here, the word "it" promotes a tempting, but honest deception. Similarly, the reader tends to presume that the "three papers" Pnin stuffs into his coat to thwart mischance (p. 26) are the just-mentioned Betty's paper, the correct lecture, and another one. This is not stated, however, and he has already been seen rearranging "various papers" in his suitcase (p. 16).

In *The Real Life of Sebastian Knight,* the narrator eagerly seeks a Madame von Graun, who pretends to be her own friend, Madame Lecerf. "Madame Lecerf" appears to the narrator four times. In the first two, we read: "She turned out to be..." and "...the lady I had seen on the previous day sidled in..."[19] The last two being with mention of "Madame Lecerf's voice"; the woman is then referred to as "she" (p. 165, 171). Thus, each appearance is fastidiously honest, even though the woman is sometimes termed "Madame Lecerf" in the ensuing conversations. Such honest deceptions could perhaps be labeled "misleadingly inadequate specification." However, they may also be seen as a special variety of "easily unnoticed precision," because it is still the precision of formulation which tends to slip by unnoticed.[20]

Nabokovian honest deception, one may conclude, subsumes a highly unusual presentation of truth. During an interview with Mr. Nabokov in Montreux, our conversation turned to the Soviet film version of *Hamlet*. Mr. Nabokov made a sour face. "All I can remember," he said, "is the terrible Moscow accent." He illustrated by nastily protracting the words "Dya-dya, dya-dya!" When asked his opinion of the Soviet Ophelia, however, Mr. Nabokov was unable to give it because, he finally admitted, he had seen only the first few minutes of the film on Swiss television. His words "All I can remember" thus proved far more true than they had seemed in giving the false impression that he had seen the entire film. Perhaps the most impressive aspect of this resourceful deception was the lack of any hesitation—the naturalness with which Mr. Nabokov's words were uttered.

Clarence Brown has suggested that Mr. Nabokov is, "like Onegin's uncle, a man of 'most honest principles.' "[21] He proceeds to assert that "Nabokov has a very Tolstoyan passion for the truth." In this sense, Mr. Nabokov's relentless use of truth in deception may be seen as less contrived—as far more natural—than one might suppose.

The three types of Nabokovian honest deception discussed above ("easily unnoticed precision," "premature key information," and "solution to a mystery hidden within its presentation") are often enriched by strategically placed, and vividly diverting, details. In what may be considered a special variety of "easily unnoticed precision," a precisely worded inadequate specification induces the reader to make an erroneous conclusion. Mr. Nabokov especially favors a presentation of premature key information which includes a specific reference to the future. In such cases, the ironic prediction may be effectively disguised in a different context.

In his "deceptive, but weirdly honest" writing, Mr. Nabokov takes remarkable pains to give only true information, even while deliberately misleading the reader. If deceived, however, the victims must often blame themselves at least partially: Mr. Nabokov has used their own perceptions against them. In this sense, as in a chess problem[22] calculated to mislead the more sophisticated solver, the reader of Nabokovian honest deceptions becomes an unwitting accomplice. Yet the author's strict integrity is not compromised: his "very Tolstoyan passion for the truth," in Clarence Brown's phrase, becomes a natural, albeit paradoxical, deceptive force. For in Nabokovian writing, the most pleasing deceptions are those that function the most naturally. They are also the most deadly.

NOTES

1. Vladimir Nabokov, *Ada* (New York, 1969), p. 143. Subsequent references will be to this edition.

2. See my *Nabokov's Deceptive World* (New York, 1971), p. 156.

3. Vladimir Nabokov, *Speak, Memory* (New York, 1966), p. 27. Subsequent references will be to this edition.

4. Vladimir Nabokov, *King, Queen, Knave* (New York, 1968), p. 99. Subsequent references will be to this edition.

5. Vladimir Nabokov, *Despair* (New York, 1966), p. 24. Subsequent references will be to this edition.

6. Vladimir Nabokov, *Lolita* (New York, 1955), p. 282. Subsequent references will be to this edition.

7. Vladimir Nabokov, *Pnin* (New York, 1965), p. 25. Subsequent references will be to this edition.

8. Several key suggestions appear even earlier. Hermann refers, for example, to "the bed upon which Lydia had been properly placed and distributed," to his "magical point of vantage," and to "the laboratorial light of a strong bed-lamp" p. 37). Even in his opening words, Hermann terms what is to follow "a certain aberration" (p. 37), and the verb forms he then employs (in retrospect only) may be seen very subtly to separate fiction from fact: "I would be in bed... I would become aware... I was standing... I would bundle Lydia to bed... I sat... I watched" (p. 37). In each case, the "would" verb form slyly describes the "aberration," and the more specific verb form, what is actually happening.

9. Carl R. Proffer, "From *Otchaianie* to *Despair*," *Slavic Review*, (June, 1968), p. 259.

10. Alfred Appel, Jr., ed., *The Annotated Lolita* (New York, 1970), p. 365.

11. Dabney Stuart, "*Laughter in The Dark:* Dimensions of Parody," *TriQuarterly*, No. 17, p. 77. Subsequent references are to Vladimir Nabokov, *Laughter in The Dark* (New York, 1961).

12. Yet another sinister allusion to Albinus' future blindness may even be concealed in Rex's attempt to persuade Margot to go to bed with him: "There's a fine view from my window when the blind is down" (p. 84). Much later, of course, when blind Albinus sleeps, Margot and Rex relentlessly compose the unusual "view" evoked by Rex.

13. *Nabokov's Deceptive World*, p. 84.

14. When I mentioned this example to Mr. Nabokov in Montreux, he seemed very fond of it.

15. Carl R. Proffer, "*Ada* as Wonderland," *Russian Literature Triquarterly*, No. 3, p. 412.

16. Vladimir Nabokov, *Pale Fire* (New York, 1966), p. 201.

17. Vladimir Nabokov, *Nabokov's Quartet* (New York, 1966), p. 10. Subsequent references will be to this edition.

18. As noted in *Nabokov's Deceptive World,* one clue that Lolita's "eye-I" has cryptographic sexual connotation is Humbert's remark: "I once read a French detective tale where the clues were actually in italics..."—which occurs just three pages after a potentially cryptographic, and italicized, Lolita's "I." (p. 189).

19. Vladimir Nabokov, *The Real Life of Sebastian Knight* (Norfolk, Conn., 1959), pp. 150, 154. Subsequent references will be to this edition.

20. An exceedingly subtle instance of "easily unnoticed precision" may be seen in the fact that Humbert Humbert rather redundantly employs the words "he said" two times in a single sentence while relating the doctor's assurances anent his supposedly potent purple pills (p. 96). Later, after Humbert's divertingly vivid vision of Lolita as a numb, unconscious victim "spread-eagled on the bed" (p. 127), we learn that the pills have failed to incapacitate her (p. 130). And of course the "skeptical shrug" (p. 97) which Humbert displays to fool the doctor while accepting the pills becomes quite ironically appropriate.

21. Clarence Brown, "Nabokov's Pushkin and Nabokov's Nabokov," *Nabokov: The Man and His Work,* L. S. Dembo, ed. (Madison, Wisc., 1967), p. 200.

22. After I mentioned to Mr. Nabokov the "Catch me calling on him again!" example treated above, he asked me if I played chess and went on to discuss the nature of chess problem composition.

William W. Rowe

PNIN'S UNCANNY LOOKING GLASS

Vladimir Nabokov's ingeniously hidden predictions[1] have lurked in some rather unlikely places. In *Despair*, it is an apparently ridiculous definition of a word: Lydia's vague notion that "mystic" somehow connects "mistake" and "stick" prefigures Hermann's fatal "stick mistake" when he murders Felix (as Carl Proffer has observed).[2] In *Laughter in the Dark*, it is two movie scenes watched by Albinus. (These subtly preview two crucial episodes much later, as Dabney Stuart has shown).[3] In *Lolita*, it is a book in Humbert's prison library entitled *Who's Who in the Limelight*. (The quotation he offers us from it foreshadows much of the ensuing novel, as Alfred Appel, Jr. has demonstrated).[4]

The walls and furnishings of Nabokovian bedrooms seem to be the area richest in such hidden prophecies. For instance, two pictures posted on Lolita's bedroom wall (one labeled "H. H."; the other, of Quilty) aptly foreshadow her two most important affairs.[5] In *The Gift*, the wallpaper of Fyodor's newly rented room ("pale yellow, with bluish tulips") soon reappears with his landlady, who is wearing a "pale yellow dress with bluish tulips."[6] Franz's newly rented room *(King, Queen, Knave)* displays above the bed a picture of "a bare-bosomed slave girl on sale," being "leered at" by "hesitant lechers."[7] Not only does this suggest the lustful sessions soon enjoyed there by Martha and initially hesitant Franz; the picture almost seems to participate in the action: "For the last time in the shabby room... The lewd bidders were appraising the big-nippled bronze-bangled slave girl for the last time" (225).

Focusing more closely, we may note that Nabokovian childhood bedrooms seem especially rich in hidden predictions. As Mr. Nabokov explains in his Foreword to *Glory:* "The perilous path that Martin finally follows into forbidden Zoorland... only continues to its illogical end the fairy-tale trail winding through the painted woods of a nursery-wall picture."[8] In *Speak, Memory* Mr. Nabokov describes the wall of his own childhood bedroom: "...a framed aquarelle showed a dusky path winding through one of those eerily dense European beechwoods..."[9] He goes on, quite revealingly, to connect this same picture with the events of his later life. "In an English fairy tale my mother had once read to me, a small boy stepped out of his bed into a picture and rode his hobbyhorse along a painted path between silent trees. While I knelt on my pillow . . . rapidly going through my prayer, I imagined the motion of climbing into the picture above my bed and plunging into that enchanted beechwood—which I did visit in due time." This characteristic passage[10] seems to explain Mr. Nabokov's interest in the fairy-tale-like prophetic potential of childhood bedrooms, as noted in *Glory,* above. It may also help to explain why he chose to translate *Alice in Wonderland* into Russian. The present paper views *Pnin* as an elusive synthesis of "Cinderella" and Lewis Carroll's *Alice*—seen through the Nabokovian looking glass of Timofey Pnin's childhood bedroom. It also seeks to pinpoint a few hidden interconnections between *Pnin* and other Nabokov works, including the preview of Timofey Pnin's migration to *Pale Fire.*

In Chapter One we follow fifty-two-year-old Pnin, precariously en route to the Cremona Women's Club. After various troubles, he has a strange heart seizure and sits down on a park bench. "Familiar shapes," we read, "became the breeding places of evil delusions."[11] Pnin recalls his childhood bedroom, when he was eleven and quite ill with a similar heart seizure. He remembers a four-section screen of polished wood that pictured "an old man hunched up on a bench, and a squirrel holding a reddish object in its front paws." As Pnin's recollection ends, we are told that a gray squirrel was "sampling a peach stone" in front of his park bench (25). Our narrator points up the parallel between Pnin's past and present by referring to "the twofold nature of his surroundings" (24). Yet the childhood bedroom also seems uncannily prophetic. For when little Pnin had attempted to discover what system of recurrence governed his wallpaper pattern: "he forthwith lost himself in a meaningless tangle of rhododendron and oak" (23). The older Pnin is now quite literally "lost" in the "rhododendrons" and "oak" (19, 20) of his park. "Probing one's childhood," Mr. Nabokov suggests in *Speak, Memory,* "is the next best to probing one's eternity" (20-21).

Eleven-year-old Pnin contemplates his wallpaper: "It stood to reason that if the evil designer—the destroyer of minds, the friend of fever—had concealed the key of the pattern with such monstrous care, that key must be as precious as life itself..." The pattern comprises "three different clusters of purple flowers and seven different oak leaves" (23). It is, in a very real sense, "as precious as life itself," because the theme of "threes" and "sevens" has luminous extension throughout the novel. In fact, the "system of recurrence" of fatidic threes and sevens is almost diabolically complex.

Pnin was born on February 3 in St. Petersburg. (67) He is very fond of a fatidical Pushkin poem dated "3:03 p.m. St. Petersburg" (67). He has three key birthdays: the heart-seizure one (21); the one he fails to recognize (67); and the one on which the novel ends (186). These last two are connected by Charles Nicol, who incisively suggests (referring to Pnin's interest in the Pushkin poem) that Pnin is unknowingly preparing, in Chapter Three, "for a Pushkinian 'future anniversary,' the birthday... when he will leave Waindell College"[12] in Chapter Seven.

Pnin is composed of seven chapters. Pnin has seven mysterious heart seizures (five are listed, 21); the sixth is in the park (19-24); the seventh is at The Pines (131).

Pnin has variously unsuccessful relationships with three women: Mira Belochkin, Liza Bogolepov, and Betty Bliss. The narrator's third meeting with Pnin occurs at "the Three Fountains" (179). There are also the "three papers" that Pnin stuffs into his coat in a desperate attempt to thwart mischance (26). And at times the hidden pattern seems to comprise an almost impossibly complex interrelation of details.[13]

Of greater importance to what the present paper will focus upon is the fact that there are three artificial squirrels in the novel and three people who are either termed, or likened to, squirrels. The artificial squirrels are: on Pnin's childhood bedroom screen (23), on Pnin's postcard to Victor (88), and the stuffed one in the Pnin apartment (177). The people are Dr. Belochkin ("squirrel" is belka in Russian; more on this later), Mira Belochkin, and Pnin himself. Researching "squirrels" in the library, Pnin takes a card-catalogue drawer "like a big nut" to a corner (76); he gives to Joan Clements his past history "in a nutshell" (33); he frequently sits "cracking nuts" with Joan at the kitchen table (40); he quite mysteriously "understands" the squirrel who wants a drink (58); and he even seems habitually squirrel-like: "At noon, as usual, Pnin washed his hands and head." (70)

Returning to Pnin's recollection in the park, we find: "He could still make out... certain parts of the nursery more tenacious of life than the rest, such as the lacquered screen, the gleam of a tumbler, the brass knobs of his bedstead..." (24) In context, these are simply the most vivid objects that Pnin recalls. However, he will soon be "holding aloft" (at the Clementses') "a tumbler" (36). The screen and bedstead knobs may be seen to reappear as the "large folding screen" and "fourposter bed" (164) in Pnin's bedroom of the house he later inhabits. The phrase "more tenacious of life" thus seems uncannily true. Similarly, the "wardrobe" of his childhood bedroom (23) may be seen to reappear as the "stuffy wardrobe in the maid's chamber" (147), where little Pnin remains hidden after his playmates have already gone home.

The cryptographic character of Pnin's childhood bedroom extends to his experience in the park. "During one melting moment, he had the sensation of holding at last the key he had sought; but, coming from very far, a rustling wind, its soft volume increasing as it ruffled the rhododendrons—now blossomless, blind—confused whatever rational pattern Timofey Pnin's surroundings had once had." As we learn later, Pnin's wife leaves him for a Dr. "Wind" (43), who "comes from very far." Pnin's wife Liza may thus be associated with the "blind" rhododendrons, which are "stirred" (25) by the "wind." Later, when Pnin recalls Liza's eyes, he pictures a "blind moist aquamarine blaze" (44).

As Pnin's recollection in the park ends, we read: "The back of the bench against which he still sprawled felt as real as his clothes, or his wallet, or the date of the Great Moscow Fire—1812." Pnin had just experienced a "Pninian quandary" involving his "clothes" and his "wallet" (16). He will soon frequently mispronounce Mrs. Thayer's name as "Mrs. Fire." The ultimate realization of this "real" feeling, however, is when Pnin repeatedly realizes that he is being "fired" from his job (169, 170). Note also that "his wallet" is mentioned alongside the (almost archly ironic) "Great Fire."

Fire seems to suggest special trouble for Pnin, which possibly relates to the "Cinderella" theme discussed below. Besides his being "fired" from his job,[14] "Mrs. Fire" points out his blunder of requesting a library book he already has (74); he slips near a fire "to crash into the poker and tongs" (43); and his bedroom at the Clementses's is cluttered with various books (which Pnin moves out) including a dictionary "('With more than 600 illustrations depicting zoos, the human body, farms, *fires—all scientifically chosen')"* (35; my italics).

When Pnin first sees this new bedroom, it is snowing outside, and this is "...reflected in the silent looking glass. Methodically

Pnin, inspected Hoecker's 'Girl with a Cat' above the bed, and Hunt's 'The Belated Kid' above the bookshelf." (34) Typically, "The Belated Kid" anticipates Liza's son Victor by Dr. Wind while she is still childless as Pnin's wife. The other cryptographic bedroom picture, in conjunction with the words "looking glass," may be seen to suggest Lewis Carroll's Alice and Cheshire Cat. It also echoes Pnin's childhood-bedroom recollection in the park, which vision is significantly associated with "the reflection of an inside object in a windowpane" plus "the outside scenery perceived through the same glass" (24). Thus, Pnin's prophetic bedroom surroundings traced above may be seen as a mysterious "looking glass" that he never quite understands. In the final chapter of the novel, the narrator (who seems to be Mr. Nabokov himself) talks with Timofey Pnin, noting in a somewhat different context "how reluctant he was to recognize his own past" (180).

Other illusions in *Pnin* to the world of Lewis Carroll's Alice teasingly recur. There is Pnin's "Duchess of Wonderland chin" (65), plus an apparently casual (more of this later) reference to "meeting a duchess" (155). We may also note the winking rabbit that Pnin can shadowgraph (13), a "live" playing card (a king, 84), plus a "Bachelor of Hearts" (151) and the repetitious "tarts" at Pnin's party (152, 171).[15] Perhaps most important is Pnin's triumphant croquet game at The Pines (which may be seen as his "Wonderland," the preserved secluded fragment of his Russian childhood past). When Pnin is "transfigured" (130), there are repeated mentions of "tea" and "chess" (132, 136). Quite ironically, the children at The Pines are rather indifferent to its "Wonderland" pleasures, only occasionally appreciating it "through a kind of interdimensional shimmer" (118). This Russian "Wonderland," it seems, is primarily for adults.

In his intriguing article on *Pnin* and "Cinderella," Charles Nicol has ably demonstrated that Pnin and Victor represent two versions of the children's story. In the earlier one (Pnin's version), "...Cinderella is befriended not by a fairy godmother but by a helpful animal, which has to be killed for its magic to take effect." (201) As Nicol observes, Pnin is befriended by a series of uncanny squirrels. This seems especially appropriate, he suggests, since Pnin's research has revealed that Cinderella's slippers were made of Russian squirrel fur in the older version.

Mr. Nicol's convincing argument may be considerably strengthened by the fact that the Russian word for squirrel is "belka." In the flashback to his childhood bedroom, sick Pnin is visited by the pediatrician Dr. Belochkin. He is the father of Mira Belochkin, Pnin's sweetheart who was "cremated" in Buchenwald (135) after marrying "a fur dealer of Russian extraction" (134). More important than these further manifestations of the "Russian squirrel fur" and "ashes" themes traced by Nicol in relation to "Cinderella," however, is the eerie possibility that Mira "Squirrel" reappears throughout the novel. Since "the exact form of her death had not been recorded," we read, "Mira kept dying a great number of deaths in one's mind, and undergoing a great number of resurrections, only to die again and again" (135). In context, this refers only to Pnin's vision-like memory of Mira, yet he is sitting on "a bench under the pines" (131) at The Pines, once again resembling the old man on his childhood bedroom screen. And it seems difficult to ignore the notion that the "Cinderella" animal must be killed for its magic to take effect. Here, unlike the park-bench scene, there is no live reappearance of the screen-painted squirrel, but Pnin does recall Mira "Squirrel." Can it be that she "undergoes a great number of resurrections," eerily reappearing as the series (noted by Nicol) of uncanny squirrels that befriend Pnin throughout the novel? For one thing, these uncanny squirrels not only befriend, but even seem to help Pnin out of trouble (as did Mira's father Dr. Belochkin).

Immediately after Pnin sees the first squirrel in the park, he recovers from his heart seizure, recovers his unobtainable suitcase, and manages to board a Cremona-bound truck (25). Similarly, when Pnin is once again "hopelessly lost," the sudden appearance of a squirrel (shot at in the forest[16]) seems almost supernaturally beneficial: "...then everything happened at once: the ant found an upright beam leading to the roof of the tower and started to ascend it with renewed zest; the sun appeared; and Pnin at the height of hopelessness, found himself on a paved road with a rusty but still glistening sign directing wayfarers 'To the Pines' " (115). En route to the library, Pnin slips twice on the path but regains his balance (73), over which recovery "a skimpy squirrel" seems to preside. Also, "a stuffed squirrel" attends the account of little Pnin's receiving an A-plus on an Algebra exam (177). There is one unhelpful squirrel, who seems to demand a drink from Pnin and who, after he has obligingly worked a water fountain, leaves "without the least sign of gratitude" (58). The gratitude, we may infer, recurs in forms Pnin fails to discern, just as he remains so "reluctant" to "recognize his own past."

We may note yet another factor suggesting that the uncanny squirrels are perhaps the fairy-tale-like reincarnations of Mira Belochkin: the theme of curious heart disorder, associated with a feeling of death-like dissociation, which Pnin tends to experience at such times. This peculiar heart condition is carefully explained by the narrator as a departure from the "discreteness" of our normal state (20), and it attends the following key scenes: Pnin's childhood sickness (when Dr. Belochkin comes, and young Pnin's bedroom is described), his recollections thereof in the park, his vision at the Cremona Women's Club of (as we realize only much later) Mira Belochkin (27), and his vision-like memory of Mira at The Pines (131). Ambrose Gordon, Jr. has termed Pnin's cardiograph "the signature" of the novel.[17]

A last addition to Charles Nicol's "Cinderella" findings may be seen in the first sentence of Chapter Seven: "My first recollection of Timofey Pnin is connected with a speck of coal dust that entered my left eye on a spring Sunday in 1911." As we soon learn, the narrator then visited Pnin's father, an opthamologist, and met little Pnin. But if the "speck of coal dust" is considered a "cinder," then the words "first recollection" may also subtly allude to the genesis of Nabokov's novel.

After describing his successful treatment, the narrator remarks: "I wonder where that speck is now? The dull, mad fact is that it *does* exist somewhere." (176) Perhaps only because this is the world of Vladimir Nabokov, one is tempted to speculate that the narrator's left-eye speck may be the same "speck" removed by Humbert from Lolita's "left eye" (45).

If this is so, the teasing cross-reference is hardly atypical. Indeed, *Pnin* contains several hidden interconnections with Mr. Nabokov's other works. In *Transparent Things,* for example, Hugh Person finds himself in "a jumble of boulders and a jungle of rhododendrons... No wonder he soon lost his way."[18] In *Pnin,* we encounter the apparently innocent sentence: "Hermann found his cane." (164) This cane, five lines later termed a "walking stick," may be seen to evoke the "stick mistake" (in *Despair,* mentioned above), wherein "Hermann" did not "find" the "stick." Similarly, there is casual mention in *Pnin* of a facial expression conveying "...a respectful, congratulatory, and slightly awed recognition of such things as dining with one's boss, being in *Who's Who,* or meeting a duchess." (155) Here, it is the "being in *Who's*

Who" (from *Lolita,* also mentioned above) which, in conjunction with "meeting a duchess," subtly serves to confirm the allusions to Lewis Carroll's *Alice* traced above, including Pnin's own "Duchess of Wonderland chin."

There are others; but for present purposes, the most important such Nabokovian interconnection involves Timofey Pnin's final departure and his reappearance in *Pale Fire* as Head of the Russian Department at Wordsmith College. This involves the highly unusual relationship between Pnin and the narrator. For when it becomes apparent that the narrator, presumably Mr. Nabokov himself, is coming to Waindell College, Pnin remarks: "I will never work under him." (170) As Nicol had observed, Pnin has a remarkable confrontation[19] with his narrator soon after this, and Pnin's punchbowl, apparently broken in the soapy dishwater, remains intact (173). This Pnian victory over his own narrator seems somewhat odd, since Mr. Nabokov has declared that his characters are "galley slaves."[20] However, it is possible (with regard to the "squirrel" and "nut" themes traced above) that within Pnin's Nabokov-imposed pattern, a "nutcracker" (dropped by Pnin into the soapy water) could not break a Cinderella-colored (158) bowl anyway. And as Mr. Nabokov has arranged it, the squirrels' help is only temporary. Helped to arrive in time at the Cremona Women's Club, for example, Pnin still brought the wrong lecture with him, as we learn from the last sentence of the novel. Mr. Nabokov's characters are indeed "galley slaves."

And this is partly why Pnin fails to detect the hidden prediction of his migration to *Pale Fire.* As both Nicol and Gordon have noted, Pnin's dream at the end of Chapter Four uncannily continues Victor's fantasy about "The King, his father" as the chapter begins.[21] Pnin's strange dream also predicts his escape to *Pale Fire:* "...Pnin saw himself fantastically cloaked, fleeing...from a chimerical palace, and then pacing a desolate strand with his dead friend Ilya Isidorovich Polyanski as they waited for some mysterious deliverance to arrive in a throbbing boat from beyond the hopeless sea" (109-110). In *Pale Fire,* the King of Zembla flees from the palace in fantastic garb and escapes in a "powerful motorboat" that awaits him "in a coastal cave" (87). Both Kings, after their escapes, will teach together at Wordsmith College in *Pale Fire.* And when Gradus finally arrives at Wordsmith, he visits both Kings but kills neither (first, Pnin in the library, 199; then Kinbote, 207). There is even a brief confusion about whether

Gradus seeks Kinbote or Pnin (200). The parallel is striking, but it is the words "mysterious deliverance" in Pnin's dream that suggest how tantalizingly close Pnin is permitted to come to understanding the significance of his dream. But Pnin does not suspect, in fact, cannot be allowed to suspect his impending escape from one Nabokov book to another.[22]

To explain this fully, we must take a final look at the wallpaper pattern of Pnin's childhood bedroom. "He had always been able to see that in the vertical plane a combination made up of three different clusters of purple flowers and seven different oak leaves was repeated a number of times with soothing exactitude, but...he could not find what system of inclusion and circumspection governed the horizontal recurrence of the pattern..."(23). As seen above, the pattern in *Pnin* of fatidical "threes" and "sevens" is almost diabolically complex, but the crucial "wallpaper" elements relating to Pnin's life are its "vertical" and "horizontal" components. For within the strangely expanding confines of Mr. Nabokov's world, his individual works may be seen as separate vertical planes, intersected by horizontal ones (therefore) composed of haunting interconnections. And while a particular character may vaguely sense that some sort of controlled pattern informs his vertical (intrabook) existence, he must remain unaware of his (interbook) horizontal potential. (Presumably, a character could only achieve such a perspective through either madness[23] or death.) Thus, Pnin can be "soothed" by the fairy-tale-like exactitude of his vertical pattern; he may even confront and defy, as Nicol suggests, its author. Yet Pnin must be limited to the "wonderment," as Barbara Monter has put it, of a Nabokov character who "strives to grasp the full pattern of the mosaic in which he himself is depicted."[24] Like any other Nabokovian "galley slave," he must remain unable to discover the authorial "system of inclusion and circumspection" that governs "the horizontal recurrence of the pattern." Pnin is finally released, but only for "further use," to quote John Shade, in Kinbote's "Pale Fire" Commentary. The escape to *Pale Fire* must remain, as glimpsed from within *Pnin,* an enigmatic, hopeful dream—or a triumphant, but unclear horizon.

NOTES

1. See my *Nabokov's Deceptive World* (New York, 1972), pp. ii, 79, 84, 99, 126, 131, 143, 147, 156.

2. Carl R. Proffer, "From *Otchaianie* to *Despair*," *Slavic Review*, June, 1968, p. 266.

3. Dabney Stuart, *"Laughter in the Dark:* dimensions of parody," *Triquarterly*, Winter, 1970, pp. 77-8.

4. Alfred Appel, Jr., ed., *The Annotated Lolita* (New York, 1970), pp. 347-52.

5. Vladimir Nabokov, *Lolita* (New York, 1955), p. 71. Subsequent references will be to this edition.

6. Vladimir Nabokov, *The Gift* (New York, 1970), p. 20.

7. Vladimir Nabokov, *King, Queen, Knave* (New York, 1968), p. 53. Subsequent references will be to this edition.

8. Vladimir Nabokov, *Glory* (New York, 1970), p. xii.

9. Vladimir Nabokov, *Speak, Memory* (New York, 1966), p. 86. Subsequent references will be to this edition.

10. Also in *Speak, Memory,* Mr. Nabokov describes the "fabulous lights" he saw (as a child in "the window of a sleeping car" on a train) as "diamonds" that he later "gave away" to his characters (24).

11. Vladimir Nabokov, *Pnin* (New York, 1965), p. 23. Subsequent references will be made to this edition.

12. Charles Nicol, "Pnin's History," *Novel*, Spring, 1971, p. 207. Subsequent page references to this article will be in the text, in parentheses.

13. For example, human anatomy seems grotesquely altered to produce a "third hand" (16) and a "third side" (21). And by a strange coincidence, Pnin's "February 3" birthday and the "3:03" Pushkin poem are mentioned in section "3" of Chapter Three; the narrator's third meeting with Pnin (at the Three Fountains) occurs in section "3" of Chapter Seven. Yet, as Alfred Appel, Jr. has suggested, Nabokovian coincidence is often not a coincidence. (*The Annotated Lolita*, p. xxviii.)

Given the almost endless complexity of such coincidences, it seems little wonder, as Mr. Nabokov once told me, that he produces only about two hundred pages of fiction per year.

14. Nabokov even makes two puns in this regard: "Boom-boom-boom" (171) and "shot" (188).

15. Since the author of this work is Vladimir Nabokov, it may not be too far-fetched to connect the following two details with Alice's abrupt alterations in size. In Pnin's bedroom at the Clementses' (which had been their daughter's) there are "height-level marks penciled on the doorjamb, beginning from a four-foot altitude" (65). Later Pnin looks "up, up, up at tall, tall, tall Victor," who is so much more grown up than Pnin had anticipated (103).

16. The hunter is apparently Praskovia's husband (119). Strangely enough, the appearances both of this squirrel and of the squirrel in the park seem to stop the "wind" (25, 115).

17. Ambrose Gordon, Jr., "The Double Pnin," in *Nabokov: The Man and His Work,* ed. L. S. Dembo (Madison, Wisconsin, 1967), p. 147.

18. Vladimir Nabokov, *Transparent Things* (New York, 1972), p. 89.

19. Poor Pnin has just learned that he will be fired, and hence, will lose the house he had proudly hoped to buy. The apparently broken bowl (a present from Victor) thus seems almost more than any fictional character should be forced to take from his author. Outraged, Pnin stares at the "blackness" beyond an open door (172) and a "quiet, lacy-winged little green insect" circles his head. Nicol terms this insect "an emblem of entomologist Nabokov... the evidence of Nabokov's presence in the scene" (208).

20. Vladimir Nabokov, "The Art of Fiction," *The Paris Review,* Summer-Fall, 1967, p. 96.

21. Nicol, p. 204; Gordon, p. 153.

22. Not the least fantastic aspect of Pnin's migration to *Pale Fire* is the haunting possibility that some trucks and even their "thunder" (190) follow him there. On the last page of *Pnin* we see them: "truck one, Pnin, truck two" (191). "Then the little sedan," we read, "boldly swung past the front truck and...there was simply no saying *what miracle might happen.*" (my italics) This happens on Tuesday. In *Pale Fire,* there is much suspicious ado about trucks: a "groaning truck" (70), Kinbote's footnote on trucks (192) and the "damned Tuesday night trucks" (206), which seem to echo, almost impossibly, Pnin's truck-filled Tuesday departure.

23. Madness for Pnin, it seems, could easily ensue from an "alas, too lucid" (24) deciphering of the referential-mania-like "evil delusions" (23) of his prophetic childhood bedroom established by the "evil designer" (23).

24. Barbara Heldt Monter, " 'Spring in Fialta': the choice that mimics chance," *Triquarterly,* Winter, 1970, p. 132.

Paul Grams

PNIN: THE BIOGRAPHER AS MEDDLER

Like Alfred Hitchcock, Nabokov has a fondness for making an occasional appearance in his own productions. To the seashore scene of *King, Queen, Knave* he and his wife pay what he calls a "visit of inspection"; at the close of *Bend Sinister* he mercifully *(auctor ex machina)* relieves Krug of his sanity. But in *Pnin* Nabokov's presence is neither incidental nor supernatural: in the final chapter he passes bodily through the looking glass into the narrative (after lurking throughout on its periphery), and meets his characters on their own ground. That last chapter reads like an autobiographical memoir—"My Recollections of Professor Pnin"—and especially so because we are urged to consider its first-person narrator Nabokov himself. Not, that is, the Nabokov who taught at Cornell and lives in Montreux, but the Nabokov denominated on the title page of *Pnin.*

The initial description of Pnin in Chapter One, for example, introduces him as "the elderly passenger" on the train who "was none other than Professor Timofey Pnin" (7)[1], where "none other" has precisely the tone of an amateur biographer's introduction of a famous personage he once encountered. The first chapter as a whole has an anecdotal flavor, narrating what Professor Cockerell on the last page calls "the story of Pnin rising to address the Cremona Women's Club and discovering he had brought the wrong lecture" (191). But "Nabokov" (author-narrator of *Pnin)* frequently oversteps the boundaries of the memoir, proving Pnin a fiction by exploring his thoughts and feelings, describing him in solitude, and abandoning his hero for occasional glances into other characters' consciousnesses.[2] The book is a kind of "fictional biography" in which the author colors in a framework of monochromatic facts with invented conversations, ruminations and novelistic details; the oscillation of narrative viewpoint and the persistent authorial intrusions (e.g., "Had I been reading about this mild old man, instead of writing about him . . . " [25]) are played off against the associations of "Nabokov" with the narrative "I." *Pnin* gets located somewhere between ordinary fact and familiar fiction.

For in the characteristically elusive way he performs essential literary tasks, Nabokov plants some of his interests and history on the person of the narrator. Pnin, an émigré, is referred to as "my friend"; "the widow of General N--" on whose estate Pnin participated in an amateur theatrical is revealed in Chapter Seven to be the narrator's aunt. In Chapter Six "a prominent Anglo-Russian writer" is about to be hired by Waindell; the narrator himself shows up for work. In Chapter Five Pnin's friend Château almost speaks the Name; observing "a score of small butterflies"—which the narrator microscopically describes—he remarks, "Pity Vladimir Vladimirovich is not here . . . He would have told us all about these enchanting insects" (128).* For Nabokov, what is hidden is interesting and important: when the unnamed narrator appears *in propria persona* to add an epilogue of personal recollections to Pnin's biography, the details he reveals about himself—his various historical whereabouts, his giving readings at émigré literary clubs, a significant pride in his lucid memory—all identify him with the name on the title page.

What complicates this "biographer-biographee" relationship is Pnin's attitude toward "Nabokov": Pnin disparages the latter's entomological abilities in Chapter Five, refuses to work under him in Chapter Six, and most confusingly, denies in Chapter Seven that "Nabokov's" recollections of their previous meetings—at Pnin's opthalmologist father's office and the amateur theatricals—are even accurate. Even the "factual framework" of this biography may be fictional. But Pnin's objections to "Nabokov's" descriptions of their childhood meetings actually provide some vindication for the narrator:

> Suddenly Pnin cried to Dr. Barakan across the table: "Now, don't believe a word he says, Georgiy Aramovich. He makes up everything. He once invented that we were schoolmates in Russia and cribbed at examinations. He is a dreadful inventor *(on uzhasniy vidumshchik)*. (185)

That Pnin's report of "Nabokov's" earlier recollection differs from the latter's—who didn't say they were schoolfellows—suggests that Pnin is the one with the inaccurate memory; but if Pnin here is telling the truth, "Nabokov's" report may well have been a lie. Then, too, "Nabokov" may be making up this scene as well. Everything spirals off into nebulous relativity; "Nabokov" is playing the Red King to Pnin's Alice.

*As described they can be only *Lycaeides samuelis* Nabokov *(L. melissa samuelis* Nab.), as Pnin and his friend cannot know.

This "who is the dreamer" conundrum is not, I think, just esthetic titillation; *Pnin* is too carefully made to seem like fictional biography. The truth of the matter may be impossible to riddle out, but the ethics of that author-character relationship (if such things can be considered) are both accessible and important. For the narrator in Chapter Seven does reveal, with enormous indirection, the reason Pnin dislikes him, and despite the "surprise and hurt" which Pnin's refusal to work under "Nabokov" caused him, it becomes apparent, once the crucial connection is made, that the narrator deserves, even if he seems not to understand, Pnin's antipathy. The link is found in the events leading up to Pnin's marriage to Liza Bogolepov. Their courtship is described thus:

> Pnin wrote her a tremendous love letter—now safe in a private collection—and she read it with tears of self pity while recovering from a pharmacopoeial attempt at suicide because of a rather silly affair with a litterateur who is now——. But no matter. Five analysts, intimate friends of hers, all said: "Pnin—and a baby at once" (45).

The unidentified allusion and the self-interrupted sentence are unusual though not importunate stylistic phenomena,[3] but when the narrator in Chapter Seven relates his personal recollection of that marriage, their meaning and purpose become luridly apparent.

At the same gathering in which he had tried to remind Pnin of their youthful encounters in Russia, "Nabokov" reports, he found that his "chief listener" was "Liza Bogolepov, a medical student who also wrote poetry":

> She asked me if she could send me for appraisal a batch of her poems . . . A few days later she sent me those poems; a fair sample of her production is the kind of stuff that émigré rhymsterettes wrote after Akhmatova . . . I wrote back telling Liza that her poems were bad and she ought to stop composing. Sometime later I saw her in another cafe . . . We walked. I suggested she let me see those poems again in some quieter place. She did. I told her they struck me as being even worse than they had seemed at first reading. She lived in the cheapest room of a decadent little hotel with no bath (180-81).

The brusque manner the narrator adopts at the end here suggests that more is going on than he perhaps wants to reveal; nonetheless it is clear a seduction takes place. He goes on: "In the result of emotions and in the course of events, the narration of which would be of no public interest whatsoever, Liza swallowed a handful of sleeping pills" (182). That *occupatio* interpolation echoes the tone of the earlier interruption, "But no matter," and confirms the identity of that "litterateur who is now..." Moreover, the narrator concludes by reporting that Liza came to him for advice about Pnin's proposal, telling him, "If I don't hear from you, I shall accept it" (182)—presumably "Nabokov" ignored her request—and then proceeds to copy out Pnin's letter offering marriage—thus revealing the ownership of that "private collection." At a subsequent meeting the narrator reports, "Liza informed me—with her usual crude candor—that she had 'told Timofey everything'; that he was 'a saint' and had 'pardoned' me" (184).

Knowing as we do the anguished soft spot in Pnin's heart for Liza, even after she abandons him, and sensing in that anguish the lugubrious but at the same time manly character of Pnin's cuckolded patience and foolishly hopeful love, we can understand Pnin's refusal to work for "Nabokov," and moreover, admire his generally polite reticence towards him. "The history of man is the history of pain" (168), remarks Pnin happily just before Hagen tells him he is losing his job; what is especially ironic about this book is that the "historian" is one of the primary sources of that pain. When Cockerell and "Nabokov" make distressingly juvenile phone calls to Pnin's shattered-dream house at the end of the book (and "Nabokov's" repeated references to "my good friend Timofey" begin to sound particularly hollow), the act is symptomatic of the whole author-character relationship.

But the narrator appears at least aware that something about his relationship with Pnin is not right—"Nabokov's" evasiveness in reporting his affair with Liza seems rather guilty, and he notes that the evening with Cockerell "somehow left me with the mental counterpart of a bad taste in the mouth" (189). For the narrator's involvement with Liza and his connection with Cockerell associate him with the whole parliament of anti-Pninians who have plagued Pnin's existence: particularly the academicians who mock and reject him and the parade of Liza's lovers, most of them psychiatrists—the two groups, ironically, against whom most of the narrator's satire is directed. That the book's last sentence, for example, can be seen as "leading into" its opening anecdote, suggests that what follows—i.e., *Pnin*—is a "Nabokovian" impersonation of Professor Timofey Pnin, superior to and more sensitive than Jack Cockerell's, but nonetheless discourteous, or more precisely, indiscrete. "Nabokov's" descriptions of Pninian idiophonics, Pninian gestures, Pninian blunders, and even Pninian pathos may therefore be the result of that "kind of fatal obsession which substitutes its own victim for that of the initial ridicule" (189). And the fact that Pnin's biographer is responsible, at least in part, for Pnin's marriage and its aftermath of hopeless suffering and embarrassment might suggest that his present recounting of Pnin's thinkings and doings, particularly in his easy superior attitude,[4] somehow violates Pnin's privacy and honor in much the same way as his past callous possession of Liza's affections did.

It is not necessary to rely on imported evaluations, however, to demonstrate that what Pnin's memorialist is performing in his "fictional biography" is, by his own standards, an unethical operation. Pnin's pain theory has already been adduced, but in the complaint to Chateau about psychiatry he reveals the essential notion behind it: "It is nothing but a kind of microcosmus of communism—all that psychiatry . . . Why not leave their private sorrows to people? Is sorrow not, one asks, the only thing in the world people really possess?" (52). That the association of communism and psychiatry here is not just an accidental intersection of Pnin's and "Nabokov's" opinions, but arises from a basic principle they share—although Pnin never articulates it—is brought out by the narrator's previous enunciation of that principle. Digressing on the strange state of consciousness that accompanies Pnin's "cardiac sensation" in Chapter One, the narrator remarks:

> I do not know if it has ever been noted before that one of the main characteristics of life is discreteness. Unless a film of flesh envelops us, we die. Man exists only insofar as he is separated from his surroundings. The cranium is a space-traveler's helmet. Stay inside or you perish. Death is divestment, death is communion. It may be wonderful to mix with the landscape, but to do so is the end of the tender ego. The sensation poor Pnin experienced was something very like that divestment, that communion (20).

Without waxing too philosophical over this somewhat macabre credo, one can note how much the notion of "discreteness" under pins the esthetics as well as the ethics of *Pnin*—or rather how little esthetic and ethical discreteness there is in the book and how cruel it is as a result. Indiscretions, of varying degrees of premeditation, are the primary anti-Pninists. Pnin's privacy is forever being invaded: by the sonic disturbances outside his various rooms, by the loud impersonations by Cockerell, by Liza's importunings and her "sordid, infantile soul," by "Nabokov's" inside knowledge of the cause of his marriage; or, on an esthetic level, by the narrator's "easy art," which places "an emblematic couple" at the end of Pnin's reverie about Mira (136), which makes Pnin's dream in Chapter Four an echo of Victor's earlier fantasy, and which interrupts a budding insight in Chapter Two with an enigmatic squirrel borrowed from Pnin's bedroom screen.

That narrative esthetic of "Nabokov" is indirectly explained by Joan Clements in an unidentified reference interrupted by tipsy panting: "But don't you think—haw—that what he is trying to do—haw—practically in all his novels—haw—is—haw—to express the fantastic recurrence of certain situations?" (159). But the more fantastic the recurrence, the greater the violation of Pnin's privacy, the greater the subjection of Pnin to "Nabokov." "Nabokov's" recollection of Pnin's father's office, for instance, includes in the waiting room three people representing the Karenins and Vronsky, merely because Dr. Pnin had once ministered, the narrator tells us, to Tolstoy; his recollection of the amateur drama has Pnin playing the "betrayed husband" after "Nabokov" declines the part—an obvious recurrence which Pnin significantly disaffirms.[5]

In other words, the liberties "Nabokov" takes in order to "fictionalize" Pnin's biography, the esthetic of "fantastic recurrence" itself, are indiscretions perpetrated on Pnin's life that take away his privacy in a way exactly opposite that which accompanies those "cardiac sensations" during which Pnin's heart expands and melts into its surroundings. And those invasions, those fictional excursions into Pnin's mind, those impersonations of Pnin by his biographer, are the literary counterparts of that obsessive imitation by which Cockerell himself is made a victim. Here the association of narrator and author becomes crucial, for only when Pnin and his biographer are seen to be dwelling in the same narrative realm—as opposed to the usual author-character relationship, where the author has an obvious, autocratic, God-like superiority—does the monstrous cruelty of that indiscretion appear. "Nabokov's" casual affair with Liza is one form of author-character cruelty: the author's directing, behind the scenes, the course and quality of his character's life—sampling, so to speak, Pnin's wife's favors himself before handing her down. A second form, an author's denying his character human discreteness, is represented by Pnin's all-permeable dwellings, and particularly by his being forced to leave the house on Todd Road—through "Nabokov's" indirect intervention. The description of that house shows exactly what he is being denied:

> The sense of living in a *discrete* building all by himself was to Pnin something singularly delightful and amazingly satisfying to a weary old want of his innermost self, battered and stunned by thirty-five years of homelessness. One of the sweetest things about the place was the silence (144, my italics).

The final drunken phone call, of course, epitomizes this second form of authorial cruelty, just as "Nabokov's" possession and use of Pnin's "tremendous love letter" epitomizes the first.

But this autocratic authority ultimately falls victim to its own obsessive ridicule, for its persistent and artifical belittling finally reduces that superior consciousness to petty-mindedness, and imaginative insights become harrassing phone calls. Perhaps the best illustration of this is what happens to one of Pnin's private images as the narrator appropriates it for his "fantastic recurrences." In Pnin's vividly remembered bedroom is:

> . . . a four-section screen of polished wood, with pyrographic designs representing a bridle path felted with fallen leaves, a lily pond, an old man hunched up on a bench, and a squirrel holding a reddish object in its front paws (23).

The squirrel with the riddling object Pnin feverishly tries to identify undergoes a strange metamorphosis as the narrator meddles with it.[6] Generally, it is the center of a constellation of images: squirrel, fever, "cardiac sensation," and some sort of search for a crucial clue. After the seizure in Chapter One, "A grey squirrel sitting on comfortable haunches on the ground before him was sampling a peach stone" (24-25). After seeing Liza in Chapter Two:

> He seemed to be quite unexpectedly (for human despair seldom leads to great truths) on the verge of a simple solution of the universe but was interrupted by an urgent request. A squirrel under a tree had seen Pnin on the path (58).

Pnin helps it *"sample* the stocky sparkling pillar of water" from a drinking fountain, thinking, "She has fever, perhaps" (58, my italics). Minor squirrels escape the projectiles of young boys immediately before Pnin loses his balance on an ice patch (73) and of Al Cook's hunting handyman before Pnin suddenly finds the road "To The Pines" (115). Playing expert croquet, Pnin is trans-figured "into a terrifically mobile, scampering, mute, sly-visaged hunchback," becoming, strangely enough, the squirrel who accom-panies the "cardiac sensation" that follows (130-31). At the end of Chapter Six, it has become a nutcracker—which does not, after all, shatter Victor's bowl. When Pnin is washing it:

> . . . The leggy thing somehow slipped out of the towel and fell like a man from a roof. He almost caught it—his fingertips actually came into contact with it in mid-air, but this only helped to propel it into the treasure-concealing foam of the sink, where an excruciating crack of broken glass followed upon the plunge (172).

The recurrences have grown fantastic: the squirrel disappears into the foliage, reduced to a shape, then a function; the febrile ex-pansion of death is interrupted, becomes a fearful flight and then a cold suicidal plunge; the sampling search devolves to a lucky find-ing, to an expert, indifferent croqueting, to a snatching that back-fires. That the degeneration of this constellation of images can be associated with the narrator's obsessive repetition of it in increas-ingly artificial guises can be partly deduced from "Nabokov's" own use of it in his recollection of Pnin's childhood home in Chapter Seven:

> . . . through the open door of the schoolroom I could see a map of Rus-sia on the wall, books on a shelf, a stuffed squirrel, and a toy mono-plane with linen wings and a rubber motor. I had a similar one but twice bigger, bought in Biarritz. After one had wound up the propeller for some time, the rubber would change its manner of twist and develop fascinating thick whorls which predicted the end of its tether (177).

The squirrel is stuffed, the interesting object is a rubber motor, and the search is merely a predictable tightening and snapping of a rubber band; the image is fully perverted, and the narrator's probe into Pnin's consciousness has become a snobbish "Nabokov" peeping into Pnin's schoolroom.

The relation of this image to the author-character problem can perhaps best be seen in the description of the clue Pnin seeks in Chapter One in a passage two paragraphs removed from "Nabok-ov's "life is discreteness" credo:

> It stood to reason that if the evil designer—the destroyer of minds, the

friend of fever—had concealed the key of the pattern with such monstrous care, that key must be as precious as life itself and, when found, would regain for Timofey Pnin his everyday health, his everyday world; and this lucid—alas, too lucid—thought forced him to persevere in the struggle (23-24).[7]

The "evil designer" here is clearly the *uzhasniy vidumshchik,* and that the "key of the pattern" is discreteness is indicated by Pnin's interrupted "simple solution of the universe" in Chapter Two:

If people are reunited in heaven (I don't believe it, but suppose), then how shall I stop it from creeping upon me, over me, that shriveled, helpless, lame thing, her soul? But this is the earth, and I am, curiously enough, alive, and there is something in me, and in life—... (58).

...—that keeps us apart, "Nabokov" would conclude. But Pnin does not, and the reason "Nabokov" has him stop short (he is, after all, writing about him) is to maintain Pnin's discreteness by preserving his innocent ignorance. For "Nabokov" is clearly no model of discretion—his designings are evil, his inventings are terrible *(vidumshchik* also means "liar," "tall-tale teller"); and they are so because in the interest of making a pattern of Pnin's life he plays too easily with Pnin's privacy. "Squirrel," Pnin's postcard to Victor explains, means "shadow-tail"; Pnin tells Château he has a "shadow behind the heart": the "reddish object" in the screen squirrel's hand is, I think, Pnin's heart. But "Nabokov's" peeping eventually makes it appear to *him* a rubber motor: his obsessive indiscretion kills Pnin for him.

But when Pnin drives off (on his birthday) "up the shining road, which one could make out the narrowing to a thread of gold in the soft mist where hill after hill made beauty of distance, and where there was simply no saying what miracle might happen" (191), he escapes forever, dead to and free from "Nabokov." "Nabokov" has set the rules ("fantastic recurrence" is one) and played the game of putting himself in his character's mind. Pnin has been a helpless victim, but he has sensed, if not recognized "Nabokov's" authorial meddling. Pnin finally drives off "in the frame of the roadway"—reminiscent of the "grobovogo vkhoda" through which Pushkin imagines himself passing into miracle-land at the end of the poem Pnin recites in Chapter Three (the end is, of course, omitted). And as Pnin escapes his own biography, he enters that afterworld of fictional characters, the world of authors and readers, the world where Humbert Humbert does indeed meander, once a year, down a green lane.[8]

NOTES

1. Vladimir Nabokov, *Pnin* (New York: Atheneum, 1967). Hereafter all page numbers are given in parentheses with the quotations.

2. At the end of Chapter Four "Nabokov" reaches a narrative zenith by describing a scene (without using his "I") which none of his characters could have been aware of: "It was a pity nobody saw the display in the empty street, where the auroral breeze wrinkled a large luminous puddle, making of the telephone wires reflected in it illegible lines of black zigzags (110). Immediately preceding this he has exercised his authorial prerogative of peering into the minds and dreams of four different characters in one paragraph: the whole sequence is almost parodically omniscient.

3. They are devices similar in purpose and ultimate effect to those in other ironic first-person narratives, such as Ford Maddox Ford's *The Good Soldier* or Nabokov's own *Despair*.

4. Consider how foolish Pnin is made to seem in the confrontation with Victor or how he fails to catch Mrs. Thayer's hint that he is going to be displaced from the Clements' house.

5. And the bus station attendant in Chapter One is transported to Russia (and back thirty-five years) to be the steward on "Nabokov's" aunt's estate in Chapter Seven. Another recurrence, considerably crueler, is the speck of coal dust "Nabokov" associates with his first purported meeting with Pnin, a diabolical counterpart to the "spatter of sun and sea . . . between your own eyelids" (44) that is associated with Pnin's memory of Liza in Chapter Two. The narrator continually steals from Pnin's experiences details for his own—or vice versa.

6. The other designs are also images of aspects of Pnin's life, and generally maintain their vibrant associations throughout the book: the bridle path—sad pun—with his relationship with Mira (82 and 133), the "lily pond" with Victor (Chapter Four throughout, e.g., "Lake," the artist—and the description of Victor's bowl on 153), and the hunched old man with Pnin in pain (20-21, 61, 131, 189-90).

7. The pattern is a repeated wallpaper design: "He could not find what system of inclusion and circumscription governed the horizontal recurrence of the pattern" (23). "Circumscription" clinches the reference to the narrator's esthetic in "horizontal recurrence." Interestingly, Krug's recognition of his fictiveness in *Bend Sinister* is described as a moment of extreme lucidity.

8. As Mark V. Boldino observes, "The double dream Pnin and Victor dream takes us to Zembla, and we actually meet Pnin again at the end of *Pale Fire* (a much more secure Pnin)."

William Carroll

NABOKOV'S SIGNS AND SYMBOLS

"My characters are galley slaves."[1]

The design of my novel is fixed in my imagination and every character follows the course I imagine for him. I am the perfect dictator in that private world insofar as I alone am responsible for its stability and truth."[2]

—Vladimir Nabokov

Being a character in one of Vladimir Nabokov's fictions is evidently not much fun. Arbitrarily created, the character leads a life inherently fragile; he is continually jostled, transported in space and time, forced into exile at the stroke of a pen, capriciously tortured, driven into madness at the last moment *(Bend Sinister),* or abruptly "cancelled." As William H. Gass puts it, Nabokov's characters "are his clowns. They blunder comically about. Clubbed by coincidence, they trip when most passionate. With rouge on their pates and wigs on their features, their fundaments honk and trousers tear. Brought eagerly, naively near, beauty in a boutonniere pees on their faces" (p. 116).[3] As flies to wanton boys are we to our authors, they kill us for their plots. Or so it seems to a series of characters in Nabokov's novels and short-stories, characters whose very position as characters-in-a-story seems to be one of the subjects of the stories in which they appear, and one of their own preoccupations there. Labyrinths, receding concentric circles, vertigo: Nabokov's fiction spawns special critical vocabularies and diseases in those who attempt to account for its persistently odd effect.

One way to a clearer perception of the aims of these fictions is to look closely at a few instances—especially at Pnin and the deranged boy in the story "Signs and Symbols"—in which a Nabokovian character's self-consciousness resembles, though in a distorted manner, our own self-consciousness as readers. I am not invoking the term "identification"; the laughter from Montreux would sweep it away anyhow. But these situations, these carefully arranged structures of self-consciousness, do seem, in curious ways, to be "archetypal" (another word Nabokov would never use). That is, our own sense of ourselves—lapsed believers in order unable to embrace disorder, dimly aware of coincidence and patterns in experience but trying to ignore their import—is often like these characters' self-awareness.

In *Pnin,* for example, Timofey Pnin tells Dr. Hagen that "the history of man is the history of pain!" (p. 167).[4] The novel demonstrates the validity of that comment as it applies to Pnin himself—beginning with Pnin's very name, in whose explosive pronunciation reverberates the word "pain,"[5] His name also alludes to an eighteenth-century Russian poet whose most famous work was *The Wail of Innocence.*[6] The outer events of Pnin's life are painful enough: political exile, flight from two totalitarian states, the hopelessness of his marriage with Liza, above all the death of Mira Belochkin (and others) in the Nazi holocaust. "In order to exist rationally, Pnin had taught himself, during the last ten years, never to remember Mira Belochkin... because, if one were quite sincere with oneself, no conscience, and hence no consciousness, could be expected to subsist in a world where such things as Mira's death were possible. One had to forget" (p. 133). And yet, of course, Pnin cannot forget. The world continually reminds him of all of this suffering, adding new refinements every day. At Waindell College, the suffering is more comic but no less real to Pnin: loafish students, dull classes, obnoxious colleagues, confusion over American arcana such as railroad timetables. The worst of his colleagues at Waindell is Jack Cockerell, who cruelly parodies everything about Pnin that is different, from his clothes to his accent. In the process, Cockerell invents or reproduces legends and anecdotes about Pnin that never happened. The novel ends with one of Cockerell's errors, that Pnin brought the wrong lecture to the Cremona Women's Club, and it begins with a different version of the same story, in which Pnin was on the wrong train. But he did arrive and give his lecture.

The pain in Pnin's life originates outside of him. His inner world of linguistic research, mythography, and Russian history is secure, comfortable, friendly. But his pain results from an uninterrupted series of cruel intrusions from the various worlds in which he must live. Perhaps the greatest intrusion, gradually revealed through the novel and most clearly seen in Chapter Seven, is made by the narrator.[7] Careful re-readers of the novel have seen that the narrator has turned up in Pnin's life suspiciously often: he helped Pnin write a letter to the *New York Times* (p. 16); he possesses one of Pnin's love letters to Liza (p. 45) and his letter of proposal to her (pp. 181-2); he too has previously been at the émigré retreat The Pines (p. 116); he has apparently had an affair with Liza before her marriage, who when dismissed by the narrator attempted suicide, then married Pnin (pp. 180-1); and it is the narrator, as *he* tells us, "a prominent Anglo-Russian writer" (p. 138), "a really fascinating lecturer" (p. 168), who has come to take over Pnin's position at Waindell, a prospect which repels Pnin: "I will never work under him" (p. 168).

Pnin's objections to the narrator appear to be twofold. In addition to the more obvious interferences mentioned above, Pnin distrusts the narrator's ability to tell the truth about him. The narrator's self-confidence—"Do I really remember his crew cut, his puffy pale face, his red ears? Yes, distinctly" (p. 175)—is not shaken by Pnin's denials. When he tries to remind Pnin of former meetings between them and amuse him and others "with the unusual lucidity and strength of my memory... he [Pnin] denied everything. He said he vaguely recalled my grandaunt but had never met me. He said that his marks in algebra had always been poor... he said that in *Zabava (Liebelei)* he had only acted the part of Christine's father. He repeated that we had never seen each other before... noticing how reluctant he was to recognize his own past, I switched to another, less personal topic" (p. 178). The trouble is exactly that Pnin cannot recognize "his own past" in the distortions and fabrications of the narrator. At a dinner in Paris, while telling other anecdotes about him, the narrator is interrupted by an angry Pnin: "Now, don't believe a word he says... He makes up everything. He once invented that we were schoolmates in Russia and cribbed at examinations. He is a dreadful inventor *(on uzhasniy vidumshchik)*" (p. 183).

Pnin, in other words, finds himself the subject of still another cruel intrusion from the outside, another invasion of his privacy. He is the subject (as we eventually realize) of a kind of biography, a version of his life told by a faulty artist, a "dreadful inventor" who adds his own details, transforms others, and plays fast and loose with the truth. Which is exactly what Nabokov—and every other artist—does. It is the very definition of an "inventor," dreadful or not. It is this power of transformation which we praise and admire in our favorite inventors. Yet Nabokov has maneuvered us into the curious position of condemning the same power in the narrator (who is necessarily distinguished from Nabokov himself). We *do* believe, with Pnin, that the narrator is "dreadful." The suffering and pain in Pnin's life have been made so powerful, so convincing, so "real," that we resent the narrator's intrusion. Vertigo sets in again when we remind ourselves that the narrator is also a fiction, that Pnin is a fiction, and that our feelings against the narrator's inventions are in a way a condemnation of Nabokov's similar power of invention, the power which has convinced us of the "reality" of these figures in the first place. And on and on in circles.

At one point, rejecting the personal intrusions of psychoanalysis, Pnin makes another wail of innocence: "Why not leave their private sorrows to people? Is sorrow not, one asks, the only thing in the world people really possess?" (p. 52). Yes, we say, our sympathy fully engaged. Yet Pnin's sorrow is not private; it is the substance of the novel. And it is the reader, as well as the narrator, who has violated Pnin's privacy. Those "private sorrows" are what have engaged us so deeply in Pnin's plight, and have engaged our anger against the narrator. Curiouser and curiouser. The act of reading the novel is thus itself an intrusion.

We are spared the worst violation of Pnin, mercifully. After the big party he gives in Chapter Six, Pnin is told by Hagen that he will be replaced in his job by the narrator. When everyone leaves, Pnin washes the dishes, which include an aquamarine glass bowl, a gift to Pnin from Victor Wind, Liza's child by her second marriage. When Liza was pregnant with Victor, Pnin "was not only ready to adopt the child when it came but was passionately eager to do so" (p. 47), and a father-son bond has grown between them; the bowl is an emblem of that bond. While washing the dishes, a distraught Pnin drops a slippery nutcracker: "He almost caught it—his fingertips actually came into contact with it in midair, but this only helped to propel it into the treasure-concealing foam of the sink, where an excruciating crack of broken glass followed the plunge" (p. 171). The pain of this moment, this apparent cruelty, is unbearable: "Pnin hurled the towel into a corner and, turning away, stood for a moment staring at the blackness beyond the threshold of the open back door. A quiet, lacy-winged little green insect circled in the glare of a strong naked lamp above Pnin's glossy bald head. He looked very old, with his toothless mouth half open and a film of tears dimming his blank, unblinking eyes." Nabokov, lurking as close to the surface as that suspicious green moth, pulls back from this worst of cruelties, though, one which seems inevitable to the reader. "Then, with a moan of anguished anticipation, he went back to the sink and, bracing himself, dipped his hand deep into the foam. A jagger of glass stung him. Gently he removed a broken goblet. The beautiful bowl was intact. He took a fresh dish towel and went on with his household work" (p. 171). The bond between Pnin and Victor, like the bowl, will remain intact throughout the novel; but this is virtually the only outside link Pnin can endure, and it is fitful and fragile at best.

As he has done in the past, Pnin makes an attempt to flee this inventor and his other intruders at Waindell. In the final scene, after a cruel anonymous phone call from Cockerell and the narrator during the night, Pnin drives out of town early (to avoid meeting the narrator). Walking in the town, the narrator sees his subject leaving. He emits "a roar of greeting," but Pnin doesn't hear him. "I hurried past the rear truck, and had another glimpse of my old friend, in tense profile, wearing a cap with ear flaps and a storm coat; but next moment the light turned green, the little white dog leaning out yapped at Sobakevich, and everything surged forward—truck one, Pnin, truck two. From where I stood I watched them recede in the frame of the roadway, between the Moorish house and the Lombardy poplar. Then the little sedan boldly swung past the front truck and, free at last, spurted up the shining road, which one could make out narrowing to a thread of gold in the soft mist where hill after hill made beauty of distance, and where there was simply no saying what miracle might happen" (pp. 189-90). A character in "flight... from his author,"[8] Pnin breaks away, "free at last." The actual scene is a fitting emblem for Pnin's life, sandwiched in between two versions of the story about the lecture: "truck one, Pnin, truck two." It also suggests his larger imprisonment in the novel, between Nabokov and the narrator.[9] He is seen in a "frame" which both emphasizes and limits his situation; a "frame" which is an artifact. But Pnin "boldly" moves out of the sequence, the rigorous pattern, and as he disappears into the mist, where distance has been made "beauty," we feel that at least one miracle has already happened. On the last page of the story of his life, on his birthday no less (February 15—p. 185), Pnin leaves us—Nabokov, narrator, reader—and recedes into a spatial, temporal, and esthetic "distance." At the novel's end, he escapes the narrator to enter the world as a living, breathing fiction.[10]

The narrator, though, leaves us with only the parody of Pnin: Jack Cockerell telling an inaccurate anecdote. When we begin to examine the narrator's stories, compare the different descriptions of the same scenes and people, and realize his interference in Pnin's life, then we must begin to wonder whether Pnin hasn't escaped us too, whether the version of Pnin we have come to believe in, through the narrator, is any more authentic than Jack Cockerell's imitation. We can take refuge in the reply that Nabokov, after all, has created all of this, that he is the master inventor. But we have been led, in the process of reading this invention, into the bizarre position of questioning the right of one "inventor" to create stories. We sense there is a moral difference between the narrator and Nabokov; and there is. But there is no esthetic difference. It is godlike to create; it is unbearably human, and inferior, to be the subject of someone else's creation. The web of human interrelationships insures that each human being will inevitably interact with others, will be, by turns, both creator and creature, master and servant. Nabokov's characters are "galley slaves" in that they know themselves subject to inhuman and autocratic powers; and we (and a few of them) know that the "galley" is both man's physical situation and the printer's proof taken from composed type. One's labor in life is analogous to labor in printed type.

Pnin's plight is sad enough, but that of the unnamed boy in the story "Signs and Symbols" is far more serious.[11] A victim of incurable derangement apparently from birth ("As a baby he looked more surprised than most babies"—p. 66), with "no desires," the boy perceives in the world about him nothing but "malignant activity that he alone could perceive" (p. 62). His parents are dull, sad people who are merely oblivious where he is paranoid. The boy lives in a closed system of signs, all of which point, malevolently, toward him. He suffers from "referential mania," as "Herman Brink" calls it. His situation thus resembles that of a character in an incredibly complex fiction, in which every single word, every image, every nuance, is carefully related to that character's life; existing only inside the system, the character cannot know what the signs are pointing to, can only dimly guess at the outside referents. Thus, in Nabokov's story, what the boy "really wanted to do was to tear a hole in his world and escape" (p. 64). Death is apparently the only way open to him; his parents, trying to visit him, learn instead of his latest suicide attempt, "a masterpiece of inventiveness." An envious fellow patient, seeing (apparently) the boy's desperate clawing motion, "thought he was learning to fly—and stopped him" (p. 64). It is inevitable that the boy's cousin is "a famous chess player," a participant in another closed system of signs. The chessmaster Luzhin, in *The Defense*,[12] like the boy here, attempts to escape his world through suicide, but fails: an eternity of dark and pale squares, another chessboard, "obligingly and inexorably spread out before him" (p. 256). As a child, we are told, Luzhin, working through classic chess games, "gradually ceased to reconstruct actually on the board and contented himself with perceiving their melody mentally through the sequence of symbols and signs" (p. 57). Nabokov clearly links the two cases together.

Referential mania is the ultimate, insane extension of the act of personification. Lunatics and poets are, as they say, of imagination all compact. The boy believes that "Phenomenal nature shadows him wherever he goes. Clouds in the staring sky transmit to one another, by means of slow signs, incredibly detailed information regarding him. His inmost thoughts are discussed at nightfall, in manual alphabet, by darkly gesticulating trees. Pebbles or stains or sun flecks form patterns representing in some awful way messages which he must intercept. Everything is a cipher and of everything he is the theme" (pp. 64-5). Signs, patterns, messages, cipher, theme: these are terms of literary analysis. The boy is the "theme" of all reality and of the story. The primary meaning of "cipher" here is "secret writing based on a system"; the system, the master writer, remains unknown. Bad literary criticism is a hunt for "keys" in this sense, making of literature something arcane and elite. But "cipher" also means, of course, "the mathematical symbol (0) denoting absence of quantity," or zero. This is the more frightening possibility; it suggests that everything is a zero, meaningless, without substance. The boy does attribute meaning, and it is this need to make such an attribution, a need we all feel, which taken to an extreme results in insanity. The intercepted messages may be in a code that reveals nothing.

After the cipher-theme comment, the unknown narrator of the story tells us of the "spies" who are "staring" and "gesticulating" at the boy: "Some of the spies are detached observers, such as glass surfaces and still pools; others, such as coats in store windows, are prejudiced witnesses, lynchers at heart; others again (running water, storms) are hysterical to the point of insanity, have a distorted opinion of him and grotesquely misinterpret his actions. He must be always on his guard and devote every minute and module of life to the decoding of the undulation of things. The very air he exhales is indexed and filed away" (p. 65). The boy conceives of three different kinds of "spies"[13] or "inventors," then, those who have created and who monitor the closed system in which he suffers. And these three correspond to the kinds of rhetorical narrators used most commonly in modern fiction since James; the boy's personifications are the personae Nabokov himself uses throughout his fiction. The "detached observers" do not intrude into their stories in obvious ways; they simply hold the mirror up to nature, as the formula has it, and their emblems here are "glass surfaces and still pools," calm, neutral reflectors of the world around them. Nabokov's earliest novels and stories, like *The Defense,* are written from this point of view. The second kind of "spies" are those "prejudiced witnesses," seen *through* the glass now, not content with passive reflection, taking some active part in the ordering of things. One thinks here of the narrators of *The Real Life of Sebastian Knight* (an ultimately beneficent "prejudice") and *Pnin* (a malevolent one). The third type of narrator is "hysterical to the point of insanity," completely unreliable, one who "grotesquely" misinterprets the subject's actions. Their emblem is not the calm reflective mirror of the "still pools" but the turbulence of "running water, storms"—a version of the pathetic fallacy. The insane narrator is Nabokov's own special province: Smurov of *The Eye,* Hermann of *Despair,* Humbert Humbert of *Lolita,* Kinbote (for the sake of argument)[14] of *Pale Fire.* Mad artists, deflected or warped imaginations, offer oblique but spectacular perspectives on the nature of art, on the idea of transformation and distortion of "reality,"[15] and Nabokov uses them with increasing frequency in his work. As avatars of the imagination, these figures are our only means of seeing the world about them. Few other narrators in modern fiction are so astonishingly, so interestingly, unreliable.

The narrator-spies represent sheer terror for the boy, however; he is another character attempting to escape from his authors. But there is no escape: "If only the interest he provokes were limited to his immediate surroundings—but alas it is not! With distance the torrents of wild scandal increase in volume and volubility. The silhouettes of his blood corpuscles, magnified a million times, flit over vast plains; and still farther, great mountains of unbearable solidity and height sum up in terms of granite and groaning firs the ultimate truth of his being" (p. 65). The "still pools," already given way to "running water, storms," are now "torrents of wild scandal." It is the extension, the completeness, of the system which is so terrifying: "a dense tangle of logically interacting illusions, making him totally inaccessible to normal minds" (p. 67). The boy is the ultimate solipsist, dying from an overdose of meaning. The existence of one object which did not seem to point to him would represent the necessary "hole in his world," through which he might now and then seek relief. But there is none.

The boy thus lives continually in a world which seems governed by an all-powerful deity disturbingly like Descartes's famous "evil genius": "I shall then suppose, not that God who is supremely good and the fountain of truth, but some evil genius not less powerful than deceitful, has employed his whole energies in deceiving me: I shall consider that the heavens, the earth, colors, figures, sound, and all other external things are nought but illusions and dreams of which this genius has availed himself in order to lay traps for my credulity."[16] The casualness of the "availed," the ubiquity of the "traps," increase the horror. Pnin has known this kind of a world, too, not only because of the narrator's actions, but as a result of childhood illnesses as well. The wallpaper in his room possessed patterns of oak leaves and purple flowers which tormented young Timofey: "he could not find what system of inclusion and circumscription governed the horizontal recurrence of the pattern" (p. 23). This childhood fascination with pattern led Luzhin to the glories and terrors of chess, but for Pnin it leads only to terror: "It stood to reason that if the evil designer—the destroyer of minds, the friend of fever—had concealed the key of the pattern with such monstrous care, that key must be as precious as life itself and, when found, would regain for Timofey Pnin his everyday health, his everyday world; and this lucid—alas, too lucid—thought forced him to persevere in the struggle" (p. 23). "Evil genius," "dreadful inventor," "evil designer," "friend of fever": this is the artist seen from within his artifact, from within a world in which paranoia is normality and the *deus absconditus* is a vain dream. Descartes imagined such a world but turned away from it; Nabokov imagined it and found a way for us to experience it with him.

"Referential mania" is a critical disease all readers of fiction suffer from. Our duty as critics is to explicate and analyze the signs—which point to a single meaning outside the work itself, as in allegory, or to another word inside the work—and the symbols—which point to various meanings simultaneously, both inside and outside the work. Over-reading is another, milder form of referential mania, and Nabokov has insured, through his rhetorical strategy, that the reader will succumb to the same mania that afflicts the boy. The story is studded with apparent signs and symbols that the gullible reader—that is, any reader—will attempt to link together in a "meaningful" pattern. Most of these signs point to the probably successful suicide of the boy. On the way to the hospital, for example, the parents take the underground train; but it "lost its life current between two stations, and for a quarter of an hour one could hear nothing but the dutiful beating of one's heart and the rustling of newspapers" (p. 63). Other things lose their "life current" and fall into darkness that day. The parents go to a bus stop, after learning of their son's latest suicide attempt: "A few feet away, under a swaying and dripping tree, a tiny half-dead unfledged bird was helplessly twitching in a puddle" (p. 63). This seems inevitably to be a "foreshadowing" of the son's death, the sort of symbolist anticipatory detail found in traditional fiction. Confronted with a similar vision in *Ada,* though, Van Veen has a more skeptical attitude, one which we might well emulate: "A dead and dry hummingbird moth lay on the window ledge of the lavatory. Thank goodness, symbols did not exist either in dreams or in the life in between" (p. 510).[17]

The rest of the parents' day is filled with similar omens. A picture of Aunt Rosa reminds the mother that "the Germans put her to death." She dimly senses a larger power behind such events; but her vagueness is the opposite of her son's hyper-sensitivity. She has no idea of any source: "she thought of the endless waves of pain that for some reason or other she and her husband had to endure; of the invisible giants hurting her boy in some unimaginable fashion; of the incalculable amount of tenderness contained in the world; of the fate of this tenderness... of neglected children... of beautiful weeds" (pp. 67-8). The existence of cruelty and death are indeed without apparent "reason," they are "unimaginable." Yet they are here, in an imagined fiction, as in the world. Nabokov gives us all sorts of signs that death is near, and we learn next how it is the fate of the "beautiful weeds" that they helplessly have "to watch the shadow of [the farmer's] simian stoop leave mangled flowers in its wake, as the monstrous darkness approaches" (p. 68).

That "darkness" seems imminent in the third and final part of the story; it is "past midnight" when the parents resolve to bring the boy home from the mental hospital, to care for him themselves. Another symbol of death appears when the mother picks up from the floor some playing cards and photographs: "knave of hearts, nine of spades, ace of spades, Elsa and her bestial beau" (p. 69). The mother is oblivious to the ace of spades, a familiar harbinger of death, but she is startled then by the telephone, ringing at "an unusual hour." It is a wrong number. "It frightened me," the mother says. The telephone rings again, again a wrong number, asking for Charlie. The mother replies: "You have the incorrect number. I will tell you what you are doing: you are turning the letter O instead of the zero" (p. 69). Absorbing the implications of *this* idea will take a moment. While it is a plausible explanation of the wrong number, the fact remains that there is no hieroglyphic difference between the letter and the number. We may recall an earlier line in the story: "Everything is a cipher and of everything he is the theme." Nabokov has placed us in the position of the boy here—is the O a letter or a number? Does it matter? Is this confusion a cipher—a clue to a hidden meaning? Or is it just null, a zero, without substance? It could be either.

The moment for our decision arrives quickly. After the second call, the father looks over the gift for his son: the ten little jars, each containing a different fruit jelly. He "re-examined with pleasure the luminous yellow, green, red little jars. His clumsy moist lips spelled out their eloquent labels: apricot, grape, beech plum, quince. He had got to crab apple, when the telephone rang again" (p. 70). And so the story ends. What has happened? Who is calling? Surely most readers of the story will feel that the hospital is calling to tell them of their son's suicide, an event the mother anticipated at the first call. This is the *third* call, a most prophetic and ominous number. The sequence of "eloquent labels," from apricot to quince, has been broken by the flat, cramped sound of "crab apple," fruit which is tart or sour while the others are luscious and ripe; it is an easy step to conclude that the sequence of wrong numbers has also been broken, by the "right" number, bringing bad news. And surely short stories aren't supposed to end with something as inconclusive as a wrong number? It seems that Nabokov has engendered in the reader (who eagerly assists him) a serious case of referential mania. A "cipher"

213

can be a nullity just as easily as it can be a key, but most readers will see it as a key; we will conclude that the third call is from the hospital. In so doing, we will have assigned a meaning to the signs based on something outside the closed system; we will have, in effect, participated with Nabokov in killing the boy. The overdose of meaning is our own; we can't accept a third random phone number, but must see the "death-pattern" completed, because that is the way our minds work. Nabokov made use of the same fact when he seemingly broke Pnin's punch bowl; but the pattern there, as here, was completed only in the reader's mind, not in the work itself. Enough for Nabokov to have suggested the possibility.

This strikes to the very nature of a created, fictional world and the kind of relationship a reader has to it. We have felt pity for the boy, sympathized with the parents, but probably separated ourselves from the boy's mania. It is our very participation in that mania, however, the need to see a completed pattern, that has "killed" the boy. It is just as plausible to argue, though, that the signs and symbols of death have no logically inherent and inescapable conclusion, that they point to nothing finally, and are as "meaning"-less as a sequence of random numbers. It is this ambiguity which makes the story so profoundly eerie. The "cipher" is constructed so that we have to supply a key, constitutionally unable to admit the possibility that there is none. As in *Pnin,* we find ourselves, as fully engaged readers, seemingly exemplifying what we would prefer to reject, and vice versa. Both fictions encourage a denial of the power that informs them. Where is the essential paradox to be located, then—in the reader or in the author?

Both (the coward's answer). There obviously *are* patterns in Nabokov's fictions.[18] In *Speak, Memory,* Nabokov himself, moreover, after relating a coincidence involving a Russian general and a match, says that "the following of such thematic designs through one's life should be, I think, the true purpose of autobiography" (p. 27).[19] We perceive similar themes in every novel, every story. As Joan Clements, speaking of an unknown author, pants in *Pnin:* "But don't you think—haw—that what he is trying to do—haw—practically in all his novels—haw—is—haw—to express the fantastic recurrence of certain situations?" (p. 158). Undoubtedly, we answer, for we have seen them. The rhetorical strategy of "Signs and Symbols" and, less clearly, of *Pnin* is first to offer "meaning" and "theme," to give us signs and the "fantastic recurrence of certain situations," and then deny or limit the pattern, to refuse to complete it and ask, with the innocence of a child, what pattern? It is yours, not mine. So we not only are *not* put off by coincidence and fantastic recurrence, by a pattern of signs; we are instead implicated in the pattern more deeply than we ever thought possible. The author's self-consciousness in these cases does *not* distance us, as critics tell us it usually does; rather, it draws us into the web of esthetic responsibility, and our anger at the cruel fates which torment Pnin and the boy deflects from the author and redounds on ourselves, his co-authors. The most remarkable thing about the whole process is that, somehow, we participate in both worlds, in that of the character and the author, creature and creator.

Nabokov tells us in *Speak, Memory* that "competition in chess problems is not really between White and Black but between the composer and the hypothetical solver (just as in a first-rate work of fiction the real clash is not between the characters but between the author and the world), so that a great part of a problem's value is due to the number of 'tries'—delusive opening moves, false scents, specious lines of play, astutely and lovingly prepared to lead the would-be solver astray" (p. 290). The metaphors Nabokov employs here—"competition," "clash,"—are, for once, misleading, for they suggest an absolute barrier between author and reader, an offputting haughtiness. Thus Gass misconstrues the distinction between game and problem: "it's ourselves the moves are made against: we are the other player. Most of Nabokov's novels... are attacks upon their readers" (p. 116). This is too crude, I think. In a game, the competition is everything; in a problem, the solver reenacts the creative process of the composer, preferably in the same sequence of moves. The solver must become, as far as is possible, the composer's double, his co-author, in effect. The relationship established between solver and composer, reader and author, is thus a bond of sharing, not an irreconcilable division. The greater authority is still on the author's side, admittedly, but in *Pnin* and "Signs and Symbols," at least, we share with Nabokov, for a moment, the incomparable eminence of the view from on high. It is a complex, and breathtaking, accomplishment. The nature of the trick is, I think, impossible to achieve in more traditional forms of fiction.

Through this labyrinthine process, finally, Nabokov has shown us what it is like to live in his world, and simultaneously reminded us of our position in our own. Ada tells Van of a similar feeling: "In 'real' life we are creatures of chance in an absolute void—unless we be artists ourselves, naturally; but in a good play I feel authored, I feel passed by the board of censors, I feel secure, with only a breathing blackness before me (instead of our Fourth-Wall Time), I feel cuddled in the embrace of puzzled Will (he thought I was you) or in that of the much more normal Anton Pavlovich, who was always passionately fond of long dark hair" (p. 426). In "Signs and Symbols" or *Pnin*—in virtually all of Nabokov's fiction—we are required to become "artists ourselves," to assign and to be assigned meaning, with the result that the "monstrous darkness" the mother in "Signs and Symbols" fears is mitigated, at least, into a "breathing blackness," one which is not merely a "void," but a blackness which may also be a cipher that is a sign, a letter (and hence a meaning) instead of a zero. All of us, everything, is "authored" in one sense or another. It is the special achievement of Nabokov's fiction that it induces a confirmation of this in us, that it represents a confirmation in itself. Better to be a "galley slave," laboring in service of the printed word, than not to feel "authored" at all. It is a very small affirmation, to be sure, but we are grateful for all such things these days.

NOTES

1. "Vladimir Nabokov: An Interview," *Paris Review,* No. 41 (Summer-Fall, 1967), p. 96.

2. "An Interview with Vladimir Nabokov," by Alfred Appel, Jr., in *Nabokov: The Man and His Work,* ed. L. S. Dembo (Madison, Wisc., Univ. of Wisconsin Press, 1967), p. 25.

3. William H. Gass, *Fiction and the Figures of Life* (New York, Vintage Books, 1972).

4. Vladimir Nabokov, *Pnin* (New York, Avon Books, 1959). Textual references are to this edition.

5. Other puns in his name: "Pun-neen" *(Pnin,* p. 26); "Think of the French word for 'tire': *punoo" (Pale Fire* [New York, G. P. Putnam's Sons, 1962] p. 268).

6. Andrew Field, *Nabokov: His Life in Art* (Boston, Little Brown, 1967), p. 139.

7. A number of critics have recently examined this aspect of the novel in greater detail. Among them: Charles Nicol, "Pnin's History," *Novel,* IV, 3 (Spring, 1971), 197-208; Paul Grams, *"Pnin:* The Biographer as Meddler," *Russian Literature Triquarterly,* No. 3 (Spring, 1972), 360-9.

8. Field, p. 132.

9. It seems that a certain "Vladimir Vladimirovich," an entomologist whose knowledge may be "merely a pose," is the narrator (p. 127).

10. Cf. the reading of this scene by Julia Bader in *Crystal Land: Artifice in Nabo-*

216

kov's English Novels (Berkeley, Univ. of California Press, 1972), pp. 86-8.

11. Vladimir Nabokov, *Nabokov's Dozen* (London, Heinemann, 1959), 62-70. Textual references are to this edition.

12. Vladimir Nabokov, *The Defense* (New York, G. P. Putnam's Sons, 1964). Textual references are to this edition.

13. "Spy" is one of the possible synonyms for the Russian word which Nabokov eventually translated as *The Eye* (New York, Phaedra, 1965). Another possibility was "watcher" ("Foreword").

14. Discretion forbids entering the controversy over whether Shade, Kinbote, or Prof. Botkin is the "primary" narrator of *Pale Fire*.

15. "One of the few words which mean nothing without quotes"—"On a Book Entitled *Lolita*," in *Lolita* (New York, G. P. Putnam's Sons, 1955), p. 314.

16. *The Philosophical Works of Descartes*, trans. E. S. Haldane and G. R. T. Ross (Cambridge, Cambridge Univ. Press, 1968), I, p. 148.

17. Vladimir Nabokov, *Ada* (New York, McGraw-Hill, 1969). Textual references are to this edition.

18. As pointed out in the articles and books by Andrew Field, Julia Bader, Charles Nicol, and Paul Grams.

19. Vladimir Nabokov, *Speak, Memory* (New York, G. P. Putnam's Sons, 1966). Textual references are to this edition.

217

A CHRONOLOGY OF *PALE FIRE*

1825

Thurgus Vseslav born in Zembla.

1845

Thurgus the Third becomes King of Zembla.

1852

Samuel Shade born.

1855

Conmal, Duke of Aros, born.

1869

Maud Shade born.

1873

Alfin Vseslav born in Zembla.

1878

(Queen) Blenda born.

1880

Conmal begins his translation of Shakespeare's works.

1888

Iris Acht is strangled in her dressing room by a fellow actor.

1889

Zule Bretwit writes letters to his cousin Ferz Bretwit.

1890

Walter Campbell born in Glasgow.[1]

1898

March (approximately): Sybil Irondell born.
July 5: John Francis Shade born.

1900

Alfin the Vague succeeds turgid Thurgus (who dies some way or another) as King of Zembla.

1902

Samuel Shade suffers a heart attack and dies.

1908

Disa's grandfather builds the Villa Paradiso in Southern France.

1909

July (approximately): John shade suffers a strange blackout. He swoons every afternoon throughout the winter.

1912

Alfin flies an umbrella-like hydroplane into the sea.

1914

Oswin Bretwit born.

1915

Odon and Count Otar are born in Zembla.

July 5: Charles Xavier Vseslav born in Onhava. Jacob Gradus born in Riga.

1916

Nodo born in Zembla.

April: Uncouth, hysterical John Shade spoons with Sybil Irondell in the gloam of the Lilac Lane.

1918

Chirstmas: Alfin the Vague dies in an airplane accident. His Queen, Blenda, rules Zembla.

1919

(First half): John Shade marries Sybil Irondell. Fleur de Fyler born.

1920

Martin Gradus dies in Riga.

1921

Charles' Zemblan nurse says to him: 'My darling, God makes hungry, the devil thirsty.'

May 18: Franklin Knight Lane dies.

1922

Walter Campbell becomes Charles' tutor. Seven-year-old Jack Grey kills his father.

1923

Bonnie Prince Charlie discovers photographs of his father's death and has bad dreams.

1928

(First half): Disa born in Southern France. She spends the first fifteen years of her life at Villa Disa.

Easter: Prince Charles discovers the joys of sodomy with Oleg, Duke of Rahl.

May (first week): Prince Charles and Oleg explore Thurgus' hidden tunnel. Monsieur Beauchamp and Mr. Campbell play chess to a draw.

Summer: Prince Charles nearly dies of pneumonia.

Fall-Winter: Prince Charles recuperates in Southern Europe.

1929

Kinbote sees a blaze of bliss gracing the visage of a young minister. (This splendor of divine vision is reflected in July 1959 on the homely face of John Shade.)

1930

Duke Conmal finishes translating Shakespeare from English into Zemblan.

1931

Oleg dies in a tobaggan accident.

1933

The Shades spend the first part of the year in Nice.

Late April (approximately): Hazel engendered on the seaside.

1934

January-February (approximately): Hazel Shade born.

1936

July 20: Prince Charlie carouses at a formal ball.

July 21: Blenda, Queen of Zembla, dies.

August: Fleur de Fyler lives with Prince Charles for three days until ousted by the Representatives of the People.

August 30: Charles Xavier Vseslav crowned King of Zembla.

1947

July 5: King Charles meets Disa, Duchess of Payn, at a masked ball.

1949

(First half): Charles the Beloved prays the night before his wedding in Onhava Cathedral. Charles marries Disa.

Summer (approximately): Maud Shade suffers a stroke and is shipped to Pinedale.

1950

Countess de Fyler perishes in the crowded vestibule of the exposition of Glass Animals. Paul Hentzner's wife leaves him.

Late January-Early February: Maud Shade dies. John Shade espies this missive scrawled on the trunk of a tree: *Life is a message scribbled in the dark.*

February (approximately): Certain objects in the Shade household go on a psychokinetic spree. John Shade awakes to find his table standing outside on the snow.

1951

Summer: Revolution flickers in Zembla with the explosion at the glass factory.

1953

King Charles banishes Queen Disa to Cap Turc ("for reasons of health").

1955

Uncle Conmal translates Kipling's "The Rhyme of the Three Sealers" and dies. King Charles begins to teach literature at Onhava University.

1956

Charles the Beloved visits Disa in Southern France. The Oxford translation of Kinbote's book on surnames is published.

October: Hazel Shade (once with Jane Provost, once alone, and once with her parents) investigates certain psychic phenomena in the Hentzner barn.

1957

John Shade publishes *Supremely Blest.* Paul H. Jr. becomes head of the English department at Wordsmith College.

March: Hazel Shade drowns herself in a lake at Lochan Neck.

1958

Summer: The Shades vacation in Italy. Hurricane Lolita sweeps from Florida to Maine.

May 1: Revolution breaks out in Zembla. Queen Disa writes King Charles a wild letter.

June 1-15 (?): The Extremists confine Charles to the palace.

June: Disa leaves the Riviera in a romantic attempt to return to Zembla. The Karlists change her mind at Stockholm.

July-August: Andronnikov and Niagarin search Onhava Palace in quest of the crown jewels.

Mid-August: The Extremists transfer the king's cot and pot to a dismal lumber room (formerly Thurgus' dressing room) on the first floor. King Charles escapes the palace through a hidden tunnel, climbs the eastern slopes of Mt. Mandevil, and flees across the sea.

Late August: Disa leaves Cap Turc again. She learns in Brussels that Charles has escaped.

September (early): Charles the Beloved visits Lavender in Lex, spends the night with gorgeous Gordon in the Grotto, and surveys the twinkling ripples of Lake Geneva.

September (later): King Charles visits Disa at the Villa Paradiso, and then goes to Paris.

September-(early) October: Charles visits the quays of Nice and Mentonne.

October 17: John Shade suffers a heart attack and glimpses the next life while lecturing at the Crashaw Club.

October 18-20 (approximately): King Charles parachutes into a field of weeds near Baltimore.

October (last two weeks): Shade recovers quickly and returns to the lectern.

November-December: Charles meets the famous American campus Preisdent, Billy Reading, cavorts in the libraries of New York and Washington, and spends a pleasant Christmas in Florida.

1959

February 5 (Thursday): Kinbote moves into the suburban house (Judge Goldsworth's) next door to the Shades.

February 9-14 (approximately): Hoping to proffer a ride campusward to his stranded neighbors, Kinbote falls down and is nearly run over by them.

February 16 (Monday): Kinbote and Shade are formally introduced in the faculty club.

February 20 (approximately): Kinbote drives Shade home from school. Sybil introduces herself to Kinbote.

February (last week): Kinbote begins to peer through his windows into Shade's house.

Spring: Odon directs a film in France.

March: As the night winds blow, Kinbote fears for his life. At Professor C's house, Kinbote watches the poet reshaping the world.

March 14: Kinbote dines at the Shades'.

March 22 (approximately): Bob the bad boarder takes a color photo of Kinbote and Shade.

March 27, Good Friday (approximately): Kinbote makes a short trip to Washington, not before seeing Shade shaving in the bathtub.

March 30: Kinbote returns home: Bad Bob is banished.

April: Kinbote and Shade stroll in the light April rain discussing prejudice.

April 2 (Thursday): Kinbote writes a letter to Disa, warning her to be more careful.

April 6 (Monday): Kinbote receives a letter (from Disa in Southern France) which quotes an early Shade poem. *[Also approximately at this time]:* He undergoes a maddening and embarrassing experience at the college indoor swimming pool and hires Balthazar, the black gardener.

May: In the course of an evening ramble with Shade, Kinbote speaks of King Charles, Disa, and Zembla.

May 23 (Saturday): Kinbote has a cozy supper at the Shades'.

June: Kinbote and Shade take nine sunset rambles.

Mid-June (morning): Kinbote presents Shade a map of Onhava Palace and stays for lunch.

June 23: Kinbote and Shade play chess (a draw), discuss God (the big G), and life after death.

June (last week): John Shade composes "The Swing."

July 1 (approximately): Disa leaves the Riviera for Italy.

July 2 (Thursday): A few minutes after midnight, Shade pens the first lines of *Pale Fire.* A playing card determines that Gradus will pursue the king.

July 3 (Friday): Shade's head creases Sybil's pillow for the three-thousand-nine-hundred-and-ninety-ninth time. Kinbote learns from Sybil that Shade has begun a really big poem.

July 4 (Saturday): Gradus the Gunman prepares to leave Zembla. Evening: Kinbote attends a party where he undergoes a series of unfortunate setbacks. Shade completes Canto One.

July 5 (Sunday): Today John Shade is sixty-one. Charles Kinbote and Jacob Gradus are both forty-four. Happy Birthday. Shade begins Canto Two (on his fourteenth index card) early in the morning. At noon, Gradus leaves Onhava on the Copenhagen plane. Kinbote arrives home at last (6:00 P. M.), where, freshly showered, he spies on Shade's party.

July 6 (Monday): Sunrise: Shade's head creases Sybil's pillow for the four-thousandth time.[2] Morning: Kinbote presents Sybil with a beribboned gift for her husband. Evening: Strolling Kinbote speaks of Zembla, while limping Shade discourses on flora and fauna. Gradus buys a brown suit and a trilby in Copenhagen.

July 7 (Tuesday): Kinbote takes *v. officinalis,* and learns from Dr. Ahlert that the Shades are planning to spend August in Cedarn, Utana. Gradus flies from Copenhagen to Paris where he visits Oswin Bretwit. Shade concludes the first twenty-four cards and two-hundred-and-ninety lines of his poem.

July 8 (Wednesday): Oswin Bretwit dies under the knife.

July 10 (Friday): Kinbote rents a cabin in Cedarn, Utana for the month of August. As Shade writes lines 406-16 on his thirty-third index card, Gradus drives from Geneva to Lex, to see Odon at Lavender's, and meets Gordon, the kingly consort. Gradus later stands at the road by where Kinbote had stood a few months previously. He returns to Geneva as Shades takes a fresh card.

July 10-14: Gradus remains fretting in Geneva.

July 11 (Saturday): Shade completes the second canto of *Pale Fire.* Kinbote disturbs the weeping Shades. Gradus visits a Finnish bathhouse, where he glimpses his bare feet.

July 12 (Sunday): Shade begins Canto Three.

July 14 (Tuesday): Dr. Sutton's daughter (the president of Sybil's women's club) accosts Kinbote in a grocery store, and calls his disagreeable and insane.

July 15 (Wednesday—St. Swithin's Day): Convivial Kinbote interrupts Shade as he reads his unfinished poem to Sybil. (Afternoon): Gradus lands at Cote d'Azur airport. Later he glimpses Niagarin break into the Villa Disa and discover a letter from the king.

July 16 (Thursday): Shade composes lines 698-746. Izumrudov visits Gradus in Nice and sends him to New York.

July 18 (Saturday): Shade fabricates lines 797-809. (Evening): Gradus takes a train from Nice to Paris.

July 19 (Sunday): Morning: Kinbote prays in two different churches. Afternoon: Shade completes Canto Three and begins Canto Four. Kinbote bursts into tears over the phone. Kinbote and Shade have a brief, inconclusive, and misleading talk.

July 20 (Monday): Evening: Gradus arrives in New York. Shade completes his nine-hundred-and-forty-eighth line and his seventy-sixth card.

July 21 (Tuesday): Morning: Jack Grey escapes from The Institute of Criminally Insane. Evening: Jack Grey unwittingly kills John Shade. Kinbote secretes *Pale Fire* under the Goldsworth girls' galoshes.

July 22 (Wednesday): Sybil consigns Shade's poem to Kinbote who sews it into the pockets of his coat.

July 22-28 (approximately): Kinbote visits Jack Grey in prison (once, perhaps twice). Jack Grey slits his own throat.

July 24 (Friday): Professor C. affirms (in a newspaper interview) that *Pale Fire* consists of disjointed drafts, none of which yields a definite text.

July 25 (Saturday): Sybil Shade asserts that her husband never intended to go beyond four parts.

July 24-27 (approximately): Sybil Shade leaves New Wye for Quebec.

July 28 (approximately): Kinbote flies from New Wye to New York.

August (first week): Kinbote procures a publisher.

August (second week, approximately): Kinbote visits Jane Provost in Chicago. Kinbote arrives in Cedarn, Utana.

August: "The Nature of Electricity," a poem by John Shade, appears posthumously in *The Beau and the Butterfly.* Sibilant Sybil Shade's translations appear in *Nouvelle revue canadienne.* Professor Hurley publishes an Appreciation of John Shade's published works.

August-October: Kinbote composes his Commentary, Foreword, and Index.

October: Kinbote reads the Letters of Franklin Lane.

October 19: Kinbote finishes the Foreword, applies the last daubs of paint to his edition of the poem, and (according to Nabokov[3]) at last surrenders utterly to the perfect safety of wooed death.

NOTES

1. I have excluded those items which appear irrelevant, and those readily available in the index (e.g., Queen Yaruga drowns in an ice-hole on the first day of 1800; Romulus Arnor is born in 1914), as well as those which are very vague (e.g., Gradus becomes a revolutionary during the thirties; Shade lectures at the Institute of Preparation for the Hereafter between (approximately) 1934 and 1940. Because Nabokov loves and lauds the odd detail, labeling any fact in his novels extraneous is a difficult and ultimately arbitrary process.

2.   We have been married forty years. At least
       Four thousand times your pillow has been creased
       By our two heads. Four hundred thousand times
       The tall clock with the hoarse Westminster chimes
       Has marked our common hour.   *(Pale Fire,* lines 275-79)

There are roughly three hundred and fifty thousand hours in forty years. This, of course, is probably an example of poetic license.

3. In an interview Nabokov said: "I think it is so nice that the day on which Kinbote committed suicide (and he certainly did after putting the last touches to his edition of the poem) happens to be both the anniversary of Pushkin's Lyceum and that of 'poor old man Swift's' death..." Interview with Vladimir Nabokov, *Nabokov: the Man and His Work,* ed. L. S. Dembo (Madison, 1967).

Nabokov might be lying, of course, but I think not. Apart from the veritable clarion of internal evidence, there is this fatidic touch (p. 157). When Kinbote discusses suicide with himself, he says: "If you rent a cell in the luminous waffle, room 1915 [the date of his birth] or 1959 [the omened date of his death], in a tall business center hotel browing the star dust, and pull up the window, and gently—not fall, not jump—but roll out..."

Alden Sprowles

PRELIMINARY ANNOTATION TO
CHARLES KINBOTE'S COMMENTARY ON "PALE FIRE"

In *Pale Fire* Nabokov establishes through the narrative testimony of a completely unreliable narrator several possible versions of "reality," mixing and undercutting the evidence to sway conviction from one version to another as the novel progresses. Although critical opinion is far from agreed upon the point, there is a definite sense that one of the versions is the "right" interpretation: the difficulty is in supporting one conclusively. The insane narrator at first appearance is Charles Kinbote, a perverted professor at Wordsmith College. His Commentary on Shade's poem slowly develops the position that he is the exiled King Charles of Zembla. While elaborate details support this idea, skeptical undertones put forth the proposition that he invents the entire story as a defense mechanism against an unhappy past, submerging his identity as Charles Botkin. Nabokov suggests peripherally that Kinbote is an anagram for Botkin, the Russian professor, but he never insists upon the identification, never provides the direct linkage.

Andrew Field[1] and Julia Bader[2] argue that Kinbote does not exist at all outside Shade's imagination, that Shade is the controlling author of the Commentary as well as the poem. Page Stegner suggests the reverse—that Kinbote is an insane genius who possibly invents Shade and writes the poem himself.[3] The difficulty with either theory is that the necessity for having a "master thumbprint" beyond Nabokov's own is unproved. Since there is never a direct statement from an internal controlling author, the proof depends on buried hints and artifical separation of genuine and artificial voices, all of which is rather spurious and pointless, as Mary McCarthy points out.[4] The acceptance of either proposition

1. Andrew Field, *Nabokov: His Life in Art* (Boston, 1967), Chapter Ten.
2. Julia Bader, *Crystal Land* (Berkeley, 1972), Chapter Three.
3. Page Stegner, *Escape into Aesthetics* (New York, 1969), p. 129.
4. Mary McCarthy, in a letter to *New York Times Book Review*, July 10, 1966.

adds nothing, indeed reduces the novel to an imaginative display by a character existing in a void, unknowable beyond his work. The Botkin-Grey theory, as first elaborated by Mary McCarthy,[5] poses no such difficulties, and can accommodate the problems bothering Field and Bader. Whichever theory is adopted, all give a definite impression that one view is correct; *Pale Fire's* intent is not to invite belief in the impossibility of ever knowing the "true reality," but rather the complexity and beauty of its manifestations, the

> *system of cells interlinked within*
> *Cells interlinked within cells interlinked*
> *Within one stem* (lines 704-706, "Pale Fire").

Nabokov introduces fiction within a fiction (specifically the Zemblan story within the Commentary's framework), and creates such an aura of reality and credibility that the interior story becomes believable and Kinbote's fantasy temporarily accepted. The interplay of the several fictions and the corresponding puzzle of their relative validity produces the curious effect of solidifying the picture of Shade and his poem. They are stable points, un-challenged facts obtaining a credibility comparable to that of the external world in novels with no internal derivative fictionalizing. Nabokov compounds the complexity by allowing his unreliable narrator to subscribe to several of Nabokov's own opinions and prejudices. These pronouncements are easily identifiable as Nabo-kov's on the basis of interviews with him and evidence in his other works, but they do not violate Kinbote's delicate characterization, nor do they limit or define his inner being. Nabokov's skill in working through a character's voice appears also in Kinbote's numerous unconscious revelations about his personality and real identity—the slips are not meant by Kinbote to deviate from his legend, but the irony is obvious. He thus allows vision through his unseeing eyes, giving the reader a fuller assessment than Kinbote intends. An interesting example is the matching games between Arcady and Zembla, arranged to suggest that these names trigger Kinbote's inventiveness and thus become incorporated into his tale. Simultaneously, his unconsciousness further develops his

---

5. Mary McCarthy, "A Bolt From the Blue," *New Republic,* June 4, 1962.

character, revealing his blindness, stupidity, obsessive viewpoint, and creative genius. While Kinbote relates his Zemblan legends, building towards his "surprise" revelation of his own royalty, he also lets the reader perceive his insanity, egocentrism, self-deception, homosexuality, and complete lack of control.

Kinbote's procedure in the Commentary offers the most obvious clues to his insanity. He rarely touches upon the poem itself, merely using a word or phrase to suggest a train of associations independent of the poem, but integral to his obsessions. He twists Shade's words to support his contention that "Pale Fire" is about King Charles' escape from Zembla and the impending assassination attempt, using spurious drafts, dubious interpretations, unproved allegations, and personal opinion to bend Shade's autobiographical and introspective poem to his purposes. Although unprovable, Nabokov lays enough clues to indicate that Kinbote did not tamper with Shade's text as given; the poem is a Fair Copy available for comparison with Kinbote's butchery of it to verify his insanity. A few examples of his inventive revision through interpretation are Kinbote's visions of Zembla in the poem and the incredible way in which Kinbote proves that the poem is living prophecy, with Shade literally creating history and events (especially in Gradus' movements) by writing them.

One difficulty resulting from Nabokov's distinctive style is the inevitable urge to emulate or parody it while criticizing him. In a logical extension of Kinbote's insane annotating (itself a byproduct of Nabokov's footnoting proclivities), all the evidence for the critical positions above follows in the form of annotation and commentary on Kinbote's Commentary. It is no doubt possible to isolate any one series of quotations and situations to argue any one point, but the act of isolation tends to deaden the spirit—part of the constant delight in reading *Pale Fire* is in the alternation and juxtaposition of themes, levels of perception, and versions of reality, and it is fit that this complexity and succession of themes and ideas be preserved. Many of the entries are obvious enough, but are necessary to indicate the wealth of details Nabokov employs for support of his artistic design. The list does not pretend to be comprehensive, merely picking some evidence for the critical ideas and dropping most of the duplication from Mary McCarthy's brilliant work, which remains the most perceptive and comprehensive criticism on the novel. Page numbers are given before each note, the first number referring to the G. P. Putnam's Sons hardcover edition (New York, 1962), the second number in parentheses referring to the Berkley Medallion paperback (New York, 1969).

GLOSSARY

13 (7). "There is a very loud amusment park right in front of my present lodgings":
   Kinbote's first intrusion into his annotation from his location at Cedarn, Utana, indicating the impure nature of his scholarship and the initial shift in orientation and "reality."

14 (8). "In a glass, darkly":
   From 1 Corinthians 13:12, though the exact wording depends on the version used ("in" or "through," "glass" or "mirror," "darkly," or "dimly"). The passage bears directly on the creative process and the definition of the "true" reality, especially as in verses 9-10 ("For our knowledge is imperfect; but when the perfect comes the imperfect will pass away"), and 12 ("For now we see in a mirror dimly, but then face to face. Now I know in part; then I shall understand fully, even as I have been fully understood").

15 (9). The first appearance of "pale fire": "As a rule, Shade destroyed drafts the moment he ceased to need them: well do I recall seeing him from my porch, on a brilliant morning, burning a whole stack of them in the pale fire of his incinerator before which he stood with bent head like an official mourner among the wind-borne black butterflies of that backyard auto-da-fé."
   This passage associates the fire with poetic inspiration, with the destruction connected with the poem, with Shade's preoccupation with death, and with the voyeuristic relationship of Kinbote with him.

18 (11). "Insert before a professional":

The sentence following this non sequitur remarks that a professional proofreader was employed. The direction survived in the final draft, obviously belying the professional nature of Kinbote's proofreader.

20 (12). "Concave inferno of ice":

A contradiction in terms, except in the *Inferno's* lake of ice surrounding Satan. Dante is more specifically applied later (see note to p. 198 [141]).

21 (13). Hurley's comment about a beauty in one of Shade's classes is later picked up by Kinbote for a little unjustifiable scandal about Shade's "other woman." Kinbote counters with remarks on his ping-pong tables, constantly identified with his homosexual ventures.

23 (14). "I explained I could not stay long as I was about to have a kind of little seminar at home followed by some table tennis with two identical twins and another boy, another boy":

Besides the ping-pong sexual innuendoes, this sentence provides an example of the word games Kinbote is fond of, the twinning of "another boy" to match the identicals and the assonance of ping-pong (which is the name the game goes by in all references but this one).

23 (14). "Henceforth I began seeing more and more of my celebrated neighbor":

Kinbote goes on to describe his first experiences as a Peeping Tom on the Shades' lives. He certainly saw more of them—peering unbidden into their house. Any doubt about the integrity, academic or otherwise, of the commentator is shredded by this innocent revelation, about which Kinbote is totally and blissfully unashamed.

24 (15). "Having, as it were, pardoned her husband for his friendship with an eccentric neighbor":

A juxtaposition joke similar to the note to p. 18 (11), since Kinbote's hypothetical "eccentric neighbor" is followed by his own crank call to his neighbor.

24 (15). Kinbote's self-delusion is shown in his remark that all Arcady envied him because of Shade's preference for his company. Gerald Emerald's comment is not at all envious—it is just derogatory (he names Kinbote the "Great Beaver"). Kinbote enjoys the *savoir-faire* with which he answers Emerald—by pulling his bowtie loose. His juvenile nature needs no other proof. Gerald Emerald is the first of the names to appear later in Zemblan history: Mary McCarthy traces the identity of Emerald, Izumrudov, Mr. Anon, and Reginald Green,[6] and Andrew Field points out that "izumrud" means "emerald" in Russian.[7]

25 (16). "You are insane":
A local lady imparts this sentiment to Kinbote, who feels so immune to the charge that he reports it to his readers. This remark also tips off that the intimations of insanity suggested by Kinbote's peculiar methods are not false.

25 (16). "Odin's Hall":
The Odin upon which Kinbote was scheduled to speak becomes transformed into Odon, Kinbote's closest Zemblan accomplice (disregarding his bedmates).

25 (16). "This friendship was the more precious for its tenderness being intentionally concealed, especially when we were not alone, by that gruffness which stems from what can be termed the dignity of the heart":
Kinbote has provided a comprehensive excuse for Shade's indifference or annoyance with him.

26 (17). "A sturdy cane that had belonged to his aunt Maud":
The cane is constantly associated with Aunt Maud, and is the first of several items that recur throughout the novel. The cane, an umbrella, and a bat all link in their repetition Maud, Shade, Gradus, and Alfin the Vague. They should not be forced into a symbolic pattern, serving rather to reinforce the "web of sense," the combinational nature of the fictional world.

---

6. Mary McCarthy, "A Bolt From the Blue," *New Republic*, June 4, 1962.
7. Andrew Field, *Nabokov: His Life in Art* (Boston, 1967), p. 312.

73 (53). "A young New Wye gardener, in whom I was interested":
The first appearance of Balthasar, Kinbote's black gardener in whom he is sexually interested and who eventually subdues Jack Grey.

75 (54). "Ultramarine glass" and "Muscovy glass":
Besides the palace and the two appearances of the theater, the Glass Works are the dominating feature of Zembla. Rarely is Zembla mentioned at any length without glass intruding, forming an almost parodic pattern. Zembla is a crystal land, however, an image produced through transparencies (imagination) and mirrors (art) making the omnipresent glass fitting as an emblem for Zembla.

77 (56). "Organizing strikes at the glass works":
All political activity originates at the Glass Works.

78 (56-7). The end of the note to line 29 has Gradus put to sleep as Shade lays down his pen for the night, seeming to suggest that Shade is the overall author. However, it is Kinbote reporting the congruence, forcing the union of the Zemblan assassin and the poem in a more subtle fashion than usual.

83 (60). The Goldsworth children are alphabetized, as is nearly everything in the house. The order has the "D" child as the oldest and "A" the youngest, involving planned parenthood by the Goldsworths. Continuing the transposition of New Wye names into Zemblan history, the youngest child's name, Alphina, is the origin for Kinbote's invention of his Zemblan father's name—Alfin.

83 (60). "A beloved Picasso: earth boy leading raincloud horse":
A Picasso painting from 1905, famous for the illusion of the boy leading the horse by the bridle—but there is no bridle. This illusion of leading is an effective metaphor for Kinbote's activity in his Commentary, referring to his control on the reader, although also applicable to the illusory connection between the poem and the Commentary.

83 (60). Kinbote sees Jack Grey's picture in Judge Goldsworth's mug album, giving rise to the immediate transfer to "Jacques d'Argus," but later becoming finalized into its anagram, Gradus.

Field and McCarthy both cover the permutations of Gradus' name and the games Nabokov plays with it.

85 (61). Kinbote describes his pattern in moving furniture as castling in chess. This is a small joke by Nabokov, since castling does bring the king and rook together, but also reverses their relative positions, which has no effect on removing the sunshine.

85 (62). Here is the explanation of Grey's motive for shooting Shade whom he mistakes for Judge Goldsworth: Kinbote mentions the revenge that many of Goldsworth's sentenced prisoners desire over him, but he immediately denies the validity of this possibility— he cannot admit it without destroying his Zemblan story: "He
> did not bring up... ridiculous stories... about this or that beast lying in prison and positively dying of *raghdirst* (thirst for revenge)—crass banalities circulated by the scurrilous and the heartless—by all those for whom romance, remoteness, sealskin-lined scarlet skies, the darkening dunes of a fabulous kingdom, simply do not exist."

This is the closest that Kinbote gets to admitting that Zembla is a fantasy, a romance designed to cover the crass banalities.

87 (63). "People who live in glass houses should not write poems":
Kinbote's twisted proverb gains its humor from his spying on the Shades, and his inevitable resort to a proverb dealing with (Zemblan, presumably) glass. Shade's retort appropriately switches "proverb" to "saws," thus furthering the pun.

90 (65). Kinbote's capacity for self-deception is well seen in Sybil's demonstrated knowledge of his peeping, yet he rationalizes his fall off the trashcan as a noise by the wind.

90 (65). "St. Swithin's Day":
July 15 is St. Swithin's Day (more usually Swith*u*n, though Swithun died on July 2. The choice of St. Swithun to mark the day is appropriate: "His shrine was splendid, but when it was
> looted by Henry VIII in 1538 its gold and jewels were found to be false.[8] See note to page 212 (152).

---

8. *The Saints,* ed. John Coulson, (New York, 1958), p. 423.

91 (66). Kinbote discovers that John Shade reads his poem to Sybil, after she had told him that Shade never reads an unfinished poem to anyone (p. 86 [62-3]). He is actually totally without Shade's confidence.

92 (67). "First time that...":
    Kinbote's ostentation is seen in his claim that his sentence is a literary first. The phenomenon he comments on—the reflection of distance and pain in the sentence structure—is present to a certain extent, but no strongly or successfully enough to warrant a note. The following sentence loses all stylistic control, and wanders very strangely until it comes to rest in "Dear Jesus, do something," as Kinbote's concentration degenerates quickly. Included in the sentence is an example of a favorite Nabokov target: the "famous avenue of all the trees mentioned in Shakespeare" is a wonderful instance of *poshlust.*

94 (68). The rejected variant contains one of Nabokov's cuts at Freud.

95 (69). Kinbote's note to "often" is a perfect example of his annotating foolishness—"often" can not possibly need annotation, and Kinbote merely uses it to jump off into another bit of Zemblan background.

97 (70). Kinbote describes the assassins as inside his head—a comment by him to indicate the pressure he is under, but unconsciously he speaks truly: "At times I thought that only by self-
    destruction could I hope to cheat the relentlessly advancing
    assassins who were in me, in my eardrums, in my pulse, in my
    skull..."
The passage mentions Kinbote's suicidal urges, tying together his invention of Gradus and his ultimate death.

98 (71). Reference to Balthasar as one of his lodgers fits nicely with the black gardener, as there is a late patristic tradition that Balthasar was a black Magus. "Heliotropium turgenevi" refers to Turgenev's *Fathers and Sons,* which has the "dusk and the garden bench, and a house of painted wood in a distant northern land."

99 (72). The variant offered here must be invented by Kinbote—it can not possibly fit into the poem or Shade's tone and central interests.

100 (72-3). Kinbote ludicrously expects Hurley's obituary for Shade to contain an etymology for Shade's mother's name. Kinbote then proceeds to give one, so that he can justify giving his own real name, Botkin, and its roots—incorrectly. He claims it to be "one who makes bottekins, fancy footwear," but it actually refers to a stiletto. He also throws in a gratuitous attack on Hurley, whom he attacks as frequently as possible—a habit also indulged with regards to Sybil Shade and Gerald Emerald.

105 (76). "Countess deFyler" and her daughter "Fleur":
Good punning names, matched in this passage by the sexual imagery into which Kinbote occasionally bursts.

106 (77). "All seven counselors, dressed in their formal splendor and carrying like plum cakes replicas of various regalia":
Plums appear frequently, another instance of a recurring pattern promoting unity and gathering their own connotations from their successive scenes. Plums' fruity, decadent, purple image is good for the pederast King Charles' tale.

107 (77). Kinbote's seal is the solitary black king, technically Solus Rex, the title of an unfinished Nabokov novel closely related in subject to *Pale Fire*. Nabokov frequently uses self-reference like this in his works (as Hurricane Lolita, p. 243 [172]).

108 (72). Kinbote scans his Zemblan verse completely mechanically, in a manner both clumsy and impossible in an Indo-European language. The three unstressed syllables are unlikely following "sagaren," and the stress on the inflected ending ("werem") is impossible. Both lines are scanned identically—most likely by counting syllables and automatically marking the accent.

112 (81). "Disa, Duchess of Payn":
Besides being an orchid genus (and one that does not survive transplantation very well) as noted on p. 213 (152), Dis, minus the feminine ending, is Dante's name for Hell and also a synonym for Pluto. "Pain" is a suitable continuation for such a start.

112 (82). "1950 Exposition of Glass Animals":
Gradus carries Zembla's predilection for glass animals abroad, pricing (but of course not buying) a crystal giraffe in Montreux (p. 198 [141]), and a violet hippopotamus at Cote d'Azur (p. 251 [178]).

117 (84-5). Kinbote is incredibly inane in trying to compute Shade's transfer of hours into grains of sand, completely missing the point and losing himself in irrelevant computation.

118 (85). The rejected draft Kinbote offers is again his own invention, it does not fit at all into the poem, and is a necessary piece for Kinbote to contain his story in the Zemblan castle.

120 (86). "Thule":
"Ultima Thule" is the name of an unfinished work by Nabokov, loosely connected to "Solus Rex," which itself reappears on p. 119 (85). Both have been translated from the original Russian and are now available. *Ultima Thule* was also the title of a novel by Henry Hadley Richardson (pseudonym for Henrietta Richardson Robertson) in 1929, about a doctor from Great Britain who displaces himself into Australia. It is unlikely that Nabokov knew of the novel.

120 (86). "Famous Glass Factory where the revolution flickered first":
The glass motif is further elaborated with "That must have been the explosion at the Glass Works in 1951—not war" (p. 145 [105]), and "an annex of the Glass Works where the Shadows happened to hold their meeting that night" (p. 150 [108]).

123 (89). The use of fire imagery with its attendant implications, is extended into the King's imagination, as well as Shade's: "And all at once that spark on that key caused a wonderful conflagration to spread in the prisoner's mind."

123 (89). Kinbote again steps out of his narrative tense to give an insight into his current state of mind outside the amusement park: "It would brighten a little these dark evenings that are destroying my brain."

123 (89). "He was a regular faunlet":

Nabokov's use of the male variant of nymphet, his invented word in *Lolita,* forms a game of semantics with his earlier novel.

127 (92). "They found Beauchamp and Campbell ending their game in a draw":

Beauchamp and Campbell are equivalent men: "Camp" can translate into the French "champ," as can "bell(e)" into "Beau." Their essential equivalency is reinforced by their equal chess ability—they draw. Later Kinbote flatters his own ability by reporting a draw between Shade and himself on p. 223 (159)— an equivalence between himself and the poet he tries to draw many times. A draw is the best resolution that Black can achieve in a Solus Rex (Solitary King) chess problem, and Kinbote (whose signet is the Black King), like Luzhin in *The Defense,* attempts to achieve this best possible solution to his life.

130 (94). Through Kinbote's voice can be heard Nabokov speaking on art: "This device which was apparently meant to enhance the effect of his tactile and tonal values had, however, something ignoble about it and disclosed not only an essential flaw in Eystein's talent, but the basic fact that "reality" is neither the subject nor the object of true art which creates its own special reality having nothing to do with the average "reality" perceived by the communal eye."

131 (95) "Somewhere an iron curtain went up":

Perhaps a reference to the Berlin Wall, erected August 13, 1961, while Nabokov was writing *Pale Fire.*

131 (95). "Nenuphar":

This means a water lilly or a plum-weevil. The latter is particularly nice, adding a different dimension to the connotations plums carry in the novel.

133 (96). "A sick bat like a cripple with a broken umbrella":

This is a gratuitous detail in King Charles' escape, but Nabokov inserts it to continue the pattern of umbrellas (linked to Alfin and Gradus), and bats (Gradus is later described as a bat).

134 (97). Kinbote's two appearances in the tunnel (also on p. 127

[92]), some thirty years apart, both lead to the theater where similar plays are being performed, both requiring Gutnish fisherman in the cast.

136 (98). Gradus also carries his umbrella faithfully, tying him in some strange way to Aunt Maud's cane and Alfin's plane misfortunes (p. 103 [75]). Kinbote becomes more overt than usual in his comment on his procedure of forcing Gradus into the poem's shape: "The force propelling him is the magic action of Shade's poem itself, the very mechanism and sweep of the verse, the powerful iambic motor."

141 (101). "Grunter (mountain farmer)":
A jest, scatological or linguistic—the farmer is defecating, for which a slang expression is "taking a grunt," and "grund" means ground or earth in Russian.

150 (108). Gradus is described as "a cross between a bat and a crab," further filling in the hooked (umbrella) and grasping (bat, crab) images.

151 (108-9). Gradus' existence, as initiated by his drawing the card designating which Shadow was to kill the King, begins at "0:05, July 2, 1959—which happens to be also the date upon which the innocent poet penned the first lines of his last poem." Kinbote gives a hint that Gradus does not exist outside the poem and its attendant circumstances. Kinbote does not start creating Gradus until Shade begins the poem, and he synchronizes the two through Shade's death and the poem's end.

151 (109). Gradus is a true Zemblan, both working and subverting the Glass Works—although neither successfully.

153 (110). "An especially brilliant impersonator of the King, the tennis ace Julius Steinmann":
Turning back to p. 153 (103) reveals that "a steinmann (a heap of stones erected as a momento of an ascent) had donned a cap of red wool in his honor." Kinbote's creative process is laid bare: Steinmann is from steinmann, which is "stone man."

155 (112). Pnin is mentioned as head of the Russian Department,

giving Nabokov another self-reference, and answering questions of where Pnin drove to when leaving Waindell. There is also a reference to Professor Botkin, who "happily" is not under Pnin.

155-6 (112). Several of Shade's opinions on literature, particularly those pertaining to over-interpretation and under-knowledge, are recognizable as Nabokov's own.

158 (113). Kinbote mentions his third ping-pong table, again clearly a homosexual reference. He also intrudes from the time of writing, with "Migraine again worse today," showing his deteriorating mental control as his Commentary proceeds.

159 (114). "My versatile gardener":
    Balthasar gives Kinbote "a much-needed rubdown," thus fulfilling partially Kinbote's sensual interest in him, although incapable of complete satisfaction (see note to p. 291 [206]).

161 (116). Kinbote says his birthday is the same as Shade's—which is also Gradus'. The identity of Gradus' life span with Kinbote's suggests that Kinbote's suicidal impulses started at birth. One suspects that he also alters his own birthdate to parallel more closely his idol's.

161 (116). "The fellow whose novels you and John think so phony":
    I suspect this to be a reference to Faulkner, who is named above.

163 (117). "See note to line 627. This reminds me of the Royal Game of the Goose, but played here with little airplanes of painted tin: a wild-goose game, rather (go to square 209)":
    This note is a complete mystery to all but Kinbote himself, as the Zemblan game is never explained and sheds no light on the story.

165 (118-9). "One of Aunt Maud's oils *(Cypress and Bat)*":
    Maud is now associated with the bat from the Zemblan tunnel.

167 (120). Kinbote indirectly tries to force his own name into a

discarded draft, this one possibly genuine: "Poor old man Swift, poor————, poor Baudelaire":

Kinbote decides the blank needs a trochee and the only one that fits nicely and needs to be concealed is his own (since Sybil, "a reader in the household," would have objected).

172 (123). "Which in these backwoods I cannot locate":
Another intrusion from Kinbote's writing location.

172 (123). Shade repeats a remark Nabokov made in *Speak, Memory* that the proper name of the particular Vanessa is Red Admirable, not Red Admiral. The Vanessa is feasting on plums.

174 (124). Nabokov's use of *Hombre,* Spanish for men, is from *Lolita,* here twisted to fit Shade, or *Ombre.*

179 (128). "Texture of time":
Prefiguring Van's preoccupation and book in *Ada.*

180 (129). Kinbote falsely identifies Bretwit as meaning "Chess Intelligence." It is much closer to brevity of wit, or nitwit.

181 (130). Dr. A——, or Ahlert, is Kinbote's name for Shade's doctor—later to be punned upon.

184 (131). Kinbote gives a one line variant of no use whatsoever, but conceivably a true one. There is a question of whether to accept this as a genuine variant, or merely one invented by Kinbote to have more credibility than his others, and induce belief in his Zemblan variants by having also an easily credible line. This is possible, considering Shade's remark that he burnt all his drafts, when he was through with them.

184 (132). For punning and innuendo reasons, the note to Line 334 is fine: "Would he ever come for me?" I used to wonder waiting and waiting, in certain amber-and-rose crepuscules, for a ping-pong friend, or for old John Shade."

186 (133). "Aunt Maud's favorite cane":
Maud's cane reappears in Shade's grip, entering him into the net of images.

187 (133-4). Kinbote inserts a cut on psychology professors which Nabokov undoubtedly sympathizes with: "required in her psychology course by a cunning professor who was collecting data on 'Autoneurynological Patterns among American university students.' "

190 (136). "There are always 'three nights' in fairy tales, and in this sad fairy tale there was a third one also":
This and the subsequent "three minutes pass" in the barn are the first set of threes to be exploited. See note to p. 198 (141).

195 (139). Kinbote includes an English Department memo referring to him as incompetent and deranged. There is no doubt about Arcady's opinion of him.

197 (141). "Lavender (the name hails from the laundry, not from the laund)":
The derivation he wants is laundry—lavendry—lavender, or launderer, washer. The name is not from the flower, the flora of the land (laund), completely inverting its expected connotations.

198 (141). Kinbote's use of Montreux is more self-referencing—Nabokov's residence is in Montreux.

198 (141). "The three index fingers of three masons":
In this scene at Villa Disa the threes proliferate, forming a parodic version of Dante's numerological use of threes in *The Divine Comedy*. It is carried further by Libitina (p. 198 [142]), where special emphasis is laid upon the "three i's" in the name of the Roman goddess of tombs and funerals—itself a continuance of the parody.

199 (142). "Gradus asked him, first in mediocre French, then in worse English, and finally in fair German":
Gradus uses three languages quite uselessly, adding another set of threes, but also laying the foundation for the joke on p. 201 (144).

199-201 (143-4) Kinbote's lustful imagination has Gordon change attire five times in the space of one scene, without breaking stride.

201 (144). "To tell him in three languages that he was wanted on the phone":
Capping the joke of the trilingual man.

202 (144). Again as a Gradus passage ends, "Shade took a fresh card," capturing Gradus in the poem by Kinbote's authority.

203 (145). Kinbote's quality of poetic judgment is made clear, where he prefers the rejected variant, probably his own invention, which is markedly inferior to Shade's choice (see the "flabbier" "Such verses as," and the clumsy "Smack of their heartless age").

204-5 (146). Villa Paradisa becomes Villa Disa, a pairing joke by Nabokov, dropping the "para" to invert Heaven into Hell.

205 (146). "May 1, 1958":
Nabokov uses one of his fatidic dates for the Zemblan Revolution, through its coincidence with May Day revealing more overtly than usual its subliminal, parodic ties with the Soviet Union.

206-7 (147-8). Disa is modeled by Kinbote upon Sybil Shade, as seen in their comparison, an ironic twist considering Sybil's and Kinbote's mutual antipathy.

208 (149). "Stood at attention":
A sample of Kinbote's sexual language.

212 (152). The joke on the Crown Jewels being hidden or lost is their parallel to Kinbote as King—as a homosexual he has lost his virility, or Crown Jewels.

214 (153). Kinbote as good as confesses that Zembla is invented for Shade: "My dear John," I replied gently and urgently, do not worry about trifles. Once transmuted by you into poetry, the stuff *will* be true, and the people *will* come alive. A poet's purified truth can cause no pain, no offense. True art is above false honor."

217 (155). "The young Negro gardener":
Refers back to Balthasar in the Foreword. An example of

Nabokov's complex, internal referencing.

219-221 (156-7). A lengthy discussion by Kinbote on suicide, his inevitable fate. He also includes a reference to using a botkin, and calls special attention to it, as if it were an important clue to something—an attempt to let the reader pierce his identity.

220 (157). "Room 1915 or 1959":
In the midst of his suicide monologue, Kinbote chooses his birth-death dates for sample room numbers.

228-9 (162-3). Kinbote creates a little scandal about Shade's "other woman," by denying its validity while feeling compelled to mention its possibility.

229 (163). Pnin is again mentioned derogatorily (note to p. 155 [112]): "A farcical pedant of whom the less said the better." Also, Professor Gordon is here, who lends his name to the faunlet at Disa's castle.

230 (163). Sybil is allergic to foods starting with "a," connecting with Hazel Shade's experience in the barn, where the ghost gave a message heavily laden with "a's" (p. 188 [135]).

235 (167). "Two tongues":
This note lists a number of paired languages, apparently because this is all that "two tongues" suggests to Kinbote. The list contains four "English-Russian entries, and no other duplication, giving indirect support for Kinbote's really being in the Russian Department. The last item in the list, "American and European," is a non-parallel construction—neither is a language and the entry has no relation to the remainder of the list.

237 (168). Another ping-pong reference.

238 (169). Shade gives his attitude toward Kinbote, although Kinbote does not recognize it as such: "That [loony] is the wrong word," he said. "One should not apply it to a person who deliberately peels off a drab and unhappy past and replaces it with a brilliant invention. That's merely turning a new leaf with the left hand."

245 (173). Another appearance of plums, here in conjunction with cherries.

246 (174). Nabokov gives a hint that a "famous old Russian *chanson de geste,* generally attributed to an anonymous bard of the twelfth century," is a Zemblan forgery. The reference is to *The Song of Igor's Campaign,* about which there is a controversy of late forgery, but in his introduction to his translation of it, Nabokov denies the validity of the forgery claim; he is convinced of the poem's validity. Hodinski, the ostensible eighteenth century forger, is first mentioned in connection with the *"Kong-skugg-sio (The Royal Mirror)"* (p. 75 [55]), the fictional embodiments of *The Song of Igor's Campaign,* as the collector of its variants, not as its forger. Kinbote either changes his views on the matter, loses consistency of imaginative creation of Zembla, or is slyly revealing the true situation late.

250 (177). Dr. "Ahlert" from earlier becomes an "alert doctor" here.

253 (179). After an attempt at castration, Gradus is laid up at Glassman Hospital.

259 (184). "The Bera Range, an erection of veined stones and shaggy firs, rose before me in all its power and pride":
Another example of Kinbote's pederasty leaking into his prose.

262 (185). The Word Golf game, which becomes a circular entry in the Index, is explained here, with Kinbote automatically picking examples turning on the novel's central concerns ("hate-love," "live-dead," "lass-male").

262 (185). Kinbote creates an appearance of integrity for his variants with his note desiring a draft reading "Zemblan king," but he explains it did not exist and he could not invent it.

266 (188). Nabokov slips in a jibe at one of his common targets—the literary worth of *Doctor Zhivago.*

267 (189). Kinbote as an anagram of Botkin is suggested by

Professor Pardon, and angrily rejected by Kinbote, who, clinging to his fantasy, prefers the more sympathetic contribution of fellow-poet Shade, who identifies Kinbote with regicide in Zemblan.

268 (189). Pnin referred to once more, in the description of how to pronounce his name ("laboriously pursing the lips," "punoo"), along with Shade's pun on "attack" and "puncturing," leading to Kinbote's continuance, "Flatman" (whose autobiographical data in the Index is perfectly correct). It should be noted that pedantic Kinbote does not make errors in matters he can look up in strange corners of libraries (as the derivation of Shakespeare's name on p. 208 [149]), but when his literary judgment is demanded, he is completely insufficient. The pronunciation device above is similar to Humbert's labial revelation of Quilty in *Lolita*.

272 (192). Kinbote is forced to admit that Zembla is Pope's, not his, by Shade's note by the side of the line containing the name. Even the name of his imaginary country is lifted from his New Wye experience, from his neighbor's scholarship and use of Pope.

274-5 (193-4). Gradus' excerpts from the *New York Times* are accurate, with the exception of the Zemblan items, of course. Nabokov picked out absurd items (as the note on the Queen, which is almost verbatim) or entries relevant to Gradus (as the costume jewelry). The names are rearranged, "Decker Glass" was originally "Thatcher," "Rachel" was "Charel," "Helman" "Lehman." Nabokov takes glee in republishing the foolishness of the tourist book and the weak literary judgment of Sandburg on Soviet literature.

276 (195). Gradus stays at the "Beverland Hotel," probably suggested by Emerald's epithet of the "Great Beaver."

280 (198). "Small Browning":
The only possible artistic choice for the gun in a novel so laden with Browning-like nuances and irony.

280 (198). "Three students lying on the grass suggested he try the Library, and all three pointed to it across the grass":

A replaying of the earlier scene with the masons on p. 198 (141).

282 (199). "A baldheaded suntanned professor":
Identified as Pnin by Nabokov in "Anniversary Notes," Supplement to *Triquarterly* (Evanston, Illinois, 1970), p. 6.

284 (200). Kinbote gives the police report on how Jack Grey got to Goldsworth's house in order to kill him—and discards it as ludicrous.

289 (204). Yet another bat appears.

291 (205). The red flannel shirt Kinbote escapes Zembla in has its original in his gardener's attire.

291 (206). Kinbote makes explicit his interest and attempts with Balthasar, noting the frustrating impotence.

293 (207). "Cradled glass":
A major Zemblan product.

295 (208). The description of Goldsworth's closet matches closely the lumber room closet through which King Charles escapes, and is probably its original.

295 (208). "The gunman gave his name as Jack Grey, no fixed abode, except the Institute for the Criminal Insane":
Kinbote rejects Grey's identity as given here, later prevailing upon the weak-minded Grey to "confess" the Zemblan conspiracy before Grey's suicide.

297 (210). Kinbote reveals that the variants he liked so much are his inventions—he predicts Sybil, the only one with knowledge of the poem's genesis and contents, will reject them: "I do not doubt that many of the statements made in this work will be brushed aside by the guilty parties when it is out. Mrs. Shade will not remember having been shown by her husband who 'showed her everything' one or two of the precious variants."

299 (211). Kinbote confesses his need to center the drama around himself, to force everything to depend on his peripheral role:
"Because of these machinations I was confronted with nightmare problems in my endeavors to make people calmly see—without having them immediately scream and hustle me—the truth of the tragedy—a tragedy in which I had not been a 'chance witness' but the protagonist, and the main, if only potential, victim."

299 (211). Grey's motive is given, his mistaking Shade for Goldsworth, connecting with the note to p. 85 (62).

300-301 (212-3). Kinbote ends on a long note of paranoia, hints of the inevitable suicide, and his intentions of transforming Zembla into a work of art, thus summing up his own egocentric concerns for "Pale Fire." His last words are on his coming assassin:
"A bigger, more respectable, more competent Gradus—"
The better "shadow" that will kill him is himself; Kinbote means "regicide" in Zemblan (p. 267 [189]), and he will commit suicide after finishing his Commentary (as confirmed by Nabokov in an interview with Alfred Appel in *Nabokov, the Man and his Work* ed. L. S. Dembo [Wisconsin, 1967] , p. 45).

309-10 (218-9). Kinbote's petty malice omits H.(urley), C.(oates?), Emerald, and most of Sybil from the Index.

310 (220). Kinbote insists on giving an exhibition of his cleverness, showing how he worked his examples in Word Golf (see Lass).

314 (223). In a last plum appearance, Thurgis' nose is "like a congested plum":
After Sterne's and Rabelais' use of noses, this becomes a good sexual crack, bringing out some of the latent connotations of plums earlier in the work.

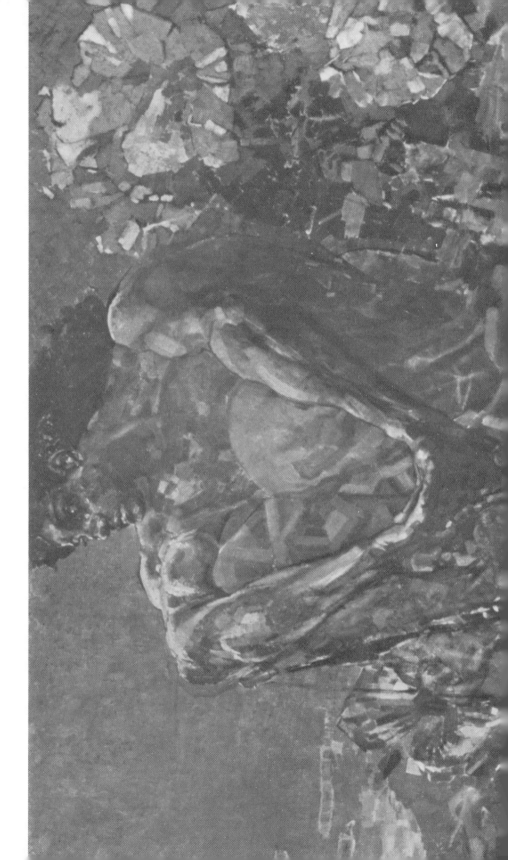

Carl R. Proffer

ADA AS WONDERLAND:
A GLOSSARY OF ALLUSIONS TO RUSSIAN LITERATURE

Antiterran readers would not find *Ada* baffling, but we on Terra suffer a curious vertigo when fifth-dimensioned in Nabokov's beautiful balloon to Ardis Hall and Kalugano. It is a world seemingly created by the bumbling brother of our God, an inept twin who has peeped over a galactic fence, but then hopelessly misarranged historical, geographical, and linguistic details when he patterned and peopled his new planet. For us, part of *Ada's* wit and charm comes from adjusting these ultramundane distortions, clarifying obscurities, elucidating allusions.

As we know from reading *Ada*, Antiterrans have three tongues. So does Nabokov. Since Russian is one which few educated Americans or Englishmen command, they are partially blind when studying *Ada*. The guide which follows is primarily for them. True, we can see through certain disguises using traditions which are closer to us—one does not have to be a Byronite to decipher "She Yawns Castle" (Chillon), or a Swinburnian to rearrange "the Burning Swine." Heinrich Muller, as the linguists say, "goes to" Henry Miller; Falknermann divides, like a bacterial cell in a *bete noire*, into Faulkner and Mann; St. Taurus and Chrion give us John Updike's *The Centaur;* Kithar Swain and "The Waistline" easily surrender T. S. Eliot; the Burning Barn episode and croquet played with "flamingoes and hedgehogs" derive from *Far from the Madding Crowd* and *Alice in Wonderland.* A fairly elementary knowledge of French changes Toulouse Los Teques to painter Lautrec; Montparnasse to Maupassant; "Bryant's castle" to Chateaubriand; and the "He traveled, he studied, he taught" which opens Part II back to "Il voyagea./ Il connut . . . / Il revint"—the opening of the penultimate chapter of Flaubert's *L'Education sentimentale.* More penetrating a bodkin is the "noble larva of the cattleya Hawkmoth . . . a seven-inch-long colossus, flesh colored"—an obvious allusion to the Cattleya Orchid which becomes a symbol of passion for Proust's Swann and Odette.

249

Nabokov's Russian distortions are harder to detect. While a few well-informed readers might know that "Ada" is the genitive form of "Hell" in Russian *(iz ada* means "from hell"—one proof that Demon Veen is Ada's father and Van her full brother), and a few will know that Sergei Aksakov wrote a novel-memoir called *A Family Chronicle* (divided, like Nabokov's, into five parts), how many, even among those who know Russian, could be expected to realize that the "Georgian tribesman . . . popping raspberries" (11/13) is a combination parody of a scene from Pushkin's *Eugene Onegin* and Robert Lowell's blundering version of Osip Mandelstam's satire on Stalin? Many of the Russian words and phrases in *Ada* are not translated. Sometimes these are bilingual puns which even a bilingualist will miss if he does not examine both members carefully. Russians may not notice that English sentences are actually translations (or adaptations) from Russian works. English song titles may be metamorphosed Russian romances—which the English speaker cannot know and the Russian speaker may well overlook.

The allusion may be a mere fleeting detail which the initiated reader uses briefly like a passing harlot. It is no great loss if one does not realize that the "elongated Persty grapes" described on page 251 are taken from a little known lyric by Pushkin. But *Ada* cannot be read intelligently if the clusters of allusions to works by Lermontov, Tolstoy, Pushkin, and Chekhov remain beyond the consciousness of the reader.

The general functions of allusion and parody of Nabokov have been treated in my own *Keys to Lolita* and Alfred Appel's *Annotated Lolita.* What follows below is a page by page explanation of Russian words, phrases, puns, anagrams, parodies, and allusions in *Ada.* * So that this guide can be used easily, every entry is keyed to both the original hardcover edition *(Ada or Ardor, A*

---

*The Penguin edition of the novel contains fifteen pages of "Notes to *Ada"* by Vivian Darkbloom. The laconic Mr. (or Ms.?) Darkbloom identifies a variety of allusions and translates much of the French and Russian. These notes are by no means comprehensive, and one senses a certain lack of authority in the annotator's occasional hesitancy and reticence.

Family Chronicle, McGraw-Hill, 1969) and the recent paperback edition (Fawcett Crest, 1970). The entry "123/1-4 (115)" means that the allusion is found on page 123, lines 1-4 of the hardcover, and on page 115 of the paperback. Because some of the items referred to are quite long, only the first and last words of each are quoted in this guide—so the reader will find it profitable to have a copy of Ada in hand as he uses it. Drugstores and drive-in beer vaults sell them.

SUMMARY OF MAIN AUTHORS ALLUDED TO:

TOLSTOY: 3/1-3, 3/7-8, 3/9, 4/14, 18/28, 19/9-10, 25/21-4, 28/27-29, 31/6, 61/8-11, 153/1, 171/15-16, 232/11-12, 240/18-19, 299/34, 323/31-32, 325/8-9, 348/6-7, 430/28-29, 490/26-27, 498/16-17, 521/27-28, 588/15.

PUSHKIN: 10/11-13, 10/15, 10/29, 11/1-22, 11/25, 31, 12/19-20, 13/5, 13/22, 107/8-10, 111/32-33, 158/6, 171/6-7, 251/24, 259/20-22, 313/33-34, 317/10-11, 398/28-29, 437/31, 443/28-31, 454/3, 481/16-17, 490/3-5, 511/33-34.

CHEKHOV: 115/16-18, 193/26-27, 193/28, 233/10-13, 235/14-18, 245/11, 272/5-10, 333/10-13, 399/15, 426/33-34, 427/4-9, 427/31-32, 428/3, 428/4-7, 429/3-4, 429/13-14, 429/15, 430/2-5, 430/23, 455/33, 498/16-17.

PASTERNAK: 13/22, 35/10, 53/23-24, 241/4, 371/15-16, 383/31, 409/6.

TURGENEV: 43/33, 105/26-27, 131/25-26, 249/2, 412/27-29.

AKSAKOV: 3/6, 149/12, 150/19-20, 151/1, 394/1, 406/18, 408/14.

GLOSSARY

3/1-3 (13). "All happy families . . ." Anna Arkadievitch Karenina.
   A reversal of the dubious generalization which begins Tolstoy's *Anna Karenina* (pub. 1875-77): "All happy families resemble one another, but each unhappy family is unhappy in its own way."
   "Arkadievitch" is a translator's joke, because it is the masculine form of the patronymic (spelled with the "t" of nineteenth-century translators); Anna's patronymic—"Arkadievna"—like her

Christian name is embraced by feminine "a's." Nabokov considers "Karenina" the wrong form for English and uses *Anna Karenin* in his own works.

3/6 (13). A family chronicle.

A Family Chronicle (Semeinaia khronika) is the title, famous in Russian literature, of Sergei A. Aksakov's nostalgic volume of memoirs about his immediate forebears (pub. 1846-56). Aksakov was descended from a Tatar named Oksak, Nabokov from a Tatar named Nabok.

Like Nabokov's family chronicle, Aksakov's is divided into five parts. The central figure of Aksakov's memoir, Stepan Bagrov, appears as a minor character in *Ada* (see note to 150/19).

3/7-8 (13). Another Tolstoy work . . . 1858.

The first two parts of Tolstoy's autobiographical trilogy (pub. 1852-54) are *Detstvo i Otrochestvo.* These translate as *Childhood and Boyhood*—not *Childhood and Fatherland*—a comic confusion of *otrochesto* and *otechestvo.*

Childhood is a frequent theme in Nabokov's prose, poetry, and prose-poetry. *Childhood (Detstvo)* is the title of a sixteen-stanza poem in Russian by Nabokov (pub. 1921).

3/9 (13). Daria ("Dolly") Durmanov.

Daria Oblonskaya, or "Dolly" as she is called, appears in the opening of *Anna Karenina* too. (She is Anna's sister-in-law.)

"Durmanov," an important name in *Ada,* comes from *durman* (a narcotic, dope), *durmanit'* (to intoxicate, dope, or stupefy).

3/10 (13). Prince Peter Zemski.

Contrary to an earlier ill-informed commentary, this name is not comic. It is, rather, close to that of the poet, critic, friend of Pushkin, and model (in one respect) for Pierre in *War and Peace,* Prince Peter Vyazemski (1792-1878).

3/16-17 (13). Severn Tories *(Severniya Territorii).*

The italicized name means "Northern Territories."

4/1 (13). Raduga.

"Rainbow."

4/3 (13). Kaluga.

A city SW of Moscow, pop. 164,000.

4/4 (13). Ladoga.

Lake Ladoga, NE of Leningrad, formerly St. Petersburg, is the largest lake in Europe.

4/14 (14). April 23, 1869.

April 23 is the day after Nabokov's own birthday. (Note also that July 21, Ada's birthday, is the day on which John Shade finishes *Pale Fire* and is shot by Gradus.) *War and Peace* was completed in 1869.

4/21 (14). The "D" . . . Demon.

The first allusion to the hero of Lermontov's narrative poem *Demon* (written in the 1830s). See note to 171/11-13.

4/25 (14). Durak Walter.

Durak means "fool," which Red Veen is.

5/9 (14). Lake Kitezh, near Luga.

Kitezh is the site of a famous old Russian church.

Luga is a form of the word for "meadow," and a town near the Nabokovs' Russian estate (see *Speak, Memory*).

7/31 (17). *Mizernoe.*

Bare, scanty.

8/18 (17). Dr. Krolik.

"Dr. Hare." Many puns are made on this name later, see for example, note to 385/8.

9/14 (18). Prince Ivan Temnosiniy.

The surname does mean "dark blue," as noted in line 18 and echoed in line 29 ("ultramarine") following an allusion to Proust's aristocratic family (Guermantes).

10/11-13 (19). A trashy ephemeron . . . famous Russian romance.

Pushkin's *Eugene Onegin.* The following paragraphs present a parodistic, unearthly version of *Onegin*. Pushkin's novelistic poem is a favorite theme for variations in Nabokov's works, beginning at least as early as *A University Poem* (1927).

10/15 (19). Prince N.

Marina is playing Tatyana in this travesty of *Onegin.* Demon bets Prince N. twenty-five rubles (a "rose-red banknote," p. 12, line 1) that he can seduce Marina-Tatyana. In Pushkin "Prince N." is Tatyana's husband *(Onegin,* VIII, XXI, 6), so if we fuse the works Demon is betting the man whom he will enhorn.

10/20 to 11/1 (19). Between two scenes.

The space between Chapter Three and Chapter Four of *Onegin* is filled by (1) tremulous Tatyana suddenly confronting Eugene in the garden, (2) digressions on love affairs by one of Pushkin's impersonations of himself.

11/1-22 (19). In the first . . . heaving breasts.

In Chapter Three of *Onegin*, Tatyana "goose-pens"a moonlight epistle, in French, to Onegin (Baron d'O), a local squire. Her Russian (hence Nabokov's "Eskimo boots") nanny clucks nearby.

The "flimsy" nightgown comes from Nabokov's description of Tatyana in a "flimsy shift" as he comments on Pushkin's drawing by a draft of EO, III, XXXII (EO Commentary, II, 396)—while the parodic violence and heaving breasts and quill pen are taken from Nabokov's contrasting description of a comical illustration of the same scene by Alexander Notbek (EO Commentary, II, 178).

11/25-31 (19). In a splendid orchard . . . fruit trees.

A parody of the berry-picking scene in *Onegin* (III, XXXIX-XL) where young girls sing a song about running away from men during their raspberry picking.

"Georgian tribesmen were popping raspberries" is a parody of two lines from Robert Lowell's ludicrous version of Osip Mandelstam's famous anti-Stalin poem:

> After each death, he is like a Georgian tribesman,
> putting a raspberry in his mouth. ("Stalin," 1934)

Stalin, of course, was a Georgian; and he appears in *Ada* as Col." St. Alin" (15/3) and "Uncle Joe" (582/20). Lowell himself appears in *Ada,* joined to Auden, as "Lowden." [More precisely translated the lines from Mandelstam are: "Every execution is a raspberry for him/ And he has the broad chest of an Ossetian."]

"Sharovars" is from *sharovary* (pants, not samovars, the well-known Russian tea-cookers).

11/32-33 (20). Dionysian . . . dance called *kurva.*

Kurva means whore. Another dig at Lowell who translates Mandelstam's *Kurva Moskva* (Moscow the Whore) as "Moscow's curving avenues."

12/7-8 (20). Her meeting . . . green tails.

In Chapters Three and Four of *Onegin,* Onegin appears from the side alley, but these spurs and tails seem fabricated.

12/15-20 (20). Last act ballet . . . belated advances.

There is a ball in the last chapter of *Onegin,* complete with Russian generals. The "metamorphosed Cinderella" is Tatyana who has changed from the impulsive ingenue whom Eugene lectured years before to a scintillating star in Petersburg society.

Pushkin's chapter and novel end suddenly when Cinderella-Tatyana walks away from Eugene, leaving him and us surprised that she has spurned the suspicious advances he makes while on his knees (VIII, XLI-XLVIII).

13/5 (20). Baron d'Onsky.

A "double" of Baron d'O. from the *Onegin* play. "Donsky" suggests Dmitri Donskoy, a medieval military hero and saint.

13/22 (21). "Eugene and Lara."

A combination of *Eugene Onegin* and Lara, the heroine of Pasternak's *Doctor Zhivago,* suggested by the fact that Tatyana's last name is "Larina." (Lenore Raven is a similar combination of Poe's "Lenore" and "The Raven.")

16/11 (23). Demon . . . crumpled wings.
Lermontov's Demon does have wings.

18/28 (25). Gavronsky.

The first reference to G. A. Vronsky, a filmmaker, and allusive namesake of Alexei Kirilich Vronsky, Anna Karenina's lover.

19/9-10 (25). 1869 (by no means a mirabilic year).

A trilingual pun: mirabilic is "mirabellic"—*mir* is "peace" (Russian), *bellum* is "war" (Latin). The publication of Tolstoy's *War and Peace* was completed in 1869.

20/22 (26). Great Revelation.

The Soviets call the October Revolution the "Great Revolution."

20/33 (26). New Believers.

The "Old Believers" were Russian schismatics. Nabokov seems to be combining the rather demonolatrous beliefs of the Old Believers with those of the Bolsheviks (pages 20-21).

25/21-24 (30). Ran away . . . same first name as hers had.

In *Anna Karenina* Dolly's children run briefly behind the bushes alone during a mushroom hunt (Part VI, Chapter V). Mushrooms are obscene fungi, and earlier in the novel (Part III, Chapter XI) the children are said to have "coarse animal inclinations." "Dolly" is the first name which Aqua and Marina share with the Oblonsky children.

28/27-29 (33). "Kareninian" . . . as deeply.

As Anna Karenina hurls herself under the train, she is suddenly horror-stricken and wonders what she is doing (Part VII, Chapter XXXI).

29/8 (33). Joan the Terrible.
Joan=John=Ivan the Terrible.

29/11 (33). Dark blue ancestor.
Prince Temnosiniy. See note to 9/14.

29/26-27 (33). *Teper' iz ada.*
A pun of the Russian for Sheherezade: she*xerizada.*

31/6 (34). Boyhood and youth.
Boyhood and *Youth (Otrochestvo* and *Iunost')* are the second and third parts of Tolstoy's autobiographical trilogy.

35/2 (37). Izbas.
Huts.

35/10 (37). Gamlet, a half-Russian village.
Gamlet is the Russian for Hamlet (note the hamlet in line 1), and the title of one of Doctor Zhivago's most famous poems.

43/8 (42). Sumerechnikov...Lumière brothers.
Sumerki means "twilight," thus a pun on the French "Light" brothers.

256

43/33 (43). *"Mimo chitatel',"* as Turgenev wrote.

Turgenev wrote things like this to the reader, but so far as I can determine, not in his peevish piece "Enough!"

45/32 (44). Russian *"hrip."*

"Hrip" means a "hoarse wheeze"—*gripp* is the flu.

53/23-24 (50). *Les Amours du Docteur Mertvago . . .* pastor.

Mertvago means "dead" (Old Russian spelling)—thus *The Loves of Doctor Dead,* a parody of *Doctor Zhivago (Zhivago* means "alive," "living") and its religious concerns.

61/8-11 (56). Special belletristic device . . . Lyovin.

Leo Tolstoy was one of the first Russian writers to use interior monologue extensively, and the first critical article in world literature on the subject of interior monologue is N. Chernyshevsky's "Leo Tolstoy's *Childhood and Boyhood,"* the same works mentioned on the opening and closing pages of *Ada.* A parodistic biography of Chernyshevsky forms one of the parts of Nabokov's other five-part novel, *The Gift.*

Lyovin is "Levin"—the hero of *Anna Karenina.*

63/6 (57). Stanislavskiana.

K. A. Stanislavsky (1863-1938) - the influential actor and director of the Moscow Art Theater.

64/6 (58). *"Angel moy"*

"My angel."

73/8 (64). V. V.

The initials of the well-known Russian poet Vladimir Vladimirovich Nabokov.

73/12-13 (64). *Kamargsky Komar* of our *muzhiks.*

Komar - mosquito. *Muzhik* - peasant. A play on the song and dance called the Kamarinsky, the purely folk version of which begins, "Oh you son of a bitch, Kamarinsky *muzhik."* With Nabokov's dash of French here.

79/20 (68). Liver . . . *pecheneg.*

A pun on *pechen'* (liver) and *pecheneg* (name of the fierce

Turkic tribesmen with whom the Russians had bloody encounters in the tenth and eleventh centuries—such as the one described in Nabokov's translation of *The Song of Igor's Campaign.*

82/17 (71). Vekchelo.
Anagram of *chelovek* - man.

92/12 (78). *Energichno.*
Energetically.

102/3 (84). *Mileyshiy.*
Dearest.

104/25-26 (86). *V skladochku . . .*case.
This rhymes with "Adochku" (little Ada).

105/25-27 (86). Turgenev's Katya.
Apparently Katya in *Fathers and Children.*

107/8-10 (88). *"Sladko!* (Sweet!" Pushkin . . . Yukon.
I have been unable to trace this one-word quote but for Nabokov's comments on Pushkin and mosquitos, see his EO Commentary, III, 280.

111/32-33 (91). Like the Marmoreal Ghost, that immemorial ghost.
An allusion to Pushkin's one-act tragedy *The Stone Guest (Kamennyi gost').* The "ghost" of Nabokov's English puns on the Russian *gost'* (guest). The marble statue of Donna Anna's deceased spouse appears at the end of the play, animated like the Bronze Statue of Peter the Great (see note to 171/6), and frightens Don Juan to death.

113/33-34 (92). *Zdrastvuyte: apofeos.*
Hello: apotheosis.

114/1-2 (93). *Les Sophismes . . .* Vieux Rose series.
An anagram: Rose-Stopchin=Rostopchin. Comtesse Sophie de Ségur (1799-1874) was *née* Rostopchine (to use the French spelling). Among her works is a volume entitled *Les Malheurs de Sophie,* published by Hachette in the "Bibliothèque rose illustrée" series. (Elsewhere in *Ada* "Hachette" is turned into "Ashette" or "little cinder," i.e., Cinderella, shading into Tatyana Larina.)

115/16-18 (93-94). "They've all gone" . . . Ranevski.

In the concluding speech of Chekhov's *The Cherry Orchard* the servant named Firs (pronounced "Fierce") says: "They've gone away... *(He sits on the divan.)* They forgot about me..." Mme Lyubov Ranevskaya is one of the main characters—Marina is type-cast.

115/31 (94). Telegas.

Not "tele-gas," but the Russian *telega* - a four-wheeled cart.

135/25-26 (106). Turgenev's *Smoke.*

A novel, published in 1867.

138/9-10 (111). *Sestra moya . . . Ladoru.*

"My sister, do you recall the hill,/ And the tall oak, and La-dore?"

143/31 (115). *"Horosho."*

Very well.

147/13 (118). *"Minirechi."*

Mini - small (Latin), *rechi* - speeches (Russian).

149/12 (119). Russian tutor . . . Aksakov ("AAA").

Sergei Aksakov was the author of another *Family Chronicle* (see note to 3/6), written before the American Automobile Association was founded.

149/34 (120). *Angelochek.*

Diminutive form of "angel."

150/19-20 (120). Aksakov . . . Bagrov's grandson.

In his *Family Chronicle* Aksakov portrays his own family under the name Bagrov. Aksakov himself was old Bagrov's grandson. And Aksakov has another work called *Childhood Years of Bagrov's Grandson.*

151/1 (120). Grandpa Bagrov wobbled in from a nap.

In Aksakov's *Family Chronicle,* Part One, Grandfather Bagrov wakes up from his nap.

152/9 (121). *Biryul'ki proshlago.*
Trifles from the past.

153/1 (122). Karamzin and Count Tolstoy.
Nikolai Karamzin (1766-1826) - a writer and historian whose Swiss experience is immortalized in his *Letters of a Russian Traveler.* Count Leo N. Tolstoy.

154/11 (123). *Traktir.*
Roadside tavern.

158/6 (126). Letter scene in Tschchaikow's opera *Onegin and Olga.*
Tchaikovsky wrote an opera called *Eugene Onegin* which Nabokov has frequently ridiculed—as he does here by suggesting that Onegin gets together with Tatyana's moon-faced sister Olga (in Pushkin's *Onegin,* Eugene calls her stupid, but does flirt). The letter scene is the same one described earlier in the play *Eugene and Lara* (13/22).

163/6 (129). *Sinok moy.*
My little son.

166/2 (131). *Lezbianochka.*
Little Lesbian.

170/9 (134). *Dura* Cordula.
"Fool" Cordula.

171/4-5 (135). Many-colored mountains . . . genius.
He has in mind the mountains of the Caucasus which inspired Pushkin, Lermontov, and Tolstoy.

171/6-7 (135). Pushkin's "Headless Horseman" poem.
An interfusion of Washington Irving's story "The Headless Horseman" and Pushkin's narrative poem "The Bronze Horseman" (written in 1833).
Headless Horseman is also the title of a novel by Mayne Reid, discussed at length in Chapter Ten of Nabokov's *Speak, Memory* (New York, 1966), 200-202.

171/11-13 (135). Allusions . . . diamond-faceted tetrameters.
Lermontov's tetrametric narrative poem *The Demon,* in which

the outcast Demon flies over the diamond mountains (see note to 180/15) of the Caucasus and falls in love with a maiden named Tamara. He seeks to regain innocence and good in her, but it ends in her death and the Demon's failure to take her soul from an eloquent angel. Nabokov repeatedly alludes to this poem in connection with Demon Veen, although the plot of the poem is less interesting than the melting fata morgana effects, the translucent tang of the demonic in Lermontov's verse.

171/15-16 (135). Tolstoy . . . tale of Murat, the Navajo chieftain.
Among Leo Tolstoy's late works is a long tale entitled *Hadji Murad* (written 1896-1904), about a gallant, rough-riding mountain chief. Here the name is fused with that of Marat, stabbed in his bath by Charlotte Corday (a scene also alluded to in *Lolita* and other Nabokov works).

180/15 (141). Diamond ring . . . like a Caucasian ridge.
In Lermontov's *Demon,* the outcast from Paradise flies high and:
Beneath him Kazbek, like the facet of a diamond
Gleamed with all its eternal snows (Part I, III, 3-4).

180/18 (141). Temporary Tamara . . . kasbek rouge.
Tamara is the temporary of Lermontov's Demon. Kazbek, one of the highest Caucasian peaks, figures prominently in Russian poetry of the Golden Age (1820-41).

180/22 (141). Caucasian perfume, Granial Maza.
Another bilingual play on I, III, 3 of Lermontov's *Demon:* "Pod nim Kazbek, kak gran' almaza." *Gran' almaza* (or Granial Maza) means "the facet of a diamond." See note to 180/15.

182/14-15 (142). P. O. Tyomkin . . . Sebastopol.
Prince Grigory Alexandrovich Potyomkin (1739-91) was in all senses of the word a favorite of Catherine the Great. The more famous battleship Potyomkin (or Potemkin) was the scene of a celebrated revolutionary encounter in Odessa (not far from Sebastopol, another Crimean town, from which Vladimir Nabokov left Russia), immortalized on film by Eisenstein, in prose by Tolstoy.
"P. O. Tyomkin, Odessa, Texas" is substituted for the English original's Coleridgian allusion "A. Person, Porlock, England" in

Nabokov's Russian translation of *Lolita*—and preceded by a comment that one does not have to be a cinematographer to guess it.

185/19-20 (145). *Pod . . . /. . . mandolini.*
    "The Blue Tango" in Russian.

187/6-7 (147). Ladies in yellow-blue Vass frocks.
    Nabokov notes that this mimics the Russian *ya lyublyu vas*—"I love you."

193/26-27 (151). Chekhov . . . 'diamonds'.
    Sonya, at the end of Chekhov's *Uncle Vanya* (produced in 1900), says: "We will rest! We will hear angels; we will see the whole sky covered with diamonds; we will see all earthly evil, all our torments disappear in the mercy with which the whole world will be filled, and our life will be peaceful, tender, sweet as a caress . . ."

193/28 (151). Uncle Van.
    Chekhov's *Uncle Vanya.*

195/26-27 (152). 'Obmanipulations' (sham . . .
    Obman is the Russian for deception, sham.

197/13 (153). Phillip Rack.
    Rak (apart from meaning "cancer") means "lobster," but its vulgate application designates that *Kama Sutra* position in which the woman kneels before the man. Rack is one of Ada's lovers (pp. 293-94), thus putting Van on the rack.

202/10 (157). Kalugano.
    Interfusion of Kaluga, Russia, and Lugano, Switzerland—one of Nabokov's current vacation and lepidoptera spots.

202/4 (157). *Kok.*
    Coca Cola.

217/26 (167). I'm Scheher . . . his Ada.
    Sheherezade. See note to 29/26-27.

219/2 (168). *Pustotsvetnost'.*
    Sterility, barrenness.

219/34 (169). *Ogon'.*
Fire.

223/28-29 (171). Baron Klim Avidov.
An anagram of "Vladimir Nabokov."

225/25-26 (173). Moronic Ozhegov . . . 52,827 words.
The Ozhegov dictionary is a standard Soviet lexicon which Nabokov periodically pans.

225/27 (173). Dr. Gerschizhevsky's reverent version.
Perhaps Herr Dr. Dmitri Chizhevsky, a Slavist who teaches in Heidelberg and is ridiculed in Nabokov's commentaries on *Eugene Onegin.*

225/29-31 (173). Four-volume Dahl . . . ethnographer.
Vladimir Dahl (Dal') [1801-1872] - the first major Russian lexicographer, also an ethnographer and short story writer from Gogol's time. His four-volume *Interpretative Dictionary of the Living Russian Language* (1864-68) is spectacularly rich in colloquialisms, dialectisms, and botanical terms. It was Nabokov's companion during his Cambridge days (see *Speak, Memory,* p. 265).

227/10-12 (174). LINKREM . . . Muscovy.
Anagram of "kremlin"—a fortress.

227/27 (174). TORFYaNUYu.
The adjective meaning "peat," accusative case.

230/12-14 (176). Dr. Krolik's cousin . . . Dr. "Rabbit."
Krolik means "hare," "zayats" *(zaets)* means "rabbit," favorites of gynecologists.

232/9 (178). *Chayku.*
Tea.

232/11-12 (178). The *ivanilich* . . . old hassock.
In Tolstoy's story "The Death of Ivan Ilich," a friend comes to pay his respects to the dead Ivan Ilich, and he sits on a hassock the lewd loose springs of which fight his behind.

232/32-33 (178). *Delikatno.*
Delicately.

232/34 to 233/1-9 (178). Griboedov's *Gore ot uma . . . that* one.

In Act I, Scene 7 of A. S. Griboedov's verse comedy *Woe from Wit* (1825), the hero, Chatsky, says to Sophia in two hexameters:

> It would often happen we'd be in the dark corner and what
>   harm might there be in that!
> Do you remember? We'd tremble, afraid the table would
>   squeak, the door . . .

The possibility for *double entendre* is clear.

233/10-13 (179). Scene with Kachalov . . . gesture.

Meaning Scene 7 in *Woe from Wit.* Kachalov was a famous Russian actor at the Moscow Art Theater.

The "Seagull Theater" is the Moscow Art Theater, founded by Stanislavsky. Its first success was Chekhov's *Seagull* (1898). In recent Soviet times the seagull sewn on the curtain has been replaced by a metal mobile representing a seagull.

235/14-18 (180). "Ada!" he cried.

This parallels and is partly a direct quotation from Act Four of Chekhov's *Three Sisters.*

> *Tuzenbakh (upset).* No. no! *(Quickly moves away, stops in the alley of trees.)* Irina!
> *Irina.* What?
> *Tuzenbakh (not knowing what to say).* I have not had coffee today. Tell them to make me some... *(Quickly walks away.)*

238/32-33 (183). *Gornishon . . . kameristochka.*

A combination of *gornichnaia* (maid) and *kornishon* (gherkin). A dimunitive of *kameristka* (lady's maid).

240/18-19 (184). Aunt Kitty . . . Tolstoy.

"Kitty" is one of the main characters in *Anna Karenina.* Her sister is married to Oblonski (Bolenski echoes this and the real aristocratic name Obolenski). In his earlier years Tolstoy was a dreadful wencher, and there are many parallels between Kitty-Lyovin and real-life Sophia Tolstoy—so in a sense Kitty did get married to Tolstoy.

241/4 (184). Sister of your Life.

Pasternak's most famous collection of poetry is entitled *My*

Sister Life (pub. 1922). It has special relevance for Demon Veen, because it is dedicated to Lermontov, and the opening poem is "In Memory of the Demon" *(Pamiati Demona)*.

245/11 (188). *The Cherry Orchard.*
An earthly play by Anton Chekhov.

245/14-23 (188). Old Demon . . . Lermontov . . . Lowden.
The iridescent wings allude to Lermontov's Demon again. In the poem the Demon does not swoop down on Tamara's castle—he visits her at night in a monastery, there implanting a satanic kiss on her labia, which makes her die.
"Lowden" is a combination of Robert Lowell and W. H. Auden.

249/2 (191). Ada is a Turgenevian maiden.
A maiden known for maintaining her maidenhood. Turgenev's novels and stories being heavily populated by virgins. (The Jane Austen miss, Fanny Price, is from *Mansfield Park.)*

249/25 (191). "Grib."
Grib means "mushroom"—and suggests Griboedov ("mushroom eater"), as well as obscene shapes.

249/33 (192). *Vodochki.*
Kinds of vodka (flavored with pepper, bison grass, etc.).

251/13 (193). *Zakusochniy stol.*
Hors-d'oeuvres table.

251/24 (193). Elongated Persty grapes.
This difficult allusion is to a not particularly well-known eight-line 1824 lyric by Pushkin—*Vinograd* ("Grapes"). *Persty* is an archaic, poetic word for "fingers." The last two lines of the poem, describing clusters of grapes, are:

> Elongated and transparent
> Like the fingers of a young maiden.

252/3 (193). Dr. Stella Ospenko's *ospedale.*
Ospenko is based on *ospa* - smallpox, *ospennyi* - variolar, i.e., pockmarked. Ospenko is in the hospital.

255/3 (196). *Ne pikhtite.*
Don't pant.

256/21 (197). Busybody Bess.
"Bes" is the Russian for "devil," "demon."

257/20-21 (198). *"Po razschyotu po moemu* (by my reckoning)."
Quoted from Famusov in Griboedov's *Woe from Wit,* Act II, Scene 1, lines 30-31. To be precise, Famusov mentions a recent widow who has not yet had a baby, but he reckons that she will give birth and that he will be at the christening. A hint at the matter of Ada's birthday and parentage.

257/23 (198). *Protestuyu . . . seriozno.*
I protest . . . seriously.

258/18 (198). Perun . . . god of thunder.
Perun was the Russian god of thunder.

259/20-22 (199). Vengerov . . . *Onegin.*
Vengerov was a celebrated literary scholar, but his real dates (1855-1920) give him less than 99 years (see Chateaubriand).
The plump, live oysters and cloisterers, are in the *Fragments of Onegin's Journey,* XXVI—Nabokov's translation goes:

> What news of oysters? They have come. O glee!
> Off flies gluttonous juventy
> to swallow from their shells
> the plump, live cloisterers
> slightly asperged with lemon. (Volume I, p. 343)

Nabokov has a paragraph on Tolstoy's description of oysters in *Anna Karenina* (Part I, Chapter 10) in his notes to this stanza.

263/27 (203). *Fal'shivo.*
False, fake.

264/26-34 (204). Lights in the rooms . . . husband.
Konstantin Romanov was a Grand Duke (during the reign of Nikolai II) who published poetry under the initials "K. R." Nabokov's contempt for the poetry is expressed in *Speak, Memory,* p. 223. These four lines are:

Uzh gasli v komnatakh ogni
Blagoukhali rozy
My seli na skam'iu v teni
Razvesistoi berezy.

Rozi are "roses," *beryozi* - "birches." —Tchaikovsky wrote music for this romance.

268/2 (205). Timur and Nabok.
Timur - Tamerlane (1336-1405). Nabok - Nabok Murza *(floreat* 1380), a Tatar prince, founder of the Nabokov clan.

272/5-10 (209). Dorn . . . on that question.
An exact quotation from Dorn's last speech in Chekhov's *The Seagull,* just before he tells Trigorin that Treplev has shot himself.

273/4 (210). *Gollivud-tozh.*
Hollywood, too. Perhaps also: Hollywoodish.

276/31 (213). Skrotomoff.
Scrotum off.

279/4 (214). *'Vyragences.'*
"French" version of the Russian *vyrazheniia* - phrases, expressions, profanity.

282/6 (217). Gamlet, the little Russian village.
Gamlet is "hamlet."

299-300/34-1 (230-31). She walked to the end of the platform.
Anna Karenina walks to the very end of a railroad platform to commit suicide. V. V.'s interior monologue, with phonetic associations determining the transitions, mimics Anna's thoughts before her suicide.

304/6 (233). Marquis Quizz Quisana.
A *kvisisana* was a cafe-restaurant in turn-of-the-century St. Petersburg.

309/27 (237). *Chervonetz.*
Ten-ruble note.

310/28-29 (238). Most Russian novelists . . . gentle birth.

Compare, in *Speak, Memory:* "No Russian writer of any repute had failed to describe *une rencontre,* a hostile meeting, always of course of the classical *duel à volonté* type . . ." (p. 151). Among the notable examples are: Pushkin (Onegin and Lensky) in *Eugene Onegin,* Lermontov (Pechorin and Grushnitsky) in *A Hero of Our Time* [both of these have been translated by Nabokov], Turgenev (Bazarov and Pavel Kirsanov) in *Fathers and Children,* Tolstoy (Pierre and Dolokhov) in *War and Peace.*

311/33 (239). *Palata.*

Ward. As in Chekhov's "Ward No. 6" ("Palata No. 6"). On p. 313 Van learns Rack is in "Ward Five."

313/33-34 (241). Like Onegin's coachman.

In a variant to I, LII. See VN's EO Commentary, II, 196.

314/9 (241). He be *tvoyu mat'.*

"Fuck your mother." The English "he be" is a phonetic approximation of the Russian "yebee" (*ebi*). The word seems a corruption of the English "yippee!"

317/10-11 (244). Your uncle has most honest standards.

The opening line of *Eugene Onegin* in Nabokov's translation is: "My uncle has most honest principles." Here Van says it to Rattner's nephew of Rattner—in *Onegin,* nephew Eugene thinks it of his rich and expiring uncle.

323/21 (248). *Tribadka.*
Lesbian.

323/31-32 (248). Mimicking Tolstoy's . . . chapter closings.
See note to 325/8-9.

325/8-9 (249). When in early September . . . he was pregnant.

A parody of Tolstoy's paragraph rhythm and chapter closings (a single-sentence paragraph providing new news). For example, Chapter VI (Part V) of *Anna Karenina* ends:

> After supper that same night the young couple left for the country.

268

Part V, Chapter XXI ends:

The doctor confirmed their supposition about Kitty. Her illness was pregnancy.

The ending of Part VII of *War and Peace:*

So the countess remained in the country and the count, taking Sonya and Natasha with him, went to Moscow at the end of January.

330/17-19 (252). Demon . . . Bessborodko . . . Bessarabia.
Bes(s) means "demon," "devil." Besborodko was a political figure under Catherine the Great.

333/6 (254). Legendary river.
The non-legendary Neva River, which flows through St. Petersburg-Leningrad.

333/10-12 (254). Deaf nun Varvara . . . Stan's principle.
In Chekhov's *Three Sisters* the "fourth" sister, i.e., their sister-in-law, is Natasha, who is not at all a nun.
Stan's principle is the Stanislavsky Method.

339/19 (259). Mr. Nekto's.
"Nekto" means "a certain person" in Russian.

341/17-18 (260). Sovereign Society of Solicitous Republics.
The Russian initials for USSR are *SSSR.*

342/32 (261). *Lapochka.*
Little paw.

344/5 (262). *The Village Eyebrow.*
The Village Voice. This English switch nearly duplicates a century-old pun-alternation in Dostoevsky's "The Crocodile" (18-65), where *Golos (The Voice)* becomes *Volos (The Hair).*

344/7 (262). Goluba University.
Columbia. But *goluba* is from the Russian for "pigeon."

344/11-12 (263). Obscene ancient Arab . . . Ben Sirine.
Sirin was Nabokov's Russian pen-name.

344/19 (263). Mandalatov.
Manda is one Russian word for private parts.

348/6-7 (265). Erotic works . . . Count Tolstoy.
"Erotic works" such as Tolstoy's "The Devil," "Father Sergius," and *The Kreutzer Sonata,* all of which center on the problem of sex.

351/6 (267). Palermontovia.
Pa - Lermontov - ia.

355/24 (271). Ritcov or Vrotic.
Suggests "erotic," and in Russian *v rotik* means "shove it in your little mouth."

357/28-29 (273). Princess Kachurin.
"To Prince S. M. Kachurin" (1947) is the title of a long Russian poem by Nabokov.

360/7-8 (274). Kneeling and wringing my hands . . . Marmlady in Dickens.
An allusion to Marmeladov kneeling before his wife (Marmlady) in Book I, Chapter 2 of Dostoevsky's *Crime and Punishment* (Dickens and Dostoevsky having many things in common).
"Dusty-trousered" alludes to "Dusty"—as Dostoevsky is dubbed by Nabokov in his translation of *Despair.*

371/15-17 (282). *Mertvago Forever.*
"Dead Forever" - another cut at Pasternak's *Doctor Zhivago*
See note to 53/23-24.

371/32 (282). "Pah!" . . . expletive.
Pah (pakh) means "groin" in Russian.

372/29 (283). N. T. S.
Perhaps irrelevant—but these are the initials of an anti-Soviet emigre organization in West Germany, the *Natsional'nyi Trudovoi Soiuz.*

386/4 (286). Audition in Sterva.
Sterva means "whore."

375/22 (285). *Krestik.*
"Little cross." An obscene anatomical arrangement. See 377/23 "a vixen's cross" and 378/1. Darkbloom suggests "little crest."

383/31 (292). *Mertvago Forever.*
See note to 371/15-16.

384/4 (292). Vieux-Rose Stopchin.
Old Rostopchin. See note to 114/1-2.

385/8 (293). Krolik . . . burrowing.
A pun—"Krolik" means "hare."

385/10 (293). Our father in hell.
Demon Veen—from Lermontov's Demon.

389/2 (296). Distance . . . Mr. Arshin.
An "arshin" is a unit of distance—28 inches.

394/1 (300). A family chronicle.
See Aksakov, note to 3/6.

394/30 (300). *Eyakulyatsiya.*
Ejaculation.

395/9-11 (301). Witnessing our *ébats . . . à la Russe.*
Pronounced this way it means "fucking"—the Russian *ebat'.*

398/28-29 (303). And the big chain around the . . . oak, *Quercus ruslan* Chât.
Quercus means oak (Latin). Chât. suggests Chateaubriand (alluded to or parodied on pages 81, 89, 106, 133, 138-39, 197, 206, 249, 343, 424-25), but it also puns to a French "cat," and in the Prologue of Pushkin's first (1820) long narrative poem *Ruslan and Ludmila* (thus *ruslan),* a very wise fairytail cat walks around an oak tree which has a golden chain around it. *Quercus* is also an important book title in Nabokov's *Invitation to a Beheading.*

399/15 (303). Sumerechnikov . . . Uncle Vanya.
Chekhov's play *Uncle Vanya* again. Sumerechnikov, as note (43/8), means "twilight."

399/23 (303). *Zdraste.*
   Hi.

401/19 (305). *Chelovek.*
   Man. (See note to 82/17.)

404/5-8 (307). March Hare. . . Krolik.
   Krolik means "hare" - plus Lewis Carroll's *Alice in Wonderland* (or *Palace in Wonderland* as in *Ada).* Let it be noted here if nowhere else that Alice images herself to be her friend Ada.
   Note also the "warren of collateral Kroliks" on 405/6.

406/18 (309). A family chronicle.
   See note to 3/6.

408/14 (311). Family Chronicle.
   See note to 3/6.

408/20 (311). Madame Trofim Fartukov.
   A comic name: "madame" plus a peasant's first name, plus the English "fart" and the Russian "fartuk" (apron).

409/6 (311). Klara Mertvago.
   Yet another dig at *Doctor Zhivago* (see notes to 371/15-16 and 13/22), the heroine of which is Lara Gishar.

410/2 (312). "Ursus."
   "The Bear" was one of the most famous restaurants in St. Petersburg.

410/12 (312). *Uha . . . ai.*
   Ai is a champagne (from Ay, France) mentioned prominently in *Onegin* as being "like a mistress," and discussed in detail in Nabokov's EO Commentary, Volume II, pp. 480-81. *Uha* is a fish soup.

410/15 (312). *Tsiganshchina . . .* Grigoriev and Glinka.
   Tsiganshchina - "gypsiness," "gypsyism" *(-shchina* is a derogatory suffix).
   Apollon Grigoriev's (1822-1864) most famous poem is "A Gypsy Hungarian Dance" (1857). See below, 413/1-6.
   Mikhail Ivanovich Glinka (1803-57), a composer, was the mentor of the famous "Mighty Five." Among his many songs is

the "Subside agitation of passion" cited on 412/12.

Nabokov has a pertinent paragraph on the "so-called *tsiganskie romansi* beloved of my generation" in his *Speak, Memory* (Chapter 11, end of section 4). He goes on to praise Fet and Tyutchev (Chapter 11, section 5).

411/33-34 and 412/106 (313). Fet's glorious . . . strings in it.

A. A. Fet (1820-92) - a lyric poet and close friend of Leo Tolstoy is really the author of a love poem *Siyala noch'* (1877)—the year *Anna Karenina* was completed. The words "Beams lay at our feet," while in Fet's poem, do not usually occur in the version which is sung—where instead there is "You and I were sitting in the drawing room" (*Sideli my s toboi v gostinoi*).

412/7-12 (313). Glinka's great amphibrachs . . . passion.

In Russian "Uimites' volneniia strasti" (1838) - M. I. Glinka's music, with N. V. Kukolnik's poem "Doubt" ("Somnenie") providing the words.

412/14 (313). "The tender kisses are forgotten."

"Zabyty nezhnye lobzaniia," words and music by Anatoly Lenin.

412/14-15 (313). "The time was early..."

"To bylo ranneiu vesnoi" - from a poem by Count Alexei Konstantinovich Tolstoy (1817-75).

412/15-16 (313). "Many songs have I heard..."

"Mnogo pesen slykhal ia v rodnoi storone" - or "Dubinushka," a revolutionary song written down by V. I. Bogdanov and revised by A. A. Olkhin. Often sung by Chaliapin before 1917.

412/17-19 (314). "There's a crag on the Ross..."

"Est' na Volge utes, dikim mokhom obros" is the first line of A. A. Navrotsky's poem "Cliff of Stenka Razin" ("Utes Stenki Razina"), written around 1864.

412/22-23 (314). In a monotone . . . dusting a bit.

"Odnozvuchno zvuchit kolokol'chik," words by I. Markarov, music by A. Gurshlev.

412/24-26 (314). Corrupted soldier dit . . . the riot.
A garbled echo of contemporary troubador Bulat Okudzhava.

412/27-29 (314). Turgenev's only memorable lyric . . . coverings.
"Utro tumannoe, utro sedoe" is from Ivan S. Turgenev's lyric poem "On The Road" ("V Doroge"), written in 1843, made into a "gypsy song" by the music of V. V. Abaza.

413/1-6 (314). Celebrated pseudo-gipsy guitar piece by Apollon Grigoriev . . . fills the canyon.
This is the first of seven stanzas by Grigoriev, a song of unhappy love in which the singer wants to know what a guitar's "sister" (i.e., his lover) desires. The "canyon" in line 4 of stanza 1 is Nabokov's invention—for the sake of the rhyme ("A noch' takaia lunnaia"). Grigoriev, a close friend of Dostoevsky, is best known as a critic.

413/16 (314). *Vinocherpiy.*
The wine steward.

413/23-24 (315). The first song . . . roses.
Konstantin Romanov's poem, cited on page 264 (see note to 264/21-34), has the first line "Uzh gasli v komnatakh ogni" and redolent roses ("Blagoukhali rozy"). In *Speak, Memory* Nabokov says: "Worst of all were the shameful gleanings from . . . Grand Duke Konstantin's lyrics of the *tsiganski* type" (p. 225).

413/25-26 (315). Favorite Fet . . . elbow.
Alludes to Fet's "Siyala noch' " (412/3-6) and the "soldier's dit" (412/25-26).

415/18 (316). *Nikak-s net.*
Absolutely not.

421/26 (321). *Spazmochka.*
Little spasm.

426/4 (324). Stan Slavsky.
Stanislavsky.

426/33-34 (324). Anton Pavlovich . . . hair.
A. P. Chekhov was married to an actress with long dark hair.

427/4-9 (324-25). Chekhov's *Four Sisters . . . The Three Sisters.*
Varvara the neurotic nun is the sister added to the version of Chekhov we are more familiar with. Masha becomes Marsha.

427/31-32 (325). Tuzenbach-Krone-Altschauer.
Nikolai Lvovich Tuzenbach-Krone-Altschauer is a main character in *Three Sisters.*

428/3 (325). *Sestra.*
Not Italian, but the Russian word for "sister."

428/4-7 (325). Irina (sobbing . . . in that speech.
This is an exact quotation of Irina (talking to Olga) in Act Three of *Three Sisters,* but Van is right—"window" precedes "ceiling."

429/3-4 (326). General Sergey Prozorov.
This is the father's name in the real play, but as noted above our Terra's Prozorov had no Varvara.

429/13-14 (326). Tchechoff . . . Nice.
In January of 1901 while *Three Sisters* was in rehearsal Chekhov lived in Nice. The address is given quite correctly.

429/15 (326). Ludicrous expository scene.
This is Nabokov's critique of the opening scene of *Three Sisters,* which was rewritten only by Nabokov.

430/2-5 (327). Fedotik . . . Skvortsov.
Real characters from *Three Sisters.* "Skvortsov" does mean "starling"—and is the name of a minor character in Nabokov's *The Gift.*

430/13 (327). Dangleleaf.
Sergei Pavlovich Diaghilev (1872-1929), Russia's most famous ballet master, was fond of young male pupils.

430/23 (327). Dawn *en robe rose et verte.*
Dawn plays Chekhov's Natasha, sister-in-law of the three sisters, who wears a "rose" dress with green sash in Act One.

275

430/28-29 (328). Didactic metaphorism of Count Tolstoy.
The following paragraph is a parody of Tolstoy's developed comparisons between (usually) phenomena in nature and human behavior.

433/13-14 (329). Tent . . . Palatka.
Palatka means "tent."

437/31 (333). Bronze Riders.
Alludes to Pushkin's narrative poem "The Bronze Rider" (or "The Bronze Horseman" as it is usually translated).

443/28-31 (337). Made himself up . . . to gravity.
A scene in Pushkin's *Boris Godunov,* where, as he is dying, Boris says to his son:

> You are a man and Tsar; *love your sister,*
> You are the only protector she has left.

My italics, Nabokov's memory.

451/11 (342). *Dyakon.*
Deacon.

454/3 (345). *"Tak ty zhenat* (so you are married)?"
Eugene Onegin says this to Tatyana's apparently fat husband (EO, Chapter Eight, XVIII, 1-4).

454/15 (345). *Bozhe moy!*
My God!

455/5 (345). *Za tvoyo zdorovie.*
Your health!

455/33 (346). Chekhovian colonel.
Colonel Vershinin in *Three Sisters,* a well-meaning cad.

456/4 (346). *Guvernantka belletristka.*
The governess writer.

456/18 (34/). Tobaks . . . dogs.
It would rhyme in Russian: *s Tobakymi* (with the Tobaks) - *s sobakami* (with dogs).

459/9 (348). *Invitation to a Climax.*
A lewd extention of Nabokov's own novel *Invitation to a Beheading.*

460/10 (349). Alone like Blok's *Incognita.*
The "unknown lady" is the first mystic, then whore-like heroine-muse of Alexander Blok's "symbolist" poetry, including the famous lyric "The Unkown Lady" (1906) where she appears foggily and gauzily in a bar.

463/8 (351). *Pravoslavnaia.*
Orthodox.

463/10 (351). *Po-russki.*
In Russian.

473/1-2 (359). *Estotskiya Vesti . . .* Screepatch.
The Estoty News. Violinist *(skripach).*

477/9 (361). "Pale Fire with Tom Cox Up."
Nabokov's annotative novel *Pale Fire.*

477/23-24 (362). Spring in Fialta.
Title of a collection of stories (and one story) by Nabokov.

477/31 (362). *Konskie deti.*
Horse children.

481/16-17 (365). "I love you with a brother's love . . . tenderly."
Here Van is rubbing Lucette's coccyx "to make pussy purr"; in EO, Eugene is pompously preaching to Tatyana and rejecting her when he uses these words (EO, Chapter Four, XVI, 3-4).

490/3-5 (372). Donna Anna . . . the Stone Cuckhold's revenge.
An allusion to Pushkin's *The Stone Guest*—in which the statue of Donna Anna's husband has its revenge on Don Juan. See note to 111/32-33.

490/26-27 (372). Father Sergius . . . famous anecdote.
The hero of Tolstoy's story "Father Sergius" (written 1890-98) axes off a symbolic finger when a divorcee with laughing eyes, bare feet, and an active imagination visits his cave and disrobes.

498/4 (377). *Pokonchila soboj.*
A misprint: *pokonchila s soboj* = put an end to herself.

498/16-17 (377-78). Decadent school . . . consumptive Anton.
Demon Veen's interpretation of Antiterran Tolstoy and tubercular Chekhov.

502/13-16 (380). And o'er the summits . . . shone.
A play on lines from Lermontov's *Demon:*

> And o'er the summits of the Caucasus
> He, banned from Paradise, flew on.
> Beneath him, like a diamond's facet,
> Mount Kazbek with snow eternal shone.

See notes to 180/15, 180/18, 180/22.

509/23-25 (385). Vrubel's wonderful picture of Father.
A painting of Lermontov's Demon by M. A. Vrubel (1856-1910), one of the most famous Russian painters. He did a series of illustrations for Lermontov's poem, but the painting entitled simply "Demon" (1890) is undoubtedly the one Nabokov has in mind. The "demented diamonds" are the Demon's eyes. See page 248 for a reproduction.

511/33-34 (387). Prince Gremin of the preposterous libretto.
A character in Tchaikovsky's opera *Eugene Onegin*—and the Antiterran Tschaikow's opus (see note to 158/6).

513/6 (388). Kosygin.
Presently a very high Soviet government official.

513/16 (388). *Korrektniy.*
Proper.

514/10 (389). *Zhidovskaya prerogativa.*
The prerogative of a Yid.

519/27 (393). Aunt Beloskunski-Belokonski.
A play on the real aristocratic name Beloselsky-Belozerski.

521/5 (394). The Vane sisters.
The title of a short story by Nabokov.

521/27-28 (395). Aleksey and Anna may have asterisked here.

Aleksey Vronsky and Anna Karenina, who in Part V, Chapter IX, move into an elaborately decorated Italian palazzo with heavy hangings on the windows, wall frescos, and a real Tintoretto (note in 521/24 the "tinted engraving"). As they are lovers, one supposes they do asterisk here.

523/34 (396). *Nu i balagur-zhe vi.*
Well what a wag you are.

526/18 (398). *Neopravdannay a zhestokost'.*
A misprint: *neopravdannaya zhestokost'.*

526/32 (399). *Golos Feniksa.*
The *Voice of Phoenix. Voice of the Phoenix.*

531/10 (402). And o'er the summits of the Basset.
A high and low parody of Lermontov's *Demon.* See note to 502/13-16.

532/16 (403). Goreloe.
"Burnt up."

547/5-6 (414). *Alice in the Camera Obscura.*
Camera Obscura is the original title of Nabokov's novel *Laughter in the Dark.*

571/17 (431). Oedipean oath of his Russian ancestry.
Eb tvoyu mat' - Love thy mother.

575/7 (434). *Blyadushki.*
Poblyadushki in Soviet Russian, "little whores."

577/29 (436). Griboyedov.
See note to 232/34.

582/18-19 (439). Old Felt and Uncle Joe.
Roosevelt and Stalin.

588/15 (444). Count Tolstoy's reminiscences.
See note to 3/7-8. See Tolstoy. [No, do you.] Insert.

Nancy Anne Zeller

The Spiral of Time in *Ada*

There is no need to prove Nabokov's interest in time and the related themes of past and memory. Subject matter alone—variations on the remembrances of an exile—would convince even the most casual reader of this, especially if he has sampled Nabokov's latest time treat, *Ada, Or Ardor: A Family Chronicle*. Many Nabokov fans, even those who have themselves published articles on earlier novels, readily admit that they found *Ada* obtuse, exasperating, and sometimes boring on first reading. Thus what *is* necessary, in fact what has been desperately required since the publication of *Ada*, is an interpretation of Nabokov's idea of time and its artistic expression, its image.

I do not plan to trace the development of Nabokov's idea of time, a topic more appropriate for the comparatist. However, it is interesting to note that the books Nabokov cites as admiring have at least one thing in common—time consciousness. One of Nabokov's greatest literary concerns is translation, thus it is significant that for his first translation into Russian he chose Lewis Carroll's *Alice in Wonderland*. Nabokov must have been as intrigued by Alice's adventures in distorted time as is the reader who knows the importance of the time-theme in Nabokov's novels. For example, the episode in *Through the Looking Glass* in which Alice learns about backward time from the White Queen immediately echoes a passage in *Ada* describing Lucette on the day she died: "Her age? (Lucinda Veen was only five hours old if one reversed the human 'time current.')"[1] Works of other writers such as Chateaubriand, Joyce, Aksakov, and Proust, all mentioned frequently by Nabokov in his own novels, emphasize the time-related themes of past and memory. Proust's conception of time in *A La Recherche Du Temps Perdu* was the major influence on Nabokov's own interest in this topic. Proust believed that trivial sensations jolt a person into remembering past events, and once an event is remembered, its significance can be reevaluated from the viewpoint of the present. Thus a greater sense of the reality of an event is obtained by linking or even merging past with present, even though for Proust this can happen only involuntarily.

We can see Proust's great influence on Nabokov when we

realize that the whole idea of memory (voluntary or involuntary) as being able to overcome time and death by fusing past to present underlies every novel that Nabokov has written. For instance, Pnin's attacks are not as a result of a heart condition but of a time condition; and when they occur, the past blends with the present.[2] Humbert recognizes Lolita as his "Riviera love," the union of his previous childhood love for Annabel with his desire for Lolita. "Everything between the two events was but a series of gropings and blunders, and false rudiments of joy. Everything they shared made one of them."[3] In a similar vein, Hermann in *Despair* insists repeatedly that it is not he but his memory that is doing the writing, and this is his explanation for slips of the pen when he refers to his wife in the past tense, or describes the scene of the murder as it was in winter (at the time of the murder) when the month was actually supposed to be June. "Thus," he says, "the future shimmers through the past,"[4] and we must conclude they actually are merged in mad Hermann's mind. Another example of such a time-blend occurs in *Pale Fire* as Gradus slowly approaches his destination. "Two silent time zones had now merged to form the standard time of one man's fate; and it is not impossible that the poet in New Wye and the thug in New York awoke that morning at the same crushed beat of their Timekeeper's stopwatch."[5] Gradus, a metaphor for all of Kinbote's past, has merged with the present. All of the above time-blends occur directly because the narrator of each novel has to recall them to write them down—they are thus remembered.

There is one other work which Nabokov admired enough to translate into English; and as we might expect, its attraction is again bound up with his interest in time: *A Hero of Our Time* by Mikhail Lermontov. As Nabokov explains in his introduction, it is the convoluted structure of *Hero* which is outstanding. He compares that structure to a poem composed by Lermontov in 1841 shortly before his death, a poem to which Nabokov gives the title "The Triple Dream," and which consists of a dream within a dream within a dream. Nabokov's interpretation of this structure and the image he assigns to the poem (And by association to *Hero* as well) will be important in our later discussion of *Ada*. Referring to the structure of the poem, Nabokov says that it:

...describes a spiral by bringing us back to the first stanza. The whorls of these five strophes have a certain structural affinity with the inter-lacings of the five stories that make up Lermontov's novel,... It will be marked by the good reader that the structural trick (now referring solely to the novel) consists in bringing Pechorin gradually nearer and nearer until he takes over; but by the time he takes over he is dead... This involute structure is responsible for blurring somewhat the time sequence of the novel. The five stories grow, revolve, reveal, and mask their contours, turn away and reappear in a new attitude or light...[6]

The image of the spiral is certainly nothing new to the reader who is familiar with Nabokov—in fact, whole articles have been devoted to it in Nabokov's criticism. L. L. Lee's "Nabokov's Great Spiral of Being"[7] applies the spiral as a general image for all Nabokovian literature. For Daniel Hughes in "Spiral and Glass "[8] it represents Nabokov's life in art. Nabokov himself refers to the spiral at length only in *Pnin* and *Speak, Memory,* but these two passages elucidate the importance of the image for him and its possible application to more specific ideas. In *Speak, Memory* Nabokov states that "Hegel's triadic series... expressed merely the essential spirality of all things in their relation to time " and "The spiral is a spiritualized circle. In the spiral form, the circle, uncoiled, unwound, has ceased to be vicious: it has been set free."[9] Events are free to recur, but on a different level, a higher level, their meaning enhanced by union with a similar past event. These recurrent events line up vertically on the spiral so that just below the present is the past and below that an even more distant past, etc. In the *Pnin* passage, the spiral is used as an image to explain the color theories of Professor Lake, Victor's art teacher. "Among the many exhilarating things Lake taught was that the order of the solar spectrum is not a closed circle but a spiral of tints from cadmium red and oranges through a strontian yellow and a pale paradisal green to cobalt blues and violets, at which point the sequence does not grade into red again but passes into another spiral, which starts with a kind of lavender grey and goes on to Cinderella shades transcending human perception."[10] Here Nabokov is applying his favorite general image to a specific idea—color—and this is precisely what I hope to do with Nabokov's idea of time in *Ada.*

What exactly *is* time to Nabokov? The question should be relatively simple to answer since the first chapter of Part Four of *Ada* is actually an essay on the subject. However, on first reading even a critical-minded Nabokov fan who realizes the importance of time in the work, may fail to grasp the core meanings of the essay because of its strategic position in the novel. Nabokov could not have picked a more inopportune moment to break into the story line as far as the reader and the narrative flow are concerned, for there is nothing more unwarranted or unwanted than a twenty-page scholarly essay when the hero and heroine are about to be reunited after a seventeen-year separation. All of which Nabokov, diabolical game player that he is, probably had in mind when he placed the essay where he did. According to a filmed interview for American educational television in 1966, Nabokov had originally intended this essay to begin his novel (which, by the way, at that time bore the tentative title *The Texture of Time)* instead of appearing near the end. But when *Ada, Or Ardor: A Family Chronicle* appeared in 1969, the only indication of time in the title was a Greek derivative—Chronos—and Nabokov left the way clear for Ada's narrator, Van Veen, to write "a kind of novella in the form of a treatise on the Texture of Time, an investigation of its veily substance, with illustrative metaphors gradually increasing, very gradually building up a logical love story, going from past to present, blossoming as a concrete story, and just as gradually reversing analogies and disintegrating again into bland abstraction "*(Ada,* 599).

Since Van Veen (V. V.=V. V. Nabokov) is clearly meant to be Nabokov's spokesman in *Ada,* we can take his views on time as presented in the essay to be those of Nabokov himself. A rejection of the future as time begins the essay with the assumption that time is nothing more than empirically perceivable on a conscious, individual basis. Van gives the example that time, for all practical purposes, did not start for him until his seventh month of life; he *remembers* an event—ceiling plaster crashing into his cradle—as the beginning of perceptual time: "The 195 days preceding that event being indistinguishable from infinite unconsciousness, are not to be included in perceptual time, so that, insofar as my mind and my pride of mind are concerned, I am today (mid-July 1922) quite exactly fifty-two..." *(Ada,* 570). Van then states his purpose in writing his Texture of Time: he wishes to separate Time from Space in order to examine its essence, and he emphasizes the difficulty involved in such a task. "I am aware that all who have tried to reach the charmed castle have got lost in obscurity, or bogged down in Space " *(Ada,* 571). This difficulty lies in language;

Van says: "I am also aware that Time is a fluid medium for the culture of metaphors " *(Ada,* 571)—a sentiment stated by Nabokov as well in the film mentioned previously. These metaphors have become so fixed in language "that we end up being unable to speak of Time without speaking of physical motion" *(Ada,* 575)— a language trap Nabokov may have (knowingly?) fallen into in writing the essay, since Van's thought on time are occasioned by the automobile trip he is making. A trip by car, speed, movement in space are plausible metaphors for the usual conception of space-time. What Van says he really wants to do is find a way to write or speak of Time using *new metaphors* which do not imply motion. The idea of a new metaphor is a difficult, but very important, concept which we will want to keep in mind.

Van then comes up with a comforting thought. Since Time is based on our perception of events, "...the only thing that hints at a sense of Time is rhythm; not the recurrent beats of the rhythm but the gap between two such beats, the gray gap between black beats: the Tender Interval " *(Ada,* 572). The beats help measure Time, but real time lies in the hollow between; and it is the essence of this Van hopes to grasp. But to do this the rhythm must be exactly right, not too fast and not too slow. "The ample rhythm causes Time to dissolve, the rapid one crowds it out " *(Ada,* 572).

The essay continues with discussions of ordinary concepts of time—evolution, directed time, and the relativist space-time—which serve to clarify Van's position, but add nothing really new and all of which Van rejects. The next important point in this essay is the explication of the Past and its nature. Sticking to his concept of time as empirically perceivable, Van sees the Past as an accumulation of sensa, and provides by his example of the model town of the previous century that the real Past exists only in the mind. These sense images form a "generous chaos out of which the genius of total recall...can pick anything he pleases..." *(Ada,* 580). Once again memory enters the picture—not the involuntary memory Proust mentioned—but Nabokov's active and very voluntary memory, attempting by an act of will to call forth images of the Past into the Present. Events of the Past usually require less clock-time to reoccur in the mind than they took when the actually happened, says Van. "The 'less' indicates that the Past is in no need of clocks and the succession of its events is not clock time, but something more in keeping with the authentic rhythm of Time."

(Ada, 583) Van-Nabokov has now arrived at one of the most important (for understanding *Ada)* points of the entire essay: to get the feel of the texture of time which exists in the gaps between past events, it is necessary "that the events to be selected for the test should be not only gaudy and graduated..., but related to each other by their main feature..." *(Ada,* 584). This requirement he illustrates by relating the events surrounding his three farewell lectures, spaced one lecture per week, and which are related by the common feature of Van's misadventures. Thus, he says, our feeling for time's texture, our only awareness of Time, comes from the rhythm of regularly-spaced events which echo one another because they all posses a common feature.

Having rejected the future earlier in the essay, Van-Nabokov has only the definition of the Present remaining, which he begins by calling the "Deliberate Present"—"three or four seconds of what can be felt as nowness. This nowness is the only reality we know;...Thus, in quite a literal sense, we may say that conscious human life lasts always only one moment, for at any moment of deliberate attention to our own flow of consciousness we cannot know if that moment will be followed by another" *(Ada,* 585). The "Deliberate Present" then, focusing in on nowness, is differentiated from what Van thinks of as "Present" when he says "Our modest Present is...the time span that one is directly and actually aware of, with the lingering freshness of the Past still perceived as part of the nowness." Here is the distinction between Deliberate Present and Present: the proximity of the Past (Past meaning not just the three or four seconds of nowness which become immediate Past by the time they are consciously perceived, but the entirety of past events). In fact, Van goes even further when he says, "What we are aware of as 'Present' is the constant building up of the Past...memory in the making" *(Ada,* 586, 595). Nabokov has arrived at the blend of Past with Present discussed earlier in this paper. This blend of past and present is for Nabokov the only real expression of time; and the new metaphor which expresses time will be voluntary memory aligning regularly recurring events, events which possess common features.

The reader may be somewhat confused by Van-Nabokovian theories on time. Certainly Nabokov never meant the essay to stand by itself as a scholarly work. On the contrary, his expressed desire was to turn abstraction into a logical love story—theories on time turned into a novel in the manner of Proust. Can we prove this is what Nabokov has done with *Ada?* I believe so. And in applying these time theories to the novel, they hopefully will become clearer.

Having investigated Nabokov's idea of time, having called to the reader's attention Nabokov's interest in the spiral as an image, it is now possible for me to arrive at the main thesis of this paper, the application of the spiral as an image to a specific idea, Nabokov's idea of time, in much the same way Nabokov himself used it in *Pnin* with the idea of color. Since *Ada* is the culmination of the time-theme in Nabokov's work and was intended by him (as we have seen expressed in the film interview as well as the quote from Van's statement about *The Texture of Time)* to be a metaphor giving life and substance to his idea of time, we shall want to deal solely with *Ada.* If we take the book as a whole to be a metaphor, it must express the elements which make up Nabokov's idea of time: blend of past and present by memory, caused by the regular rhythm of events which have obvious similarities.

This, we see by examining the structure of *Ada,* is actually the case. A short summary of the story would be appropriate. The chronicle relates the history of the love affair between Van Veen and his cousin / sister, Ada, and the story-line is structured around the periods of time Van and Ada were able to be together. The series begins with the summer of 1884: hero and heroine meet and fall in love; their romps through the arbors of Ardis are ended by Van's return to school in the fall. The romance is only resumed four years later in 1888. That summer ends with Van going off to seek revenge against the two men who seduced Ada, and there is another separation of four years. Van and Ada are reunited in the winter of 1892-1893, and this happy period of their joint lives is ended by family decree. Ada marries Andrey Vinelander; Van continues his studies; and eventually air, fire, and water destroy (in the deaths of Demon, Marina, and Lucette) the family objection to the union of brother and sister. In 1905, twelve years later, Van and Ada succeed in getting together again at the Three Swans Hotel, during the Vinelander's stay in Europe. The possibility of a life together ends, however, when Ada's husband is taken seriously ill. Ada, who cannot refuse to care for any hurt animal, plays nurse for her husband until his death seventeen years later in the summer of 1922. Any information the reader gleans about Ada's film career or Van's studies in psychology and time or Lucette's death by drowning is meant by Nabokov to be filler between the major events of the book—the gray gap between black beats. In addition Nabokov has made clear to the reader that Van is actively *remembering* these events for the purpose of writing his memoirs.

The events described in *Ada* seem at first glance to be the kind of regularly recurring event required by Nabokov's idea of time. The reader can see that the periods of separation have a certain rhythm: four years, four years, twelve years, seventeen years (17!). All are multiples of four, except the last. Where one would expect (assuming regular recurrence) sixteen years, we get instead seventeen. If *Ada* is indeed a metaphor for Nabokov's idea of time, it certainly is a shame that one little flaw should mar the obvious comparison. But is it a flaw? Imagine for a moment that the last period of separation were sixteen years as we expect it to be, and notice how succinctly everything would fall into place. Nabokov's idea of time calls for memory aligning regularly recurring events which have a common feature. *Ada* is Van's memory aligning regularly recurring meetings between Van and Ada the common feature of which is their love.

If it is still not clear as to the intent in making *Ada* a metaphor, perhaps an image would serve to illustrate this conception of time. As the following diagram shows, the spiral is the obvious choice:

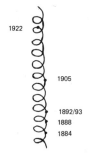

Each loop of the spiral represents four years, and by using the spiral as an image it is possible to represent visually the way Van's memory aligns the events vertically. Thus each meeting between Van and Ada, except the last, echoes their first meeting, and the memory of the previous meetings enhances the one following. In every case, except the last, Van is able to see in the Ada of 1888, 1892, and 1905 his memories of the little girl he had first loved in 1884. Each new meeting carries with it memories of the past—the past mingles with the present. The only trouble with this scheme is that the final meeting in 1922 does not align with the others, because seventeen is not a multiple of four. As might be expected the meeting is offkey in other respects as well. When Van arrives at the Three Swans Hotel it has been completely redecorated and there are hardly any remnants of his 1905 stay there with Ada. Van tries to recapture the past by reserving the same suite of rooms in the hotel: 508-509-510, but even these have changed beyond recognition and the town as well seems noisier than he remembered. One hopeful note is injected: the lake, although not exactly as it had been in 1905, is beautiful enough to engage his attention; and the telephone call from Ada reawakens his memories:

> Now it so happened that she had never—never, at least, in adult life—spoken to him by phone; hence, the phone had preserved the very essence, the bright vibration of her vocal cords,...It was the timbre of their past, as if the past had put through that call. Goldenly, youthfully, it bubbled with all the melodius characteristics he knew—or better say recollected...That telephone voice, by resurrecting the past and linking it up with the present formed the centerpiece in his deepest perception of tangible time, the glittering "now" that was the only reality of Time's texture *(Ada,* 591-592).

But Ada's voice was the only thing that had not changed. She now wore a corset; her hair had been bobbed and dyed bronze; her lavish use of cosmetics could not disguise the wrinkles and raised veins. "Nothing remained of her gangling grace...their shared birthmarks had got lost among the freckles of age" *(Ada,* 592, 594). To make matters worse Ada could not stay because she had to retrieve her luggage and maids from a neighboring town. "Had they lived together these seventeen wretched years, they would have been spared the shock and the humiliation; their aging would have been a gradual adjustment, as imperceptible as Time itself " *(Ada,* 594-595).

So the problem in their meeting after seventeen years was that the rhythm of time had been lost. "Time means succession and succession, change / Hence timelessness is bound to disarrange / schedules of sentiment."[11] This reference to *Pale Fire* is justified by Nabokov himself, who makes three references to John Shade in the last section of *Ada* alone. One of these references points directly to the lines quoted here as if Nabokov were trying to head the reader in the right direction. And seventeen years without any events occurring rhythmically is near to timelessness according to Nabokov's idea of time. It is significant that this longest separation is treated by Nabokov in only one and a half pages (Remember "The amply rhythm causes Time to dissolve"). The meeting between Van and Ada in 1922 does not retain the rhythm of the multiples of four, and thus does not echo all previous meetings. Obviously something must be done to save the novel as a metaphor for time. Van wakes up the next morning having decided to follow Ada, only to discover her standing on her balcony one floor below him (Room 410) observing the view. "He saw her bronze bob, her white neck and arms, the pale flowers on her flimsy peignoir, her bare legs, her high-heeled silver slippers. Pensively, youngly, voluptuously, she was scratching her thigh at the rise of the right buttock: Ladore's pink signature on vellum at mosquito dusk" *(Ada,* 598). One floor below—one year below— was the Ada of his youth, (and to clinch our spiral image) Van "left the balcony and ran down a short spiral staircase to the *fourth* floor " *(Ada,* 598). In spite of the apparent contradiction, Van realigns their schedules of sentiment by retreating back down the spiral; the seventeen-year separation is turned into sixteen; rhythm is restored; and Ada is indeed the metaphor for Nabokov's idea of time. The image of the spiral has helped us to arrive at an understanding of a complex idea.

The metaphor is carried to completion in Part Five (an echo of the five books of Lermontov's *Hero* and the five strophes of his poem?), which describes the remaining forty-seven years of Van and Ada's life together. Van as the narrator has described his life in terms of Ada—we might even say that Ada is a metaphor for Van's past, while Van is a metaphor for the present. Part Five, then, describes their gradual blend into one another, just as past and present blend to form real time.

By the way, who dies first? Ada, Van, Ada. Vaniada. Nobody. Each hoped to go first, so as to concede, by implication, a longer life to the other, and each wished to go last, in order to spare the other the anguish, or worries of widowhood. Actually, the question of mortal precedence has now hardly any importance. I mean, the hero and heroine should get so close to each other by the time the horror begins, so *organically* close, that they overlap, intergrade, interache, and even if Vaniada's end is described in the epilogue, we, writers and readers, should be unable to make out (myopic, myopic) who exactly survives, Dava or Vada, Anda or Vanda *(Ada,* 621).

Stylistically, this is exactly what Nabokov achieves. Up until Part Five it was possible to tell the sections in which Van lets Ada take over the writing. But by the end of the book, this becomes impossible. The description of their physical pain could apply to Van or Ada or both. And Nabokov's use of the word "Vaniada" is clear enough to even the reader who does not know that in Russian this would mean "Van and Ada". "One can even surmise that if our time-racked, flat-lying couple ever intended to die they would die, as it were, *into* the finished book, into Eden or Hades, into the prose of the book or the poetry of its blurb " *(Ada,* 625).The last description of Van and Ada—two old people lying together in one bed propping up the finished manuscript of *Ada*—echoes the first description of Van and Ada discovering family secrets in a scrap book in the attic of Ardis Hall. Just as Lermontov did in *Hero of Our Time,* Nabokov spirals the reader to an ending only temporally different from the beginning. All during the book Van and Ada have been getting nearer and nearer to the present of the reader. When on the next to last page the voice of the editor takes over, it is clear that both have died and that *Ada,* the book, is the blend of Van and Ada; the blend of past and present—the metaphor for Nabokov's idea of time.

NOTES

1. Vladimir Nabokov, *Ada, Or Ardor: A Family Chronicle* (New York: McGraw-Hill, 1969), p. 516. Further references to this book will be cited in the text as *(Ada,* page no.).

2. Vladimir Nabokov, *Pnin* (New York: Avon, 1959), p. 132.

3. Vladimir Nabokov, *Lolita* (New York: Berkley Medallion Books, 1955), p. 39.

4. Vladimir Nabokov, *Despair* (New York: Capricorn Books, 1965/66), p. 47.

5. Vladimir Nabokov, *Pale Fire* (New York: Berkley Medallion Books, 1962), p. 192.

6. Mikhail Lermontov, *A Hero of Our Time,* trans. with an introduction by Vladimir Nabokov in collaboration with Dmitri Nabokov (Garden City, N.Y.: Doubleday Anchor Books, 1958), p. vi-vii.

7. L. L. Lee, "Vladimir Nabokov's Great Spiral of Being," *Western Humanities Review* 18: pp. 225-236.

8. Daniel Hughes, "Nabokov: Spiral and Glass," *Novel,* Vol. I: pp. 178-185.

9. Vladimir Nabokov, *Speak, Memory* (New York; Pyramid Books, 1966), p. 203.

10. Vladimir Nabokov, *Pnin* (Great Britain: Cox & Wyman Ltd., 1971), p. 80.

11. Vladimir Nabokov, *Pale Fire* (New York: Berkley Medallion Books, 1962), p. 38.

Francis Bulhof

DUTCH FOOTNOTES TO NABOKOV'S *ADA*

For those readers of *Ada* who are not familiar with the Dutch language, the following notes may be useful. The name of *Ada's* protagonist, Van Veen, is a common last name in the Netherlands, pronounced "Vahn Vane," the "Van" part corresponding to English "of," and "Veen" meaning "marshland" or "fen." Van is never a first name in Dutch. The name Van Veen has probably to be seen in connection with the art dealers family name Duveen, of which the first syllable means "of" in French, of course. The French etymology of the Duveen's name is questionable though. Around the town of Meppel, in Drenthe, where the Duveen family originated, there are a great many towns with names such as Nijeveen, Kolderveen, Wapserveen, etc.

If one wants to see a family tree full of incestuous intra-marriages one should take a look at the chart facing page 3 of James Henry Duveen's *The Rise of the House of Duveen,* New York, Knopf, 1957.

On page 60-61 of the Fawcett Crest paperback edition, uncle Dan is reading an article on oystering in a Dutch magazine with the help of a small dictionary. The words "vestpocket wordbook," p. 61, are reminiscent of the Dutch original "vestzakwoordenboek," while the word "groote" (in the pre-1934 spelling) means "big" or "great," to the dismay of uncle Dan.

The paragraph on p. 266-267, which deals with the town of Ruinen is the most elusive. Ruinen is a small town a couple of miles away from Meppel. Only in a wider sense it is "somewhat near Zwolle," as the text has it. It has nothing to do with ruins. In Dutch the association is with "ruin," meaning "gelding." But Nabokov does not know everything. Dudok was a real architect, whose main works are not to be found in the province of Friesland but among other places in Hilversum.

Finally, the painter Jeroen Bosch, who has more than one epiphany in *Ada,* turns up on p. 333 as Jeroen Anth(o)niszoon van Aken, the Umlaut being an erroneous spelling for the Dutch Aeken, old form for Aix-la-Chapelle.

William Rowe

MISPRINTS

Introducing his *Eugene Onegin* translation, Mr. Nabokov insists that an artist's "end product" should reign supreme: "Even obvious misprints should be treated gingerly; after all, they may be supposed to have been left uncorrected by the author" (I, p. 15-16). Thus, a "treacherous misprint" (II, p. 393) which turns "delight" into "poison" (in Tatiana's Letter) is faithfully reproduced in the 1837 Russian language edition accompanying the *EO* translation.

With regard to his own fiction. Mr. Nabokov has insisted that the final word of *Bend Sinister* (which ends: "A good night for mothing.") is not a misprint. John Shade (in mountain-fountain) finds "Life Everlasting—based on a misprint!" (N.Y. 1966, p. 44). Kinbote notes a supposed reference to Keats in the account of a sports event, plus an episode involving "korona, vorona, korova—crown, crow, cow" (p. 184), dubbing them "vivid misprints" (p. 84).

Some Nabokovian misprints seem vivid enough "to have been left uncorrected by the author." We read, for example, that a "terrifically mobile, scampering" Pnin "teemed" (N.Y., 1965, p. 130) with Madame Bolotov at croquet. And in *Laughter in The Dark* (which begins, "Once upon a time"), we find: "A window opened in the fourth story" (N.Y., 1966, p. 156). But what is one to make, in *Nikolai Gogol,* of a young villager playing the balalaika, who "sits on a log with crossed legs (in brand new high boots) surrounded by sunset midgets and country girls?" (N.Y., 1961, p. 81). In *The Real Life of Sebastian Knight,* one finds: "It is not quite evening yet, but the air is golden and midgets are performing a primitive native dance in a sunbeam" (Norfolk, Conn., 1959, p. 138).

Also in *Bend Sinister,* the word "playful" is playfully corrected (in the text to "planful;" (London, 1960, p. 133) and some countries on a map are referred to in such a way ("the one that is blue on the map and the one that is fallow" [p. 80]) as to make the reader wonder: yellow? Finally, a passage said to be "garbled" from a different work contains the following: "fo whom they belong... and turther" (p. 134). The "f" and "t" were transposed in an edition four years later (N.Y., 1964, p. 134); one wonders by whom.

A similar case may be seen in "An Affair of Honor," which contains mention of "the lame sentence: 'One of us much perish' " *(Nabokov's Quartet,* [N.Y., 1966], p. 20). Like "garbled," above, the word "lame" seems to suggest that the "h" in "much" is correct.

In "The Vane Sisters," we read of an eccentric librarian who searches for "miraculous misprints" such as the substitution of "l" for the second "h" in "hither." *(Ibid.,* p. 84). In "Ultima Thule" (as printed both in *A Russian Beauty And Other Stories* [N.Y. 1973, p. 152] and in *The New Yorker* [April 7, 1973, p. 38]) we see, among other objects on the beach, "a shiver of garnet-red glass." Since the Russian original was *oskolok* (a "splinter" or "fragment"), an "h" seems here to have been substituted for an "l" ("sliver"). *(Vesna v Fial'te* [N.Y., 1956, p. 277]). However, an uncommon meaning of the English word "shiver" is "splinter" or "fragment."

GODS

To Peter Lubin's proleptic tmesis (Shakespeare's "pale his ineffectual fire") may perhaps be added George Meredith's proleptic allusion to *Ada* (in *The Egoist):* "But a solitary soul dragging a log, must make the log a God to rejoice in the burden" (N.Y., 1910, p. 65).

Two other Nabokovian Gods are "dog" ("How do God and Devil combine to form a live dog?"—*Despair* [N.Y., 1966, p. 56]) and "bog" (from a play on bog, "God" in Russian, and "swamp," combining to form "the bog-gods" of St. Petersburg—*Nikolai Gogol* [p. 11]. From God, log-dog-bog.

"Gut" (p. 212) (God in Zemblan) and "Gott" *(Bend Sinister,* p. 111) possibly comprise part of another pattern.

SNAKES, CIGARETTES AND LAPS

Like a snake, Emma Bovary's corset-string writhes about her hips. Prior to sleeping with Humbert, Lolita tries on "the slow snake of a brilliant belt" (N.Y., 1955, p. 122). When

Martha *(King, Queen, Knave)* first sleeps with Franz: "In the rickety wardrobe a blue black-spotted tie slithered off its twig like a snake" (N.Y., 1968, p. 98). When Paul *(Laughter in The Dark)* accidentally learns of Albinus' affair with Margot, he hangs up the telephone receiver "as though he had inadvertently caught hold of a snake" (N.Y., 1966, p. 40).

After Van first possesses Ada, there is mention of the "post-coital cigarette" (N.Y., 1969, p. 120). In retrospect, this seems to confirm just-accomplished furtive sex in both *Despair* ("Lydia lay smoking" [p. 114]) and *Laughter* ("Margot was lying supine, smoking lustily" [p. 97]).

In *The Defense*, Luzhin seats his future wife on his lap, has a facial spasm and relaxes oddly. He then "greedily" (N.Y., 1964, p. 106) lights a cigarette, and we see "a half-open drawer from which, snakelike, a green, red-spotted tie came crawling" (p. 107).

While wearing her "lolita" (p. 77) skirt, Ada sits upon, and nearly detonates, Van's "hard lap" (pp. 86-7). Four years later, Lucette similarly sits on Van's lap, and Ada is troubled by thoughts "more faintly remembered" than "a green snake in a dark paradise" (pp. 280-1). Van relives the past by pretending that Lucette is Ada, yet the narration strikingly recalls the famous lap episode in Lolita. Van feels a "golden flood of swelling joy" (p. 281)—Humbert acutely feels a "golden load" (p. 61). Van watches Ada's bracelet and her lips in the sun (p. 281)—Humbert looks at Lolita's "sloppy anklet" (p. 62) and: "the sun was on her lips." Lolita's skirt is "balooning" (p. 60)—Van (with Lucette) remembers Ada's "lolita" (p. 281) skirt as "so swooney-baloony" (p. 60). Moreover, the "Eden-red apple" eaten by Lolita on Humbert's lap seems strangely related to Ada's haunting memory ("a green snake in a dark paradise"), presumably, of sitting on Van's lap in her "lolita" skirt.

In *Laughter*, Margot sits on Rex's lap while reading to blind Albinus (p. 142). In *King, Queen, Knave*, Martha sits on Franz's lap, "... and the fact that she had gained weight and was quite bottom-heavy made things all the more cozy" (p. 155). And in *Bend Sinister*, Krug dreams "... that he was surreptitiously enjoying Mariette while she sat, wincing a little, in his lap during the rehearsal of a play in which she was supposed to be his daughter" (p. 154). A preview of *Lolita?* Humbert later remarks: "... I liked the cool feel of armchair leather against my massive nakedness as I held her in my lap" (p. 167).

Carl R. Proffer

THINGS ABOUT *LOOK AT THE HARLEQUINS!*
Some Marginal Notes

LATH's ultimate annotation will probably be longer than the novel itself, and the author of this annotation will no doubt go directly from the reference room to a padded cell. In the grano-blastic texture of the novel Nabokov recapitulates all of his previous novels and styles, as is suggested by the transparent titles in the Narrator's prefatory list of works. My shorter marginal notes include the following (all page references to the first American edition, Vladimir Nabokov, *Look at the Harlequins!* [New York: McGraw-Hill Book Co., 1974]):

(3-4). Gogol's *Inspector.* . . . nightmare . . . . *rêve?*
Gogol's play (1836) has been interpreted, by Belinsky and by Nabokov, as a "dream play." The Town Mayor does dream of big black rats. The etymology is fanciful.

(9). [First paragraph]
See the opening paragraph of *Lolita.*

(23). Rodential Gadara.
A reference to the Gadarene swine bedeviled and drowned in Luke, 8, 26-39. The passage is famous in Russian literature because it was used by Dostoevsky as the epigraph to *The Devils.*

(29). Pushkin . . . feet.
Pushkin's beloved, famous feet are in *Eugene Onegin,* 1, 32-34.

(30). Mirana Palace.
See the Hotel Mirana in *Lolita,* Chapter 2, etc.

(53). The three lovers . . . Pushkin's mad gambler.
Pushkin's gambler, Hermann, is the hero of "The Queen of

Spades." Three secret cards are the keys to his failure.

(57). Prostakov-Skotinin, a Russian comedy name.
Names of two major characters in Fonvizin's eighteenth-century play *The Minor.*

(58). Defenestrate the poor chess player.
The fate of Luzhin, hero of Nabokov's *The Defense.*

(59). Iris . . . lessons.
The Emma Bovary piano lesson rendezvous technique. See *Madame Bovary,* Chapter V, Part III.

(61). Novella in verse *Polnolunie.*
Eugene Onegin was called a "novel in verse" and otherwise has no connection to *The Defense.*

(62-63). *Beloved . . . Your Jules . . .* whole letter in French.
A distant parody of Tatyana's letter to Eugene Onegin, also translated from the French.

(65). April 23, 1930.
Nabokov's birthday is April 22. Note that the Narrator changes the language in which he writes on April 23 (p. 124), a time of birth and metamorphosis. See notes on *Ada.*

(76). Shipogradov.
Ivan Bunin was Russia's only Nobel Laureate.

(77). "A pretty bauble always gladden us."
That is, "A thing of beauty is a joy forever."

(78). Clockwork doll.
A version of Dolly Haze.

(81). [Dictation scene]
The whole scene is based on a similar situation in Dostoevsky's life—when he first used a stenographer (for *The Gambler),* and married her, which is what the Russian reader expects here.

(88). Dr. Moreau's island zoo.

In H. G. Wells's *The Island of Dr. Moreau.*

(88). Boyan Bookshop.

Boyan was the most famous, legendary, bard of ancient Rus. See Nabokov's translation *The Song of Igor's Campaign.*

(90). "Bronze Horseman" Publishing House.

The colophon of the real émigré publishing house "Petropolis" was the Bronze Horseman—the Falconet statue of Peter the Great, used in Pushkin's "The Bronze Horseman."

(94). *Hero of Our Era*

Lermontov's *A Hero of Our Time* (which Nabokov has translated).

(94). *Prime Numbers.*

There was an émigré periodical called *Numbers (Chisla).*

(94). *Princess Mary* is out, I mean *Mary.*

Princess Mary is one of the sections of *A Hero of Our Time;* *Mary* is a Nabokov novel.

(95). Your *Tamara,* not Lermontov's.

Lermontov's Tamara appears in his poem *The Demon;* one of Nabokov's in *Speak, Memory.* See notes on *Ada*, above.

(96). Demon. Vrubel has portrayed him.

See illustration, page 248 above, and notes on *Ada.*

(97). V. Irisin.

V. Sirin, Nabokov's pen-name.

(99). *The Dare (Podarok Otchizne).*

Combines Nabokov's *Glory* (in Russian, *Podvig*—something daring) and *The Gift (Dar), Podarok Otchizne* being a "gift to the fatherland."

(99). Turgenev Publishing House.

There was, and is, a real émigré Chekhov Publishing House.

(100). Biography of Dostoevski.

In *The Gift* it is actually a biography of Chernysehvski, one of Dostoevski's, and Nabokov's, greatest enemies.

(101). Chernolyubov-Dobroshevski.

N. Chernyshevski and N. Dobrolyubov, two famous but untalented literary and social critics; the former is a hero in *The Gift.*

(113). Prudery . . . moans.

Possibly an allusion to Pushkin's poem to his cold wife, "No, I set no value on stormy pleasures."

(115). *Le Petit Diable Boiteux.*

Le Diable boiteux is a novel by Lesage.

(116). Adam Atropovich.

G. Adamovich was an émigré critic, atrophied.

(117). The Mother . . . corny Soviet film.

From Gorky's novel *The Mother.*

(120). Great scarab.

Alludes to Kafka's *Metamorphosis,* a take-off on Dostoevski's "The Crocodile."

(124). Neochomsk . . . linguistics.

Contemporary linguist N. Chomsky.

(125). Word for a pigling . . . *The Carrick.*

An ordinary full-grown young pig plays a strange role in Gogol's story *The Carrick (The Overcoat),* as noted by Nabokov in his book on Gogol.

(138ff.)

The style and intonation of this section closely approximate that of *Lolita* (Lo, Quilty, Humbert Humbert).

(140). *Krasnaia Niva.*

The real Soviet literary journal was *Krasnaia Nov' (Red Virgin Soil).* There was an older magazine called simply *Niva.*

(142). Swivington.

"Swive" has been replaced by a more onomatopoetic four-letter word. The whole section continues the replay of *Lolita.*

(150). Myrna Soloway . . . "Soloveychik."
In Russian "Solovei" means "nightingale."

(155). Learning to drive.
This section replays a marvelous section of *Pnin.*

(156). *The Invisible Lath.*
Suggests: *Transparent Things* and *Look at the Harlequins!*

(159). Gerard Adamson . . . very fast girl.
Edmund Wilson and Mary McCarthy.

(161). Emma.
Emma Bovary.

(166-67).
More replay of *Lolita,* with Lo and big Haze.

(169). Ada Bredow.
New incarnation of Ada from *Ada.*

(170). Isabel Lee.
Annabel Leigh, Annabel Lee, Lolita.

(183ff).
Still more replay of *Lolita,* this time using the screen play.

(184). Glass . . . Riviera souvenir.
The Riviera sunglasses which wander psychologically and physically through *Lolita.*

(186). Charles Dodgson.
Lewis Carroll, who liked to photograph little girls.

(193). Rose Brown.
There is a Ruby Black in *Ada,* also a maid.

(194). Allan Garden...Virginia.
Ada and Van reincarnated, and reversed.

(208). *Sharovars.*
Russian: "pants."

(209). *Kotleta po kievski.*
Soviet cutlets are not cutlets. See *The Moscow Gourmet,* published by Ardis, Ann Arbor.

(210). Nobody, according to Gogol, knows.
In Gogol's *Nose* (knows), set in St. Petersburg, the narrator keeps repeating, at crucial points, that nobody knows what happened next. At St. Petersburg is a foggy town.

(211). House on Gertsen St.
The Nabokov house is (was) on Gertsen (Herzen) Street.

(215ff.). [Blurb]
A replay of *Ada,* particularly the ending.

(217). Fyodor Mihaylovich.
Dostoevski.

(218). Kingdom by the Sea.
That is, *Lolita.*

(223). Substance of Space.
Parallels the Texture of Time in *Ada.*

(230). Private . . . (Dick Cockburn, a staunch friend of mine).
I wouldn't dare touch this one.

(246). Gavrila Petrovich Kamenev.
(1772-1803). A minor poet, who so far as is generally known, did not forge the tedious epic "poem" which constitutes one of Russia's few claims to having literature before Pushkin.

(246). *Le Tramway ivre.*
A combination of Rimbaud and Nikolai Gumilev. The latter's

famous "Streetcar Gone Astray" is translated in *Russian Literature Triquarterly,* No. 1 (Fall 1971).

(253). Ceylon and Jamaica, the sibling islands.
    Why sibling? —Tea and coffee.

A *LOLITA* CROSSWORD PUZZLE BY KERRY AHEARN

ACROSS

1 diminutive for Lolita
3 the nymphet's surname
6 a college where HH lectures
10 diminutive for Humbert
11 initials: child-bride of a famous author
13 Charlotte's maiden name
16 the tongue's second step
17 Swine and Potts gave him HH's room key
18 the days of cohabitating with Charlotte
19 Charlie Holmes's last occupation
20 garment HH never mentions
22 Ned Litam's preference
25 Lolita's Christian name
28 *Who's Who* actor
30 John Ray's qualification
31 listed as author of *Hansel and Gretel*
32 the tongue's first step
33 "deep-voiced" HH/Berthe in the fantasy visit to summer camp
36 maker of the auto which spirits Lolita away from the hospital
38 initials: Renaissance French poet HH quotes one Friday
40 hotel where HH first possesses his darling
42 sister of an Elphinstone nurse
43 auto licenses: letters from one, numbers from another
45 initials: Lolita's father
47 a female Ramsdale classmate
49 nickname for HH's .32 automatic
51 *Who's Who* actress
52 Beardsley School's substitute for the academic "R"
53 pop. 1001

55 initials: female Ramsdale classmate
59 HH's mistake in the name of the lake
60 initials: Ramsdale classmate "who has let strangers touch her"
61 a Beardsley girl, a nymphet herself
62 HH thought of fleeing here with Lolita
63 Papa's Purple Pills: HH calls them Vitamin ____
65 Dolly never calls Charlotte this
66 Mrs. Schiller's final answer to HH
68 the tongue's tap
69 the summer camp
70 overly inquisitive Beardsley neighbor
72 the playwright always smoked them
73 acronym: refrigerator transit company; also, HH's refuge
74 Lolita's friend, Poet in the Beardsley play

DOWN

1 informed HH that his second wife was dead
2 HH's reason for writing these "confessions"
3 Miss Pratt asks HH to allow Lolita to play a part in it
4 time of day HH is seduced
5 first part of Dolly HH caresses
7 animal to which HH likens himself, Valeria, and Taxovich
8 Prof. Humbertoldi's nickname for his roly-poly adversary

ACROSS	DOWN
1 Lola	1 Les
3 Haze	2 Love
6 Cantrip	3 Hunted Enchanters
10 Hum	4 AM
11 VP	5 Eye
13 Becker	7 Ape
16 Lee	8 Rom
17 Tom	9 Pavor
18 50	12 Pets
19 GI	13 BM
20 Tie	15 Red
22 Lads	16 Lightning
25 Dolores	21 Poe
28 Pym	22 Leigh
30 PHD	23 AS
31 Roe	24 Sport
32 Lo	26 Or
33 DP	27 Lore
36 GM	29 MD
38 RB	34 Past
40 Enchanted Hunters	35 NH
42 Ann	37 Mushroom
43 SHI564	39 Bea
45 HH	41 342
47 MG	42 AM
49 Chum	44 56
51 Quine	46 Tums
52 D	48 Cue
53 Soda	49 Carmen
55 MC	50 McFate
59 Our	52 D
60 SF	54 Duo
61 Eva	56 Ivor
62 Mexico	57 Rita
63 X	58 10
65 Mom	61 End
66 No	63 X
68 Ta	64 Car
70 East	67 MM
72 Dromes	69 Q
74 Mona	71 AA

KEY TO *LOLITA* CROSSWORD PUZZLE